JOSEPH

Wolpe

Key Figures in Counselling and Psychotherapy

Series editor: Windy Dryden

The *Key Figures in Counselling and Psychotherapy* series of books provides a concise, accessible introduction to the lives, contributions and influence of the leading innovators whose theoretical and practical work has had a profound impact on counselling and psychotherapy. The series includes comprehensive overviews of:

Sigmund Freud
by Michael Jacobs

Eric Berne
by Ian Stewart

Carl Rogers
by Brian Thorne

Melanie Klein
by Julia Segal

Fritz Perls
by Petrūska Clarkson and Jennifer Mackewn

Aaron T. Beck
by Marjorie E. Weishaar

Albert Ellis
by Joseph Yankura and Windy Dryden

Joseph Wolpe
by Roger Poppen

George Kelly
by Fay Fransella

D. W. Winnicott
by Michael Jacobs

JOSEPH Wolpe

Roger Poppen

SAGE Publications
London • Thousand Oaks • New Delhi

SAGE Publications Ltd
6 Bonhill Street
London EC2A 4PU

SAGE Publications Inc
2455 Teller Road
Thousand Oaks, California 91320

SAGE Publications India Pvt Ltd
32, M-Block Market
Greater Kailash – I
New Delhi 110 048

British Library Cataloguing in Publication data

A catalogue record for this book is available
from the British Library.

ISBN 0 8039 8666 1
ISBN 0 8039 8667 X (pbk)

Library of Congress catalog card number 95-071355

Typeset by Mayhew Typesetting, Rhayader, Powys
Printed in Great Britain by Biddles Ltd, Guildford, Surrey

Contents

Acknowledgments

I would like to thank several people for the time and information that they generously shared with me. Foremost is Joseph Wolpe himself, whose candor and cooperation were immensely helpful. Leo Reyna and Alan Goldstein provided valuable material and context, as did Cyril Franks and Dorothy Susskind. At a distance of more than three decades, I thank Albert Bandura and Arnold Lazarus for turning my interests toward behavior therapy in graduate school. Finally, I appreciate the guidance and patience of Windy Dryden, the series editor.

1

The Life of Joseph Wolpe

The gray tabby quietly licked her forepaw as she sat on the metal grid floor of a small wire mesh cage. She paused and raised her head at the raucous noise of an automobile 'hooter' attached to the side of the cage, but displayed no other concern. She had heard it several times on a previous day and now was quite used to it. However, this time as the noise ended, a brief jolt of electric current surged through her feet. The cat leaped up with a yowl, her trajectory stopped by the top of the cage. She crouched to one side, ears flattened, fur puffed out, sides heaving, claws extended, her eyes wide and staring.

A bespectacled young man in a white laboratory coat, standing next to the cage, also watched intently. He lifted his hand from the switch that controlled the low amperage electric current and began to write on his clipboard: 'Trial 1: vocalization, piloerection, mydriasis . . .' After several long minutes the tabby's ears perked up, her coat smoothed. She stretched and slowly began to move about the small cage. Again the hooter sounded. The man in the laboratory coat watched the cat as she froze in place, her eyes widening, as he extended his finger toward the electric switch.

After about a dozen pairings of the hooter and electric shock over two successive days, the once calm tabby now shrank from the laboratory assistant's hand when he arrived at the living cage and yowled in the carrying cage as she was brought to the experimental room. The young man had to take care to avoid her flailing paws as he maneuvered her through the small opening on the top of the experimental cage. Latching the cage door, he took up his position next to the electrical apparatus. The tabby took up her usual position, crouched tensely in a corner of the cage, eyes wide, ears flattened, and tail twitching. On this occasion something new had been added: in the middle of the cage floor, not more than 12 inches from the cat's nose, were a few small pellets of ground beef. She appeared not to notice. An entire two hours continued in this fashion, the cat almost motionless, the young man watching intently. He noted, 'tension, crouching, mydriasis, refusal to eat . . .'

The next day it was the same, even though the tabby had now not eaten for 48 hours.

The first part of the young man's task had been completed; he had produced a neurotic reaction in this animal, as he would in about a dozen others. Now his challenge was to cure them.

Roots

The young man who had watched the cats so intently, Joseph Wolpe, was born in the early years of the First World War in Johannesburg, a burgeoning city in the gold fields of the newly formed Union of South Africa. His grandparents were Jews who had emigrated from Lithuania with their children to this region at the beginning of the twentieth century. Lithuania for centuries had been a haven for Jewish refugees from pogroms in Russia and the Ukraine, forming a citadel of Jewish scholarship and enterprise (Dawidowicz, 1989, pp. 38–48). Though suffering periodic restrictions during Polish and Russian struggles for control of the region, Jewish culture had flourished. Education, both Talmudic and secular, was highly prized; the Lithuanian Jew, or *litvak*, was said to be characterized by an emotional reserve and an intellectual quickness (Dawidowicz, 1989, p. 46). At the close of the nineteenth century, some Jewish leaders had sufficient power to participate in Marxist-based efforts to promote social and democratic reforms for Lithuania, fueling harsh anti-Semitic reprisals by the Russian czar (Sabaliunas, 1990, pp. 1–19). Persecution of Jews escalated after the czar's overthrow as Bolsheviks and Polish nationals battled for political dominance.

South Africa was a land steeped in ethnic and religious conflict as virulent as in eastern Europe (Kruger, 1969; Sparks, 1990). The Afrikaners, descendants of seventeenth-century Dutch colonists, maintained a reclusive agrarian culture based on the belief of their divinely ordained dominion over non-white races. The great conflict at the beginning of the twentieth century, however, was not between white and black but between Afrikaner and English, who had gained hegemony over the Cape colony in 1814. The Afrikaners had avoided English settlers and resisted English laws, which abolished slavery and granted some legal rights to non-whites, by migrating northward to the vast plains of the interior. In the 'great trek,' beginning in 1836, they developed military skills and leaders in battles with indigenous black African peoples, and they successfully resisted English attempts to take over their newly formed states. However, the discovery of diamonds in the 1860s and gold in the 1880s brought floods of immigrants to their territory and intensified

English interest in the area. The English mounted a costly offensive, the Boer War, which, while militarily successful, only intensified Afrikaner cohesiveness and singularity of purpose. In subsequent political settlements, beginning with the union of the South African colonies in 1910, Afrikaners maintained a prepotent position, ensuring policies of white racial dominance. Even so, some Afrikaner elements sought more drastic solutions. There was organized support for Germany in the years before the First World War, reflected in the statement of an Afrikaner leader that he would not have his country run by 'Englishmen, niggers, and Jews' (Walker, 1957, p. 655). During this period there were strong but eventually unsuccessful attempts to have Jews classified as 'Asiatics,' which would have limited immigration and restricted activities of residents.

Johannesburg began as a wide-open gold-rush town and rapidly grew into a busy metropolis. English settlers supplied the capital and skills needed for industry and commerce, dominating business as the Afrikaners dominated politics. While the English were more tolerant than the Afrikaner, there remained an anti-Semitic strain, particularly among the 'aristocracy' of the city.

> They built grand homes a sanitary distance from the hurly-burly of Ferreira's Camp [the gold fields], and an English gentlemen's club, all leather and silence, where they could gather alone without blacks and Boers and Jews . . . (Sparks, 1990, p. 124)

This was the milieu into which Joseph Wolpe was born in 1915. The oldest child of an industrious book-keeper, he had two sisters, Marian and Margery, and a brother, Harold. The scholarly *litvak* tradition was especially strong in the family of his mother, Sarah. Though of more working-class origins, his father, Michael, also had a profound respect for education. Several years before Joseph's birth, Michael had purchased the ponderous *Webster's New International Dictionary* and a 25-volume world history encyclopedia intended for the education of his children. Michael Wolpe was a liberal in his political views and passed his concern for the wellbeing of others to his children. Harold, 10 years Joseph's junior, became a noted political activist. A sociologist and a lawyer, he defended participants in Nelson Mandela's anti-apartheid movement, enduring imprisonment and effecting a dramatic escape to continue his work in England. Formal religion was of concern only to Joseph's maternal grandmother, who lived with the family and from whom the youngster gained a general theistic belief but no specific doctrine. Assimilated into the middle-class English culture of Johannesburg, the family experienced little overt anti-Semitism but could not escape the pervasive cultural focus on race and class.

Joseph was an avid reader from an early age, sometimes preferring the company of books to that of his playmates. He was occasionally late for school because of reading in the morning, and on school holidays he would read as many as two books a day. His parents prized his precocious verbal skills, instilling in him a strong confidence in his intellectual ability. He was found to need eyeglasses his first year of elementary school, but often avoided wearing them because he felt they were unattractive. Somewhat shy, he could be embarrassed by the chutzpah of his mother as she bargained with merchants when he accompanied her on shopping trips. Joseph was fond of sports, particularly football (soccer), which he played with neighborhood children.

At the close of his elementary school days, young Joseph was impressed by the 'Greyfriars' stories of adventure in an English public school, serialized in a boys' magazine. Attracted to the image of comrades in their caps and blazers overcoming rivals on the playing field, he chose to attend the Parktown Boys' High School, which followed the English model, far from his own home. He refused the bicycle which his parents offered if he went to the neighborhood school; instead he commuted daily by bus and tram to the other side of the city. His chances of glory on the football field were diminished on the first day of high school when he was struck by a motorcycle and suffered concussion and a broken leg. Although he could not qualify for the school's football and track teams, he remained a faithful fan and cheered on his more athletic comrades. Academic competition proved to be his forte, and he received numerous prizes for outstanding performance in a wide variety of subjects, including Latin, mathematics, and geography. His ability and diligence were such that he graduated first in his class, reinforcing his self-confidence and his family's pride in his intellectual skills.

During high school, Joseph developed a particular attraction to chemistry. This was a subject that required not just reading and recitation about abstractions, but active participation with the subject matter. He rapidly surpassed the school's chemistry curriculum and devoured college-level textbooks. He set up a laboratory at home, with materials loaned by his professors, to perform experiments on his own. The orderliness of chemical relations and the possibility of discovering new ones were tremendously appealing. He would become, he decided, a chemistry researcher. To his parents, who were pragmatic people, this was a dubious profession. After some discussion it was agreed that Joseph would pursue medicine; this would provide him with a sound income and respected social standing, as well as permitting the option of chemical research. Thus, at age 18, he matriculated at the University of the Witwatersrand, which followed the English practice of a six-year medical program following high school. Wolpe entered college a shy young man, confident of his academic abilities but reserved and unsure in social relationships.

Discovery

University was a new world for the young Joseph Wolpe, both socially and intellectually. It was his first time living away from home, and after his years in the all-male high school he acquired a girl-friend straight away, a beautiful young woman in the class ahead of his. He poured so much time and attention into this affair that he actually failed his first-year chemistry course. After the romantic flame extinguished he settled down a bit, but his academic performance never reached the heights that it had in high school. When grades were posted, his were often in the lower tier of students. Nevertheless, he maintained the utmost confidence in himself, sure that his knowledge of a subject was greater than that manifested on the timed written examinations which determined grades. His parents, whose pride in his earlier academic success helped build his self-confidence, continued their support of his efforts despite his lower grades.

After his flirtation, the main diversion from his medical studies was a coterie of male friends who stayed up late into the night engaging in discussions of philosophy. Wolpe was particularly interested in epistemology; he read all of Kant's *Critiques* and then investigated his intellectual forbear, David Hume. Perhaps the subjectivism of these works was unsatisfactory, for Wolpe turned to contemporary philosophers of a more empiricist and positivist view, such as Bertrand Russell and Alfred North Whitehead. The difficulties which Hume and Kant had in reconciling their systems with the religious dogmas of their day, and the outright atheism of the later writers, led Wolpe to abandon his vague theistic views in favor of a totally materialist outlook.

As he completed his medical studies, Wolpe maintained an interest in a number of specialities, including internal medicine, anesthesiology, and immunology. Psychiatry seemed only a distant possibility. Wolpe's acceptance of Freudian theory had waxed and waned throughout his medical studies. It had been taught routinely as part of the curriculum but Wolpe initially had regarded it as rubbish. However, several personal experiences altered his assessment. At one point, after talking with a friend he was left with a peculiar depersonalized 'hollow' feeling, and began to fear he was a schizophrenic. Only after several weeks did this fear dissipate, but the experience reinforced his interest in psychiatric phenomena. As an intern he was involved with the treatment of a young woman psychiatric patient. She reported a dream in which she was swimming toward a man on a distant shore which she could never reach. On advice from a colleague, Wolpe made the interpretation that she desired to meet a man like her father. Within a few minutes she began to display a marked worsening of her symptoms, which Wolpe felt resulted from her defenses against this powerful insight. Such experiences, supported by discussions with friends and colleagues, kindled his interest in reading Freud more extensively, and Wolpe even began a program of recording and analyzing his own dreams.

Wolpe completed his medical studies shortly before the advent of the Second World War and he volunteered for the Cape Corps as a medical officer. In 1942 he was assigned to the military hospital at Kimberley, which received a large number of 'war neurosis' cases. According to prevailing Freudian theory, neuroses were the result of repressed memories of traumatic experiences and the recommended treatment was their release through sodium pentothal infusion, a much briefer method than traditional psychoanalysis. It was with great interest that Wolpe observed and participated in the treatment of these patients. Overall, the results were unsatisfactory; despite dramatic revelations and some immediate improvements, no lasting results of 'narcoanalysis' were observed. In addition, Wolpe's reading of the sociologist Malinowski's *Sex and Repression in Savage Society* (1927) and Valentine's *Psychology of Early Childhood* (1943) led him to question the validity of Oedipal theory (Wolpe, 1958, p. vii). He began a search for an alternative to Freud. The fact that the Russian allies did not accept Freud piqued his interest in their theory of neurotic disorders, which led him to the work of Pavlov.

Throughout this period at Kimberley, Wolpe was a regular participant in a discussion group of several young medical corpsmen hosted by Abe Edelstein, who, as a married officer, had his own apartment. This was a welcome change from the single officers' spartan quarters, and the late night discussions were reminiscent of his college years. A favored topic concerned the causes of disordered behavior, and the works of Karl Marx and Ivan Pavlov were thoroughly analyzed. The possibility that Pavlov's research on 'experimental neurosis' might provide an alternative to Freud's theories of psychopathology was tantalizing, though just how that might be worked out was not resolved. Wolpe was impressed with the precision of Pavlov's methods but did not accept his speculations about cortical pathology as the basis of experimental neurosis.

After two years Wolpe was transferred from Kimberley to another base, but his direction towards psychiatry seemed certain. On leave at a resort near Cape Town in 1945, he visited the Edelsteins, who now lived in this city. Cynthia Edelstein had begun a master's degree program in psychology at Cape Town University, and told Wolpe about her major professor, James G. Taylor, an expert on conditioning and learning. A meeting was arranged and Taylor, upon hearing of Wolpe's interest in Pavlov, recommended that he read Clark Hull's recently published *Principles of Behavior*. Hull's rigorous, systematic and comprehensive theory had tremendous appeal to Wolpe. Here was a psychological approximation to the periodic table of elements, in which manifest behavior was synthesized out of the interaction of its various components. Hull's theory, unlike Pavlov's, did not speculate about physiology, but Wolpe's medically trained eye saw the underlying operation of neural connections. Like that of Pavlov, Hull's theory reinforced the idea that principles applicable to human behavior could be developed via animal models. Although it did not address neurosis as such, it set Wolpe thinking about applications to maladaptive behavior. It was the beginning of an alternative to Freudian theory.

Upon his discharge from the army in 1946, Wolpe returned to the University of the Witwatersrand to pursue an MD degree in the Department of Psychiatry. This was a research degree, requiring the completion of an experimental dissertation. Wolpe was determined to follow the leads of Pavlov and Hull in developing an empirical foundation for psychiatry. In preparation, he plunged into the experimental psychology literature, reading all he could find about learning and perception. Fortuitously, the end of the year saw the arrival of Leo J. Reyna on the faculty of the Department of Psychology for a three-year appointment. About the same age as Wolpe, Reyna had just completed his PhD dissertation at the University of Iowa where he had studied with Kenneth Spence, Hull's distinguished collaborator. Wolpe attended Reyna's seminars on Hullian theory and became part of an informal group of psychology students interested in conditioning. Well-versed in the intricacies of Hullian theory as well as a wide range of issues in psychology, Reyna provided valuable guidance and feedback for Wolpe's developing ideas. Reyna served as a 'reader' on Wolpe's dissertation committee in the psychiatry department, but was in reality his major professor for the actual conduct and write-up of the experiment. The two men formed a close relationship which has continued to the present time.

Reyna's dissertation at Iowa had concerned 'extinction,' or the elimination of learned behavior (Reyna, 1946). He impressed upon Wolpe the importance of this topic for psychiatric practice, which was concerned with the elimination of undesirable thoughts, actions, and feelings. Hull and other learning theorists had dealt extensively with the factors related to extinction, and developed theories of inhibitory processes to account for it. Yet Pavlov and other researchers had reported that experimental neurosis was notably difficult, if not impossible, to eliminate. Thus, an experiment on the production and elimination of neurosis appeared to have immense theoretical as well as practical significance.

Performing such an experiment posed the difficult question of which species and procedures to employ. Wolpe assiduously combed the literature for guidance. Pavlov (1927) had described a variety of methods to generate experimental neuroses in his dogs, but he reported wide individual differences and no procedure seemed generally applicable. Researchers at Cornell University reported consistent results with sheep and goats (for example Anderson and Liddell, 1935), but ovines were large animals requiring farm facilities for their maintenance. Rats were the favored subjects of Hullian researchers, but there was little in the literature to suggest that rodents were susceptible to experimental neurosis. The solution was found in *Behavior and Neurosis* by Jules Masserman (1943). Masserman reported consistent production of neurotic disturbances in common house cats when they were administered an electric shock as they opened a covered food dish. As a bonus, Masserman had couched his experiments in terms of Freudian theory involving conflict between motivational states. Here then was an opportunity to test Freudian theory against an alternative theory formulated by himself. Cats were in plentiful supply as research animals in the medical school. Supported by a small grant to purchase food for the animals, Wolpe paid for the construction of the needed equipment out of his own pocket. He began the experiment in the middle of 1947 and submitted the completed project less than a year later (Wolpe, 1948).

The year 1948 was a milestone in Wolpe's personal as well as professional life, for it was in May of that year that he married Stella Ettman. He had been attracted to her two years previously when he met her at a party given by Cynthia Edelstein. A strong, self-supporting young woman, raised by her father, she had been a high school English teacher but had come to Johannesburg when her father died. She worked as a secretary for a labour union with the wife of Leo Reyna. Wolpe's previous attempts to develop serious relationships with women had come to naught and Abe

Edelstein had counseled him to be less ardent in his pursuit of Stella. This advice apparently worked, as he courted her for a year before proposing marriage. She was very taken with this intense young researcher, and she contributed her English and secretarial skills as he wrote up his dissertation, but she demurred on his proposal of marriage. Impatient, he chanced to meet a previous girl-friend and made a date with her. When he informed Stella of this she told him to break his date, that he could consider himself engaged. They married two months later.

Cat Therapy

The grey tabby assumed her usual crouched position in the experimental cage but, instead of retiring to the corner of the room, Wolpe reached into the cage with a small wooden spatula and offered a morsel of ground beef to the animal. He had reasoned that since anxiety inhibited eating, then eating could be employed to overcome anxiety, a principle he called 'reciprocal inhibition.' But the animal made no response. He withdrew for a few minutes and then tried again. The cat eyed the bit of meat before her nose but backed away. Wolpe persisted, but so did the cat, and even after several sessions she continued to refuse to eat in the cage where she had been shocked.

The following day, the animal was not placed in the experimental cage, but left on the floor of the laboratory where she was offered bits of meat. The tabby retreated to a corner of the room and refused to eat. The next day, Wolpe brought her to a room next to the experimental room. After a few minutes, the cat began to move around, but still she avoided the proffered morsels. The following day, he brought her to a room in a different part of the building and placed her on the floor with the bits of meat. After cautiously exploring the room, the tabby approached the food, sniffed, and quickly gobbled a morsel. After several seconds, she ate another, and then another. The researcher let out a sigh and smiled as she ate the entire complement of meat pellets that he had placed on the floor. The next session she ate in the room next to the experimental room, and, in successive sessions, inside the door of the experimental room, and then closer and closer to the experimental cage, and then inside the cage itself. Gone was the wide-eyed stare, the crouching and trembling. Gone also was her cringing at his approach and her reluctance to enter the cage.

But there was one more test. Wolpe tapped the button which sounded the hooter, resulting in a very brief noise, and immediately dropped a morsel in front of the tabby. The animal crouched, staring, fur on end. Wolpe watched the clock on the wall; in less than a minute the cat slowly moved toward the food, ate it, and appeared to become calmer. The procedure was repeated, and the animal's reaction to the hooter became less pronounced each time. On subsequent sessions, Wolpe progressively increased the duration of the hooter, until finally the tabby showed no adverse reactions at all to a full 30-second blast, but rather looked around for the food to be delivered. She had been cured of her experimental neurosis.

Professional Development

Upon completion of his dissertation, Wolpe endeavored to establish himself as a contributor to Hullian learning theory and to earn some remuneration for his hard work. Encouraged by Reyna, he reworked his dissertation into a book-length manuscript entitled *Conditioning and Neurosis*. In it he reviewed the entire history of experimental neurosis, critiquing the myriad theories and formulating his own account that extended Hull's learning theory to maladaptive behavior. At Reyna's behest, he ambitiously sent the manuscript to Hull himself for review and, he hoped, recommendation for publication by Appleton-Century-Crofts, whose burgeoning 'Century Psychology Series' had published both Hull's *Principles of Behavior* (1943) and B.F. Skinner's dissertation, *The Behavior of Organisms* (1938). Hull, ill and pressured to complete his own forthcoming books, passed it along to his current publisher which asked Kenneth Spence to review it. Spence reported that there was little market for such a work, an opinion concurred in by Kenneth MacCorquodale for another publisher.

However, the following year saw the publication of two books extending Hullian theory to maladaptive behavior by two of Hull's own students, Neal Miller (Dollard and Miller, 1950) and O.H. Mowrer (1950). Their books gained wide influence, indicating the timeliness of this idea. Perhaps it was Wolpe's lack of a track record as an experimenter, or the vagueness of his formulations, or just that he was an unknown from the other side of the globe, that prevented his being the first to publish an extrapolation of Hull's theory to human neurosis. But despite their higher standing as experimenters and theorists, neither Miller nor Mowrer developed a therapy program that had the impact of Wolpe's. For treatment they could only recommend psychoanalysis, couched in Hullian terms, and Mowrer later departed from learning theory altogether in developing a program of group psychotherapy.

Still determined to make his mark as a Hullian theorist, Wolpe prepared a series of papers which presented a 'neurophysiological view' of several learning phenomena. Hull for the most part had avoided specification of neural structures, preferring to develop functional and mathematical statements of hypothetical processes to account for empirical data. Wolpe proposed to fill the space between observed stimuli and responses with chains of neurons having various arrangements of facilitatory and inhibitory synaptic connections. These were elegant wiring diagrams based on logic rather than actual anatomic structures. Published in the *Psychological Review* (Wolpe, 1949; 1950; 1952c,d,e; 1953a,b), the articles had little impact. They were referred to in a footnote as one of 'many speculative models' by Ernest Hilgard (1956, p. 454) in his comprehensive *Theories of Learning*. These works stand as a statement of Wolpe's allegiance to a physical determinist point of view, in contrast to a mentalistic approach.

With fame and fortune as a learning theorist eluding him, Wolpe started a private psychiatric practice in Johannesburg to support his new bride. However, it was her employment as a secretary that provided most of their income, because Wolpe's maverick ideas placed him outside the established referral network of psychiatrists and physicians. Eschewing traditional Freudian practice, he was determined to develop his own procedures based on his belief that anxiety was a conditioned response that could be directly disconnected from its controlling stimuli by evoking a stronger competing response. He saw only a few patients, sent by Reyna or personal friends in the medical community, and these he treated with methods that were less than satisfactory to the patients and himself. But with the same persistent self-confidence by which he knew that he was better than his grades on examination papers in college, and backed by Stella's encouragement, he spent two arduous years forging the basic structure of a new therapy system.

While rejecting Freud's theory and methods per se, Wolpe's approach retained some general influences. These included the intensive analysis of each individual case to discover the factors which underlay the manifest symptoms. Anxiety was the primary pathogenic factor in both systems. Anecdotal report of individual cases provided the main support for theory and illustration of clinical practices for both Freud and Wolpe. The notion that experiential events caused pathology in an otherwise 'normal' person was also common to both, though Wolpe rejected the Freudian emphasis on infantile and childhood sexual conflicts which warped the entire personality.

That anxiety could be overcome in the laboratory seemed clear enough. The question was, how could this process be accomplished in the multifarious situations in which neurotic patients found themselves? What method could be employed to overcome anxious arousal? Drawing directly from his dissertation experiment with cats, and from Mary Cover Jones' classic treatment of 'Little Peter' (Jones, 1924), Wolpe briefly considered the use of eating as a therapeutic tool (1958, p. x). He speculated that the reported benefits of insulin shock therapy might have been due to the patients' increased appetite and resultant eating. But faced with the impracticality of pairing anxiety-evoking situations with food, he soon gave up this line of reasoning.

He had at this time as a patient a young man who was afraid of scrutiny by strangers. What emotion could be employed to oppose this timid, fearful response? Perhaps recalling his own experiences as a shy, bookish youth, Wolpe reasoned that a feeling of defiance, of mustering oneself and railing against the fearful situations, would be effective in overcoming anxiety. Thus he instructed the young man to go to the public library, where there were 'strangers' in varying numbers depending on location and time of day, and to arouse within himself feelings of anger and to imagine shouting defiance at those who evoked fear in him. The young man did as he was told and happily reported back that he was much relieved. Similar tactics were employed with other patients having social fears, with generally positive results.

In late 1949, before his departure for the United States, Reyna presented Wolpe with a newly published book. Andrew Salter's *Conditioned Reflex Therapy* (1949) detailed a clinical approach loosely based on Pavlov's theories. A New York psychologist in private practice, Salter provided numerous case vignettes illustrating his use of 'excitatory' exercises for patients with excessively 'inhibitory' personalities. Salter's methods were akin to his own and Wolpe merged some of them into his practice, developing what he came to call 'assertive responses.' He sometimes recommended that patients read pertinent parts of Salter's book. Salter also described the use of a personality test as a diagnostic tool. Wolpe saw the value of such assessment, and began to employ personality tests not only as a diagnostic procedure but also as a gauge of therapeutic outcome.

Salter described interventions for a very broad range of problems but it became obvious to Wolpe that, while assertive responses were useful for anxiety evoked by many interpersonal situations, they were not appropriate for non-social fears. Expressing defiance toward fearsome but inanimate situations did not make sense and did not produce much change. Searching for a wider repertoire of responses to counteract anxiety, Wolpe discovered Edmund Jacobson's *Progressive Relaxation: A Psychological and Clinical Investigation of Muscular States and Their Significance in Psychological and Medical Practice* (1938). Jacobson, a physician and physiologist at the University of Chicago, provided detailed instructions on a muscular tense–release procedure. Although he did not use the term neurosis, Jacobson used his relaxation procedure with patients having a wide variety of ailments, such as hypertension, colitis, tics, phobias, and general anxiety. Fitting easily into Wolpe's theory of reciprocal inhibition (see Chapter 2), relaxation seemed an obvious anxiety-inhibitor. Jacobson's method involved scores of training exercises practiced over many months, resulting in a deep and profound state of relaxation. To this, Wolpe added the instructions that patients were to engage in relaxation in fear-provoking circumstances. However, in many instances, the anxiety proved overwhelming. Moreover, it was usually impossible for the patient to adopt the supine relaxed postures in actual fearsome situations. Nor was it possible to achieve a state of profound relaxation immediately prior to the occurrence of anxiety-evoking circumstances, which were often unpredictable.

To solve these problems, Wolpe began experimenting with hypnosis, using the induction method of Wolberg (1948). Wolpe was familiar with Hull's *Hypnosis and Suggestibility: An Experimental Approach* (1933), which presented a behavioral account of hypnotic phenomena. Hull proposed that the hypnotist's words served as conditioned stimuli to evoke responses from the subject. Salter (1944, 1949) had elaborated this approach, developing clinical procedures of 'autohypnosis' and a theory involving Pavlovian conditioning in the patient's daily routine. Wolpe took a simpler tack; he saw hypnosis as a tool whereby the therapist's verbal description of an anxiety-provoking situation could substitute for the actual event, allowing treatment to occur in the therapist's office. In addition, this allowed control of the magnitude of the anxiety response so that it could be overcome by relaxation. Wolpe also thought that hypnosis could be useful in enhancing the state of relaxation and in decreasing relaxation training time. Following a Pavlovian model, he paired a hypnotically suggested mild anxiety-evoking scene with the hypnotically enhanced state of relaxation, and found that the patient remained calm. Wolpe noted that in Pavlov's laboratory it was common practice to present only one such pairing a day, but this would lead to a prohibitively large number of treatment sessions when many anxiety scenes were involved. In his first trial of this procedure it was with some trepidation that Wolpe presented a second scene, and then a third, while the patient remained calm and relaxed. Thus was born the technique of 'systematic desensitization,' in which the deeply relaxed patient was asked to imagine a slightly upsetting scene while remaining calm, and then was presented with progressively more arousing scenes, just as the cats had eaten in the presence of progressively longer durations of the hooter. With time and experience, Wolpe found less and less need for hypnotic induction procedures, realizing that desensitization could stand on its own.

In addition to assertion and relaxation, Wolpe reasoned that sexual arousal was effective in overcoming anxiety in real-life sexual situations, as long as those situations were arranged in a progressive order. This triumvirate of relaxation, assertion and sexual arousal provided a clinical armamentarium to deal with a broad spectrum of disorders (1954).

The next few years brought a measure of success as Wolpe's acumen and industriousness began to pay off. The effectiveness of his methods earned him an increasingly successful practice, largely through referrals by satisfied patients. Many of these patients had lengthy histories of unsuccessful treatment by psychoanalysis and other traditional psychiatric methods. It was apparent that Wolpe had developed an alternative to Freudian theory and practice which often succeeded when psychoanalysis had failed, and was more efficient than the multi-year enterprise of classic psychoanalysis to boot. Almost single-handedly he had melded the theories of Pavlov and Hull with the clinical practices of Jacobson and Salter into an effective therapeutic system – which contrasted with the ineffectiveness of psychoanalysis.

Wolpe shared his formulations with the world in publications describing his theory, methods, and outcomes (1952a,b; 1954; 1955; 1956a,b). He reported success rates of around 90 percent of his cases, covering a wide variety of neurotic disorders. These publications coincided with an influential attack on traditional psychotherapy by Eysenck (1952) and formed the heart of an alternative therapeutic system. The advent of Wolpe's system shifted what began as an 'is not – is too' argument about the effectiveness of psychotherapy to more productive questions concerning relative outcomes of different therapies, and then to questions about the factors responsible for therapeutic effects (see Chapter 4). There was an element of fortunate timing, as Wolpe appeared on the scene just as the hook was extended to drag Freud off center stage.

In 1955, at the age of 40, Wolpe seemed comfortably set. He had two sons, David, born in 1951, and Allan, born in 1954. His practice was going well and he had secured a part-time academic appointment at his alma mater. There he met Stanley Rachman, who was working on his PhD in psychology. To a great extent, Rachman filled the intellectual gap left by Reyna's departure, only now Wolpe was in the mentor's role. Wolpe trained Rachman in his clinical methods and Rachman began a small clinical practice of his own. An undergraduate psychology student at the university, Arnold Lazarus, was also eager to learn this new approach to therapy and spent many hours not only at university but in the Wolpe household as well, sharing meals and playing with the children. Wolpe was reasonably secure financially, respected professionally, and had the opportunity to do both practice and teaching. But broader horizons beckoned. Before leaving the country Reyna had told him, 'You are too big for South Africa.' He had received more than 100 requests for reprints of his article describing his new approach to psychotherapy (1954), most from the United States, and Hans Eysenck had written, enlisting his participation in his crusade against traditional psychotherapy.

Reyna, who had gone to Boston University, urged Wolpe to come to the United States. He tried to obtain an invitation for Wolpe to come to Boston but was not successful. However, Reyna shared Wolpe's articles with a colleague, John Brodbeck, who in 1955 was one of the first group of fellows at Stanford University's new Center for Advanced Studies in the Behavioral Sciences. Impressed, Brodbeck proposed Wolpe for a fellowship to the Center. He notified Wolpe in Johannesburg of this proposal and asked for his resumé. Wolpe sent off the material and sat back to wait. Nothing was heard for several months, until a visiting psychiatrist from New York encouraged Wolpe to be assertive and inquire into the matter. Wolpe wrote the Center and learned by return mail that he had indeed been accepted as a Fellow for the year 1956/7.

The Great Trek

Some 50 years after his grandparents had arrived with their children, seeking freedom and opportunity in the land of gold and diamonds, Wolpe, with Stella and their small sons, sailed for the Golden State of California. On their journey, they visited London, the capital of the former empire which had colonized both countries, and over the next decade they were to retrace their steps more than once before settling in Philadelphia, the city where American liberty was born. It was fitting that this key contributor to the revolution in psychotherapy followed a geographical path shadowed by political revolutionaries.

London
At Eysenck's invitation, Wolpe visited the citadel of anti-Freudian rhetoric on his way to and from the United States. Hans Jurgen Eysenck had completed his PhD in 1940 at the University of London under the famed Sir Cyril Burt. Like Burt, Eysenck was

interested in the biological and genetic bases of behavior, but he integrated this approach with Hullian learning theory. These systems became the foundation for his encyclopedic research into personality and psychopathology. During the Second World War, Eysenck attended informal seminars held by Alexander Herzberg, a German psychoanalyst who had fled the Nazis (Kazdin, 1979, pp. 160–7). Herzberg had developed an unorthodox treatment method which, in contrast to the 'talking cure,' prescribed active participation by the patient in a series of graduated tasks related to his or her symptoms (Herzberg, 1945). Eysenck decided that the graduated task method was better explained by learning than by psychodynamic theory.

After the end of World War II, Eysenck became head of the Department of Psychology in the Institute of Psychiatry at the Maudsley Hospital, a psychiatric teaching facility associated with the University of London. There he collected a group of clinical researchers who, beginning in the early 1950s, employed graduated tasks, massed practice, and other techniques which they derived from learning theory (for example Jones, 1956; Meyer, 1957; Shapiro, 1957; Yates, 1958b). In 1952, Eysenck launched his far-reaching attack on psychoanalytic therapy and encouraged Wolpe to join him as an ally in this battle. During his visit, Wolpe's seminars on his techniques were eagerly attended by the Maudsley staff, who added them to their repertoire and proceeded to do critical analyses of them. Wolpe profited from discussing Eysenck's theories of personality and incorporated some of their features into his own system.

Stanford, California

The Center for Advanced Studies in the Behavioral Sciences, nestled in the northern California hills behind the Stanford University campus, was an idyllic place for quiet reflection and active production. A group of Fellows was invited each year to meet each other and follow their muse. No specific outcome was required and support was generous. Among those present in Wolpe's group were the noted philosophers Karl Popper and Charles Wallace, and psychologists Fred Attneave, Daniel Berlyne, Ernest Hilgard, and Edward Newcomb. No direct collaboration occurred but Wolpe developed friendships that endured for many years; he credited his colleagues for their critical contributions as he developed his manuscript. Stella and the boys also fell in love with the climate, both physical and social, of the Stanford area.

Wolpe seized the opportunity the Center offered, collating and adding to his previous writings to produce the manuscript that was published the following year by Stanford University Press – *Psychotherapy by Reciprocal Inhibition* (1958). Wolpe toured the San Francisco bay area, meeting with professional psychologists and faculty members of the many universities in the area. At the University of California at Berkeley he was particularly pleased to meet the noted cognitive learning theorist Edward C. Tolman, and Mary Cover Jones, whom he esteemed as a pioneer in the new psychotherapy. Encouraged by the positive reception of his ideas, Wolpe embarked on a lecture tour, taking the Sunset Limited train throughout the southern United States, speaking to numerous professional groups and college faculties. At the University of Virginia, Ian Stevenson, Chairman of the Department of Psychiatry, offered him a position, but Wolpe decided to see what other options might be open to him. All too soon the year was over and the family reluctantly left California to return to South Africa.

Back in Johannesburg in late 1957, Wolpe again took up clinical practice and teaching, resuming his collaboration with Rachman and Lazarus, who was now a graduate student in the psychology department. Upon completing his PhD in 1956, Rachman had taken over the treatment of some of Wolpe's patients during the latter's stay in California. Rachman and Lazarus both engaged in the practice of Wolpe's methods and were the first persons, after Wolpe himself, to publish a clinical report of their effectiveness (Lazarus and Rachman, 1957). In 1959 Rachman left for England to work with Eysenck at the Maudsley. Wolpe supervised Lazarus' doctoral dissertation, an experiment notable for several innovations (Lazarus, 1961). It was the first study to do a prospective comparison of systematic desensitization and 'dynamic' therapy, the first to employ direct observations of behavior as an outcome measure, and the first to try group desensitization. Lazarus (1958) was also the first to use the term 'behavior therapy' to differentiate the empirical, learning-theory-based treatment from the traditional psychodynamic variety.

Eysenck picked up the term 'behavior therapy' in an article contrasting this new approach with Freudian psychotherapy (Eysenck, 1959a). In 1960, Eysenck edited a book with this title, which drew together the various techniques developed by the Maudsley group, Wolpe, and others. The chapter on desensitization was written by Lazarus and Rachman (1960).

Charlottesville, Virginia

After their warm acceptance in California, the dearth of intellectual stimulation, provinciality, overt racism and underlying anti-Semitism that characterized much of society in Johannesburg were all too apparent to Joseph and Stella. They thought seriously about returning to the United States. Ian Stevenson had been persistent in his offers, increasing the salary each time Wolpe refused. After much deliberation, Wolpe and his family moved to Charlottesville, Virginia in January 1960.

There he was regarded as a representative of the new behavioral approach to psychotherapy and was accorded polite respect if not warm acceptance in the psychoanalytically-dominated Department of Psychiatry. He had few specific teaching duties other than supervising a few residents; he devoted most of his time to seeing patients and to writing, as well as presenting seminars and demonstrations of his methods to academic and professional audiences. He added to the growing polemic chorus of behavior therapy against psychoanalysis (1960a,b; 1961a,b,c; Wolpe and Rachman, 1960; see Chapter 4), increasing his isolation in the Department, which had a gentlemanly agreement to accommodate all points of view. While Stevenson was enthusiastic about the new behavior therapy he was not about to join the revolution against Freud. Rather he envisioned an amalgamation of the new and the old in a kind of super therapy. Wolpe was further dismayed to learn that Stevenson's penchant for the nontraditional extended to beliefs in parapsychology and reincarnation. Although they collaborated on a paper describing the treatment of homosexuality (Stevenson and Wolpe, 1960), Stevenson was not a bedfellow with whom Wolpe felt comfortable. In addition, Charlottesville society was steeped in the tradition of the old Confederacy; its attitudes towards class and race were not much different from those of Johannesburg. Despite periodic consultations with Reyna, who traveled down from Boston, Wolpe was very much on his own. It was clear that Charlottesville was not the promised land.

Wolpe's major accomplishment at Virginia was the organization of a conference in the spring of 1962, with the help of Stevenson and Reyna, entitled *The Conditioning Therapies: The Challenge in Psychotherapy* (Wolpe et al., 1964). The conference was an eclectic affair which spanned the past, present, and future of the rapidly developing field of behavior therapy. The past was represented by Howard Liddell and W. Horsley Gantt, who described their Pavlovian experimental neurosis research, and by Andrew Salter, who described his Pavlovian theory of therapy. The future was represented by Peter J. Lang, who presented his controlled experiments into the efficacy of systematic desensitization employing snake-avoidant college students, and by Arthur J. Bachrach, who spoke of the clinical relevance of operant conditioning concepts and

procedures. Stevenson's comments about the need of research comparing psychotherapies also proved prophetic.

After the conference, Salter suggested to Wolpe that they form a
conditioning therapy center in New York City. But the two strongly
opinionated men could not reach agreement on the appropriate
theoretical foundation for such an undertaking. Salter insisted on
his Pavlovian interpretations of excitation and inhibition, while
Wolpe maintained his Hullian orientation. While Wolpe had been
open in citing Salter's contributions to his thinking, the older man
remained concerned with his own pioneer status and the two parted
with some negative feelings. Salter returned to his practice in New
York and Wolpe continued his search for a center to teach and
practice behavior therapy.

Wolpe decided to give London another look. He had maintained
a cordial correspondence with Eysenck. Aubrey Lewis, Chair of the
Psychiatry Department of the University of London, whom Wolpe
met at the American Psychiatric Association convention, also
encouraged him to try to develop a center in London. So Wolpe
undertook a one-year unpaid leave of absence from Virginia
beginning in the summer of 1962. But the year was a bleak one as
Wolpe was forced to support his family with earnings from a
hastily arranged private practice in London. Wolpe had the idea of
a facility for the treatment of patients who had been unsuccessful
with other forms of psychotherapy. Eysenck provided him with
introductions to some representatives of government and business,
but financial arrangements for a treatment center could not be
worked out. The Maudsley Hospital itself was well stocked with
Eysenck's group of clinical researchers who had begun to provide
training for psychologists and psychiatrists interested in the new
behavior therapy. There appeared to be no additional room in
England for a person with Wolpe's interests and skills. Other than
an article (1963a) that he contributed to the first edition of
Eysenck's new journal, *Behaviour Research and Therapy*, Wolpe
had little to show for this excursion.

To make matters worse, upon returning to Charlottesville in
1963, Wolpe found that Stevenson had left on sabbatical and that
departmental politics were quite under the control of the psycho-
dynamically-oriented faculty. Wolpe's teaching duties were dras-
tically curtailed and he was, more than ever, an outsider. He busied
himself with his practice, speaking, writing, and in looking for a new
position. He completed a number of expository articles on behavior
therapy for various audiences (1963b; 1964a,b,c,d,e; 1965a,b;
1966a,b), edited the conference proceedings for a book (Wolpe et
al., 1964), and did some reviews and critical commentaries (1964f,g;

1965c,d). He performed a quantitative analysis of desensitization data (1963c), collaborated in the construction of a fear survey schedule (Wolpe and Lang, 1964), and described the use of behavior therapy with sexual disorders (1964h), drug addiction (1965e), and stuttering (1966c). Notably, he engaged in a correspondence collaboration with his former student Arnold Lazarus, putting together a practical textbook of behavior therapy techniques (Wolpe and Lazarus, 1966). What for most people would be considered a very productive period, Wolpe regarded as marking time. He continued to look for a chance to set up a behavior therapy treatment and training center.

A beginning effort was the 'June Institute.' Wolpe had received numerous inquiries from practicing clinicians and psychology graduate students concerning training in behavior therapy methods. In the summer of 1965, he offered his first one-month behavior therapy training seminar. There were over a dozen participants, coming from Europe and Latin America as well as the United States. The first group included Joseph Cautela, Alan Goldstein, and Dorothy Susskind, who were later to make their own notable contributions to behavior therapy. The experience of Goldstein is illustrative of those heady early days. A graduate student in clinical psychology, Goldstein was discouraged with the psychodynamic model and found an exciting alternative in Wolpe's 1958 book. He wrote to Wolpe, who was cordial in reply, and Goldstein soon moved his young family to Virginia while he studied with Wolpe. The Institute was conducted with Wolpe lecturing on theoretical and technical issues in the mornings, and in the afternoon serving as co-therapist with students, or observing therapy conducted by pairs of participants, with volunteer patients. Evenings were spent in socializing and discussion, a highlight being the South African curries prepared by Wolpe himself, while Stella served as a mother hen for all involved. This pleasant experience reinforced Wolpe's determination to find a favourable environment for his training program.

The 1965 American Psychiatric Association convention in New York offered several possibilities. After a meeting he had organized for persons interested in behavior therapy, Wolpe had a drink with R. Bruce Sloane, who was about to become Chairman of the Psychiatry Department at Temple University. Sloane had trained at London's Maudsley Hospital where he had become acquainted with Eysenck and his group. Sloane was interested in broadening the psychoanalytic focus of the Temple Department and invited Wolpe to visit him. Martin Orne of the University of Pennsylvania also expressed interest in Wolpe joining them, and Joel Elkes invited Wolpe to visit him at Johns Hopkins in Baltimore.

Philadelphia, Pennsylvania

Wolpe went to Philadelphia for an interview at Temple University School of Medicine, and then to Hopkins. The psychoanalytic faculty of Temple's Department of Psychiatry rejected Wolpe, but he was invited to meet with the Dean and an appointment in the Department of Behavioral Sciences was discussed. Despite the opposition of the psychiatry faculty, which was nothing new, Wolpe was impressed with the level of intellectual activity at Temple, as well as the Philadelphia area in general, and so accepted a position in Behavioral Sciences. Within six months Sloane had effected a shakeup in the Psychiatry Department and Wolpe was cross-appointed in both departments. With Sloane's help, a Behavior Therapy Unit was organized in 1966. At last it seemed that Wolpe's dream of a behavior therapy training and treatment center would be realized.

The Behavior Therapy Unit was established as an outpatient treatment program at the Eastern Pennsylvania Psychiatric Institute (EPPI), a state-financed facility under the auspices of Temple University. As a condition of his appointment, Wolpe negotiated a position for his former student Arnold Lazarus to assist in the development and conduct of the Unit. Lazarus had taken over Wolpe's practice when the latter left South Africa for Virginia. He later followed Wolpe's footsteps to Stanford, in 1963, where he had a one-year visiting appointment in the Department of Psychology. When his contract expired with no offer of a tenured position, Lazarus returned to South Africa where he maintained a clinical practice and inquired about positions in the United States. He then joined David Fischer, whom he met while at Stanford, at the Behavior Therapy Institute, a small group practice near San Francisco, California, but continued to seek a more prestigious position. Although Wolpe and Lazarus had not worked together since Lazarus' dissertation nearly a decade earlier, their long-distance collaboration on the textbook had gone well and Wolpe anticipated an effective partnership in developing the Behavior Therapy Unit at Temple.

Instead, Wolpe described the year after Lazarus' arrival as 'the worst year of my life.' Given the bleak times he had experienced in Johannesburg starting his practice, or in Charlottesville or London, this was a surprising statement. In the earlier situations Wolpe had been sustained by the hope for something better in the future, but at

Temple his long-held dream was at last within his grasp, only to be rudely shattered by someone whom he had mentored and thought he could trust. Wolpe's deeply felt certitude, which had enabled him to stand alone so many years against the forces of the traditional psychotherapists, perhaps worked against his establishing a collaborative relationship. He had expected Lazarus to be a junior partner, something of the student he had been so many years earlier, while Lazarus saw himself as surpassing his former teacher. Lazarus had begun to criticize Wolpe's conditioning model as the foundation of behavior therapy and espoused a broader approach (Lazarus, 1966; 1967). To most it appeared that the rift was based on a theoretical dispute between the originator of an approach and his student who wanted to go in a new direction, similar to the rift between Freud and Jung. But for Wolpe, it was not theoretical or technical differences that caused the split; he felt that Lazarus behaved in ways that made personal and professional interactions impossible. By the middle of 1968 the two were not speaking to each other, passing each other silently in the halls of the Unit. This unpleasant situation lasted until 1970 when Lazarus was denied tenure at Temple and departed (Wolpe was not on the tenure committee, but certainly lent whatever influence he had to oppose the appointment). Cyril Franks, who had taken his degree with Eysenck at the Maudsley, and who was at Rutgers University in New Jersey, befriended Lazarus and secured a position for him there.

After the split with Lazarus, Wolpe quickly put together his own textbook, *The Practice of Behavior Therapy* (1969), to replace their earlier joint effort. With Reyna's mediation, a letter of agreement was drawn up which specified the contributions of each. Lazarus followed soon after with a text of his own, *Behavior Therapy and Beyond* (1971), in which he caricatured Wolpe's position as narrow, mechanistic conditioning that neglected relationship and cognitive factors.

Despite this shaky beginning, the Behavior Therapy Unit produced many notable accomplishments. The June Institute continued each summer for the next decade and a half, enrolling about 30 participants each year. In addition, about 10 students were accepted each year into the doctoral programs of the Departments of Psychology and Psychiatry. Wolpe initially obtained some National Institutes of Health training grant funds for students, but he never mastered the grant-application writing skills for training or research support which formed the backbone of the American medical and psychological academic enterprise. Thus the Unit was always at the mercy of administrators who controlled the purse strings.

Throughout the 1970s, state and federal support for research and training in mental health was fairly generous and consistent, and the Behavior Therapy Unit flourished.

A number of persons connected with the Unit were successful in obtaining research grants and conducting clinical studies of issues within behavior therapy. Foremost was the Department Chair himself, R. Bruce Sloane, whose recruitment of Wolpe was motivated in part by a desire to conduct a controlled comparison of psychoanalytic and behavior therapy (see Chapter 4). Planning for this landmark study began immediately after Wolpe arrived at Temple. Neil Yorkston, another Maudsley export, soon joined the team. Wolpe served as the senior behavior therapist on the project, with Michael Serber (a new member of the Psychiatry Department faculty) and Arnold Lazarus participating as the other two behavior therapists.

Alan Goldstein was hired when Lazarus left, becoming Wolpe's 'right-hand man' in the Unit. Goldstein was but the first of a number of researchers, including Diane Chambless, Edna Foa, and Gail Steketee, who secured research grants to conduct widely influential studies on the behavioral assessment and treatment of agoraphobic and obsessive–compulsive disorders. Wolpe, for the most part, was not directly involved in these formal research programs. He continued to provide training at the June Institutes and clinical supervision for some psychiatric residents and psychology doctoral interns. His primary activity was writing and speaking to professional audiences throughout the United States, Europe and Latin America, providing critical guidance for the rapidly expanding field of behavior therapy. Whether the audience numbered five or five hundred, Wolpe was ready to speak on behalf of behavior therapy. Some observers noted that his speeches, which focused on research results, tended to be rather dull, but he was exceptionally effective in discussion formats and talking one-on-one. His contributions to the development of professional behavior therapy in several countries have been gratefully acknowledged (Distinguished Scientific Award, 1980; Seiden, 1994). Stella continued to be a sustaining influence during good times and bad, and accompanied him on trips whenever possible.

In 1979, Wolpe was recognized with the 'Distinguished Scientific Award for the Applications of Psychology' from the American Psychological Association:

> For his outstanding contribution to the understanding and modification of abnormal behavior, and in particular his pioneering work that led to the establishment of behavior therapy. He played a vital role in developing the theory and practice of behavior therapy, currently one of the

most widely employed of the therapeutic procedures. Wolpe's therapeutic methods, especially desensitization, have been successfully used to reduce fear and distress in thousands of patients. His achievements are all the more remarkable for having been accomplished while in geographical and intellectual isolation. (Distinguished Scientific Award, 1980)

After this pinnacle, the Behavior Therapy Unit suffered a decline. The 1980 presidential election in the United States presaged a major shift in national priorities, as funding for education and mental health decreased markedly. Clinical operations at the Behavior Therapy Unit became more dependent on patient fees, which were insufficient to sustain day-to-day operations, let alone training activities. Wolpe's colleagues with research grants provided the lifeblood for EPPI and assumed an increasingly important role. Moreover, in 1982, Wolpe reached the mandatory retirement age of 67; he was allowed to continue as an 'exception,' but at reduced pay and, undoubtedly, at reduced status. A final blow was the break-up of his relationship with Alan Goldstein. Wolpe felt that Goldstein's research program in effect had created a separate, autonomous unit that threatened the original one. In addition, a personal disagreement between the two men made it impossible for them to work together and, with regret, Goldstein left EPPI to set up an independent program of research and practice in the Philadelphia area.

Los Angeles, California

Finally, Stella, in poor health, prevailed upon her husband to step back from the fray. She had wanted to return to California ever since their days at Stanford. Their sons David, an actor and play-wright, and Allen, a physician, both lived in southern California. An offer of an emeritus position from Pepperdine University provided Wolpe with a comfortable environment in which to continue his writing and travels, and in 1988 they moved to Los Angeles. Unfortunately, Stella died of lymphoma a short time after their move. Saddened by the loss of his strong partner of 40 years, Wolpe was no less determined to continue the work he had begun in California 30 years earlier. He maintained a vigorous pace of writing and speaking on behalf of behavior therapy.

Concurrent Developments in Behavior Therapy

An old proverb states, 'A rising tide raises all boats.' In the two decades after Wolpe's first visit to the United States and the publication of *Psychotherapy by Reciprocal Inhibition*, there was a flood of contributions to the new behavior therapy. Wolpe's eminence increased with its growth. Some of these developments were variations on Wolpe's ideas and methods, while others were completely independent. Whether replication, modification, disputation, or novel contribution, these expansions comprised a broad intellectual and professional environment in which Wolpe refined his own theories and practices. Four of the most important areas of progress were the growth of 'behavior modification,' the experimental study of systematic desensitization, the establishment of a professional organization for behavior therapy, and the 'cognitive revolution.'

Behavior Modification

During the 1960s, the operant conditioning theory and methods of B.F. Skinner (1938; Ferster and Skinner, 1957) had flourished in many American university departments of experimental psychology. This tradition emphasized the direct empirical demonstration of relationships between environmental factors and behavior, and eschewed the inference of hypothetical psychological or neurological constructs, such as employed in Hullian or Pavlovian theory, to explain such relationships (Skinner, 1950). Skinner's vision extended beyond the animal laboratory, and, in response to the horrors of the Second World War, he speculated on the societal importance of operant conditioning (Skinner, 1948; 1953). Although Skinner offered no specific programs to remedy individual or social problems, many other investigators began to explore the relevance of his system for human behavior. The first efforts were directed toward the conveniently measured motoric performance of human subjects in larger versions of the experimental chamber that Skinner devised to train rats and pigeons, such as the work of Ogden Lindsley with psychotic inpatients (Lindsley, 1956), or that of Sidney Bijou with nursery school children (Bijou, 1957). Incidentally, it was in this context that the term 'behavior therapy' first appeared (Skinner et al., 1953), though it did not gain currency until its later use by Eysenck (1960).

Applications of operant methods were soon directed toward more socially relevant behaviors and environments. Given the importance of environmental factors in Skinner's system, it was only natural that operant conditioners began their clinical efforts with individuals over whom a great deal of control already existed, such as schizophrenic patients in mental institutions (Allyon, 1963) or retarded children in classrooms (Bijou et al., 1966). Typically, these were people for whom conventional psychiatric and psychological services were ineffective or nonexistent. Thus there was little entrenched opposition to early operant conditioning treatment programs, and centers of training and application proliferated throughout the United States.

Because of its focus on relatively circumscribed 'target' behaviors, the operant approach was labeled 'behavior modification' (for example, Ullman and Krasner, 1965). The operant treatment of psychotic, retarded, autistic, and other institutionalized patient groups nicely complemented the Wolpian focus on outpatient neurotics, providing a broad spectrum of learning-based therapies for a wide range of clinical problems. Wolpe's theories and methods were integrated into this wider framework by textbook authors and university training programs, and the terms 'behavior modification' and 'behavior therapy' began to be used interchangeably to denote this broader system.

But in the early 1970s, 'behavior modification' was subjected to critical scrutiny following increasing concern about patient rights and confusion about invasive medical procedures such as lobotomy and electroconvulsive shock (Subcommittee on Constitutional Rights, 1974; Stoltz, 1977). As a result, the more benign-sounding 'behavior therapy' became the generic term for the field. Those maintaining a strict operant orthodoxy reserved the term 'applied behavior analysis' to designate their speciality (Baer et al., 1968). The *Journal of Applied Behavior Analysis* was founded in 1968, an offshoot of the more basic science *Journal of the Experimental Analysis of Behavior* begun a decade earlier.

Reyna, who had become friends with Skinner in Boston, kept Wolpe apprised of developments in the applied operant field and Wolpe supported its inclusion under the rubric of behavior therapy. They had invited Arthur Bachrach to the 1962 'conditioning therapies' conference at Virginia; he described the early operant conditioning work of Teodoro Allyon with schizophrenic inpatients (Bachrach, 1964), and Wolpe consulted with Bachrach in the pioneering operant behavioral treatment of an anorexic patient (Bachrach et al., 1965). Another operant conditioning proponent, Joseph Cautela, participated in the first June Institute in Charlottesville (Cautela, 1990). Cautela had completed his doctorate in experimental psychology under Reyna at Boston University and had worked with Ogden Lindsley, Skinner's student and colleague (Cautela, 1990). From these two influences Cautela developed a 'covert conditioning' model of learning and therapy, according to which imaginal performance and consequences lead to changes in overt behavior (Cautela, 1972). Although Wolpe did not agree with all of Cautela's theoretical interpretations, the two maintained a positive relationship and Wolpe included covert conditioning procedures in his behavior therapy textbooks.

In fact, Wolpe included a cursory chapter on operant principles and techniques in all editions of his behavior therapy textbooks, emphasizing their use for psychotic, autistic, and delinquent populations. However, he maintained they were of relatively minor importance for the emotional problems which characterized neurotic disorders, and that effects attributed to reinforcement were better explained by reciprocal inhibition. Regardless of theoretical differences, Wolpe maintained congenial relationships with those promoting the operant approach.

Experimental Studies of Systematic Desensitization
Topics for psychology doctoral dissertations often follow trends as particular theories and methodologies wax and wane in popularity. A favored topic for clinical doctoral dissertations in the 1950s was the relationship between scores on an anxiety questionnaire and some aspect of conditioning as a test of predictions from Hullian theory (Spence and Taylor, 1953). This vein had been about mined out when David Lazovik and Peter J. Lang at the University of Pittsburgh struck a new lode with their experimentally controlled investigation of systematic desensitization treatment for fear of snakes in college students (Lazovik and Lang, 1960; Lang and Lazovik, 1963; Lang, 1964). Systematic desensitization was a clearly specified clinical technique which could be analyzed into its component parts and compared with placebo or alternative techniques. College students with circumscribed fears were far more numerous and convenient than actual neurotic patients and were of more obvious clinical relevance than cats or rats. Their overt responses to feared situations could be directly observed, and they could provide subjective reports and physiologic measures. 'Analogue research,' as this endeavor was termed, was the perfect medium to test propositions about treatment effectiveness and predictions from Wolpe's or alternative theories.

Wolpe's theories and procedures were in the right place at the right time as the post-war demand for doctoral training in psychology mushroomed. Over the next decade hundreds of analogue studies appeared. Some, such as the dissertations of Gordon Paul (1966) at the University of Illinois and Gerald Davison (1968) at Stanford, were carefully crafted paragons of experimental rigor, while others were of lesser quality. A discussion of the major issues connected with analogue research will be provided in Chapter 4; the important point here is that this line of inquiry strongly reinforced Wolpe's fundamental role in behavior therapy. While Wolpe neither invented nor employed the analogue research paradigm, it established systematic desensitization as the first empirically validated clinical intervention and the benchmark against which other procedures were compared. It was a mixed blessing, however. On the one hand, analogue research made Wolpe a 'household name' in psychology departments and textbooks throughout the world, but on the other, it reinforced the notion that he contributed only a simple treatment for simple problems.

Professional Organizations and Journals

Dorothy Susskind, another participant in Wolpe's first June Institute in Charlottesville, was a psychologist in private practice in New York City in the early 1960s. Although Wolpe's lone practice in Johannesburg was a decade earlier and half a globe distant, the acceptance of behavior therapy among the professional community in New York was no different. Susskind felt the need for an organization which could provide a means of communication and mutual support among behavior therapists. She was acquainted with Cyril Franks, at Rutgers University in New Jersey, across the river from New York City, and, in 1965, invited him and others in the area interested in behavior therapy to meet at her apartment on a regular basis to discuss treatments and develop strategies to promote behavior therapy (Cautela, 1990; Franks, 1993). Participants included Andrew Salter and Herbert Fensterheim in New York, Joseph Cautela from Boston, and Leonard Krasner and Gerald Davison, who had left Stanford University to take positions at the University of New York in Stony Brook. Wolpe and Lazarus, both now in Philadelphia, also took part on a regular basis, although their personal animosity added an uncomfortable note to the meetings.

While in London, Franks had been involved with the British Association for the Advancement of Science, an organization that provided publicity for scientific achievements, and from this he derived the name Association for the Advancement of the Behavioral Therapies (AABT) for the group meeting in Susskind's apartment. The group sponsored symposia, often in the format of debates with psychotherapists, published a newsletter, with Franks as editor, and organized a special interest group within the American Psychological Association (APA). AABT held its first national convention concurrently with the APA annual convention in 1967. Franks served as the first President with Susskind as Executive Secretary. In recognition of his pioneering status and the prestige of his medical background, Franks encouraged Wolpe to stand for President of AABT in 1968. To Wolpe's chagrin, Lazarus followed him in this post in 1969. Somewhat ironically, the same year saw the name of the organization changed to the 'Association for the Advancement of Behavior Therapy,' rather than 'Therapies,' in response to an article pointing to the common heritage of learning theory (Wilson and Evans, 1967).

The growing membership of AABT was comprised primarily of academic and clinical psychologists, and Wolpe wished to promote something similar within the psychiatric community. Accordingly, he founded the Behavior Therapy and Research Society in 1970, which met in conjunction with the annual conventions of the 'other APA,' the American Psychiatric Association. It was dedicated to promoting research and developing the profession of behavior therapy within psychiatry. He and Reyna began the *Journal of Behavior Therapy and Experimental Psychiatry* as the official publication of this society. In the same year, the *AABT Newsletter* evolved into the journal *Behavior Therapy*, with Franks as first editor, although its editorship has changed regularly, reflecting growth and changes within AABT. The Behavior Therapy and Research Society did not achieve its desired niche in psychiatry, which seemed to overleap the developing science of behavior in its transition from the psychoanalytic couch to chemical treatment of behavior. However, the Society continued under the guidance of Wolpe and Reyna to publish the *Journal*, to sponsor discussion panels at AABT, and to designate a roster of 'clinical fellows' who met training standards in the practice of behavior therapy.

The Cognitive Revolution

Having struck a telling if not fatal blow to psychoanalysis, Wolpe was soon faced with another challenge toward which he directed his critical efforts. This challenge concerned the role of cognition in the control of neurotic behavior and the necessity of cognitive interventions for effective therapy (see Chapter 4). Research and debate on cognitive factors resulted in a proliferation of theories and therapy programs. This was regarded as growth or maturation of behavior therapy by those espousing cognitive approaches. But Wolpe, for the most part, viewed these efforts as unnecessary or counterproductive.

Historically, tension within psychology over the role of internal processes had existed ever since John B. Watson (1913) coined the term 'behaviorism' in his attack on 'mentalism.' In its broadest outline, behaviorism was concerned with the formulation of principles which explained, predicted, and allowed control of the interaction of an organism with its environment, hence the label 'stimulus–response psychology.' Three major though not mutually exclusive points of view contended for primacy within behavioristic psychology: one held that sufficient lawful relationships existed between the environment and overt behavior for investigation of internal processes to be unnecessary; another held that physiologic (neurologic or genetic) structures and activity were essential to account for behavior; and the third held that hypothetical mediating functions were required to express the relationship between environment and behavior. The student of learning theory will recognize the first viewpoint as that of B.F. Skinner, the second as that of Pavlov and Watson, and the third as that of Hull and Spence. Within experimental psychology, focused as it was on animal learning, these formulations dominated cognitive theories, such as those of Tolman or the Gestalt tradition. Wolpe, consistent with his medical training, favored the physiologic view; as noted earlier, he sought to translate Hull's hypothetical constructs into neurophysiologic terms.

The 1960s saw a resurgence of interest in cognitive processes which was related to several factors: more research was conducted with verbal human rather than animal subjects; expanding computer capabilities provided information-processing models for human behavior; and the cultural zeitgeist of individuality and freedom contended with the determinism implied by behaviorism. Influential books included *Plans and the Structure of Behavior* by the group of Fellows who followed Wolpe's tenure at the Center for Advanced Studies two years later (Miller et al., 1960), and Ulrich Neisser's *Cognitive Psychology* (1967). Experimental cognitive psychology provided abundant methods, data, and concepts concerning cognitive structures and processes involved in perception and memory. However, little of this was employed directly by 'cognitive behavior' therapists. Instead, they developed a variety of cognitive formulations related to clinical phenomena such as anxiety and depression, united only by the view that conditioning models were at best inadequate, and at worst irrelevant, for the explanation and modification of human behavior.

Another factor contributing to the interest in cognition may also have been a tradition of revolution. Wolpe and Eysenck conceived of behavior therapy as a revolt against psychotherapy, entirely overturning the old, and this fervor seemed to characterize behavior therapy. Developments that could appear to be evolutionary modifications and accretions were presented in revolutionary terms by the 'young turks.' The contingencies of the profession rewarded innovation and creation of separate programs more than systematic development and building on precedent. Thus it was that the rapidly growing interest in cognitive processes and procedures was announced as a 'cognitive revolution,' overturning the recently established behavior therapy 'traditions' (Mahoney, 1977; Franks and Rosenbaum, 1983).

A host of clinical researchers and theorists who started within the conditioning tradition evolved into cognitive theorists, producing a Babel of cognitive behavior therapy systems. Albert Bandura's research on modeling led to a cognitive theory that supplanted conditioning models (Bandura, 1965; 1969, pp. 118–51). He later produced 'self-efficacy' theory (Bandura, 1977) which provided a cognitive framework for many behavioral and cognitive interventions. Arnold Lazarus developed 'broad spectrum' and 'multimodal' therapy, though his 'technical eclecticism' ranged beyond cognitive as well as conditioning theory (Lazarus, 1966; 1971; 1976). Marvin Goldfried (1971) and Richard Suinn (Suinn and Richardson, 1971) both emphasized the cognitive elements in systematic desensitization which they elaborated into therapy programs called 'systematic rational restructuring' (Goldfried, 1979) and 'anxiety management training' (Suinn and Richardson, 1971). Other cognitive therapies had their roots in operant conditioning theory, including Joseph Cautela's 'covert conditioning' (Cautela, 1972; Cautela and Wall, 1980) and Donald Meichenbaum's 'self-instruction therapy' and 'stress inoculation training' (Meichenbaum, 1973; 1977). Skinner's early musing on self-control (Skinner, 1953, pp. 228–9) was the seed for a number of self-management programs involving cognitive factors (for example Kanfer, 1970; Mahoney and Thoreson, 1974; Mahoney, 1977).

Two major contributors from outside the behavioral tradition were the rational–emotive therapy (RET) of Albert Ellis (1962) and the cognitive therapy of Aaron Beck (1972). Both men were formally trained in psychoanalysis and had begun their clinical practice as psychodynamic therapists, but both independently had rejected the emphasis on deeply buried unconscious determinants of behavior in favor of conscious, cognitive factors.

Ellis (1957) had conducted a comparative study of an early version of RET that was mentioned favorably by Eysenck in the same article in which he extolled Wolpe's initial work. Eysenck noted, 'Ellis does not attempt to derive his rational psychotherapy from learning theory, but this should not be impossible' (Eysenck, 1961b, p. 719). Instead, Ellis developed his system without regard to learning theory (Ellis, 1962; Ellis and Harper, 1965). He founded his Institute for Rational Living in New York City, where he conducted therapist training and workshops in RET. A colorful and forceful writer and speaker, Ellis produced numerous works for popular as well as professional audiences, promoting a general philosophy for living as opposed to a mere psychotherapy program

(Dryden and Ellis, 1988). Many behavior therapists noted the behavioral features of some of his methods and adopted elements of his theory and procedures, although Ellis was critical of this watered-down approach (Ellis, 1980).

Beck was an academic clinician and researcher at the University of Pennsylvania in Philadelphia, close in distance though far in spirit from Wolpe at Temple. Beck's early interest was in cognitive distortions related to depression (Beck, 1963; 1972) which he expanded to include anxiety disorders (Beck, 1976; Beck and Emery, 1985). He and his colleagues initiated an influential series of outcome studies for the cognitive behavioral treatment of depression (Rush et al., 1977) culminating in the first large-scale clinical trial of a psychotherapeutic intervention (Elkin et al., 1985). Beck (1970) was quick to recognize areas of similarity between cognitive therapy and behavior therapy and explicitly included behavioral treatments in his program for depression (Beck et al., 1979). Beck's congeniality and rigorous empirical studies did much to forge the connections between cognitive and behavior therapies.

Both Ellis and Beck were invited frequently to speak at the annual conventions of AABT. The magnitude of the cognitive revolution is indicated by the fact that there was a movement in this organization to change its name to the Association for Behavior and Cognitive Therapy. By vote of its membership in 1993, this name change was rejected.

Wolpe, who had stood alone against the psychoanalysts in Johannesburg and Charlottesville, was not about to back down from this challenge, and turned his writing and speaking efforts toward criticizing cognitive revolutionaries. He maintained that he had adequately included cognitions in his therapy system, such as the clarification of misconceptions for anxiety based on misinformation. He objected to the philosophical implications of a mental sphere of existence apart from the physical universe, maintaining that cognitive phenomena were ultimately reducible to neurophysiologic processes explained by conditioning. He concluded that cognitive factors were important in the disorders of some patients and conditioning factors were preeminent in others, and that wholesale cognitive treatment of patients without regard to this distinction was countertherapeutic (see Chapter 4).

Summary and Conclusions

Born to the *litvak* tradition of scholarly analysis and exposition in a family of Lithuanian immigrants, Joseph Wolpe was raised in the reserved English tradition in the newly formed Union of South

Africa. A bookish youth, accustomed to independent study, he won recognition from family and teachers for his intellectual accomplishments, forging a supreme self-confidence that sustained him in times of adversity and opposition. As a young medical student he enjoyed philosophical and theoretical debate on the foundations of human behavior, favoring physicalist, empiricist, determinist, and associationist points of view. Put off by Freudian theory in the medical curriculum, he briefly embraced it as a medical officer doing psychiatric duty during World War II, only to become disenchanted with its effectiveness as a therapy. Discovery of the research of Pavlov and Hull provided an exciting theoretical alternative to Freud's theory of neurosis, but no alternative therapeutic application was immediately obvious. Under the tutelage of Leo Reyna, his own theories on the causes and cures of neurosis crystallized as he completed his doctoral dissertation research, performing a systematic replication of Jules Masserman's experiments on anxiety in cats. This convinced him of the superiority of an associationist conditioning model over Freudian conflict theory and provided ideas for therapeutic intervention.

Wolpe devoted the next few years to working out neurological models of Hullian concepts and putting his theories into practice as a clinician. His first two years of practice were decidedly lean; outside the mainstream of the psychoanalytic-dominated professional community, he was sustained by his belief in the possibility of a learning-based psychotherapy and his wife Stella's encouragement. He melded his theory of anxiety conditioning and reciprocal inhibition with the writings of Andrew Salter and Edmund Jacobson into a novel program of assessment and treatment. Soon he was achieving results unprecedented in the psychotherapeutic literature. His publications on learning theory received a tepid response but his clinical outcome reports excited great interest. His program was based on the respected science of learning, his procedures were clearly specified, and his goals of therapy were clearly stated and usually achieved. This was truly a revolutionary accomplishment!

The post-war era was primed for this development. Hans Eysenck served as a Joshua to psychotherapy's Jericho and Wolpe's first book, *Psychotherapy by Reciprocal Inhibition*, provided the ammunition for a new wave of clinicians who took up the movement that became known as behavior therapy. Wolpe settled at the Eastern Pennsylvania Psychiatric Institute of Temple University in the mid 1960s. There he was a key figure in the landmark *Psychotherapy versus Behavior Therapy* study and engaged in practice, training, traveling, speaking, and writing on behalf of this burgeoning new field. Over the next two decades, hundreds of professionals were trained by Wolpe personally, many more hundreds experimented with his procedures in their doctoral and post-doctoral research; thousands heard him speak and more thousands read his publications. Behavior therapy took the lead in developing empirically-based treatment, forcing traditional psycho-therapy to acknowledge the effectiveness of this newcomer and to sharpen its efforts to demonstrate its own worth.

In the last decade, in his 'emeritus' role, Wolpe's pace of speaking and writing has hardly slowed. He remains open to new techniques and data but is critical of attempts to 'integrate' behavior therapy with psychodynamic or mentalistic approaches. As in his college days, he is committed to a materialist, determinist philosophy of human nature, and he enjoys a good debate.

2

Major Contributions to Theory

Rather than the chemist of his childhood plans, Wolpe may be seen as an alchemist, transmuting learning theory into clinical theory and practice. Wolpe's formulations were rooted in his studies of Freudian and animal learning theories, and were augmented by his clinical observations and by results of behavior therapy research. This chapter is divided into two main sections: the first reviews Wolpe's theory of the etiology of neurosis; the second provides his theoretical foundations for therapy. An approximate historical format is followed, with changes and developments over time noted as appropriate.

I. The Etiology of Neurosis

Herbert Spencer, Darwin's contemporary, extended the concept of natural selection to individual behavior, suggesting that an organism's environment selects actions that produce pleasure and reduce pain (Schwartz and Reisberg, 1991, pp. 8–9). The principles of maximizing pleasure and minimizing pain permitted the organism to adapt to the demands of a constantly changing environment, promoting its well-being and survival. Maladaptive behavior, however, posed a puzzle. How was it that an individual, in the absence of neurologic defect, would act against its own best interest? Two influential lines of investigation, which had great impact on Wolpe, were begun by Sigmund Freud and Ivan Pavlov.

Freud is credited with applying the principles of pleasure and pain to human behavior and demoting humankind from the position of special creation of God to that of just another species struggling for survival. For Freud, neurosis was a human condition which arose from unconscious intrapsychic conflicts between basic animal instincts and the pressures of living in a civilized society. Freud identified *anxiety* as the result of such conflicts and neurotic symptoms as the ways in which people tried to resolve them. Psychoanalysis was a process of achieving conscious insight into the conflicts and redirecting the instincts into less destructive channels.

As noted in Chapter 1, Wolpe studied and embraced psychoanalysis for a short period during his medical and psychiatric training before ultimately rejecting it, primarily because it did not produce effective outcomes. However, the idea of anxiety, acquired as a result of some kind of experience, serving as the core of neurosis, and motivating the formation of symptoms, retained its appeal.

Experimental animal psychology was based on the Darwinian premise of continuity between species, implying that the study of learning in other species was informative for the human condition. Pavlov's discovery of 'experimental neurosis' implied that neurosis was not a uniquely human condition. The animal laboratory offered the possibility of analyzing the topography and physiology of neurotic behavior, specifying the conditions which precipitated it, and determining effective treatments. Studies of experimental neurosis proliferated but the phenomenon was inconsistent and treatment was elusive (Liddell, 1964). Pavlov proposed that neurosis resulted from conflicting 'excitatory' and 'inhibitory' cortical arousal which, in conjunction with the animal's genetic 'type' of nervous system, produced a neurologic deficit. Wolpe felt there was no evidence for cortical damage and searched the literature to see if there were any consistent principles by which to organize the disparate experimental neurosis data.

The concept of conflict was a recurring theme in both Freudian and Pavlovian theories. These two lines of investigation were merged in the eating inhibition procedure of Dimmick et al. (1939), which was expanded by Jules Masserman (1943). These experimenters trained cats to raise the lid of a box containing food in response to a visual/auditory signal; the animals were then administered an electric shock as they opened the food box. The conflict between the drives of hunger and safety, according to these authors, was responsible for the resulting experimental neurosis. Wolpe proposed an alternative concept, namely conditioned anxiety. Hull's student O.H. Mowrer (1939; 1940) had proposed that anxiety was a conditioned form of the pain response to a noxious stimulus. Wolpe's dissertation set out to compare these two theories.

Conflict Versus Aversive Conditioning

A more detailed look at Wolpe's cat experiment, described briefly in Chapter 1, shows the foundations of his theory. Wolpe (1952a; 1958, pp. 50–60) employed an apparatus and procedure similar to Masserman's (1943). A 'conflict' group of six cats were provided with an auditory conditioned stimulus (CS) followed by delivery of food in a small box. After eight to 16 sessions of about 20 trials each, these animals were subjected to electric shock following the CS and food delivery. Shock trials were repeated until they ceased approaching the food box at the CS; only two or three shocks were required for most animals, but nine shocks over three sessions were required for one cat. Wolpe's innovation was a non-conflict group, in which six other cats did not receive the food approach training but were simply shocked following a two- to three-second presentation of the auditory CS. These animals were subjected to between five and 10 trials of CS-shock pairings at irregular intervals, and five of them received a second series one to three days later.

The immediate reaction to the shock was agitated motor activity including clawing at the cage, vocalization, and autonomic activity such as mydriasis (pupil dilation), piloerection (fur standing on end), rapid respiration, and sometimes urination or defecation. In addition, all animals resisted being put into the experimental cage and, most importantly, they refused to eat freely available food in the cage, even after three days of starvation. Idiosyncratic patterns of anxiety were also noted. Symptoms were intensified when the auditory stimulus was presented. Wolpe concluded that neurotic behavior had been acquired in both the group faced with 'conflict' between food and shock and the group having no conflict, indicating that conflict was unnecessary for neurosis production and that Pavlovian conditioning with a noxious stimulus was sufficient.

Wolpe then took the step which had eluded many other researchers – curing the neurosis. Elaborating on the concept of reciprocal inhibition (see below), he reasoned that since eating was inhibited by anxiety, feeding could be used to overcome anxious arousal. The first procedure he tried was to augment the eating response in the experimental cage. Nine animals were offered food by hand, which he assumed was associated with approach since animals were fed by hand in their home cages. The other three animals (all in the 'conflict' group) were forced by a movable barrier (Masserman's 'forced solution') to remain next to the full food box. Four of the hand-fed cats and all of the 'forced' cats eventually began to eat; as they did so Wolpe reported that they began to move freely about the cage and progressively displayed fewer anxiety symptoms.

For the five recalcitrant animals, Wolpe developed the procedure of feeding them in locations which progressively resembled the room housing the experimental cage. He identified three rooms (labeled B, C, and D) which in his judgment systematically differed from the experimental room (A) on several visual, auditory, and proximity stimulus dimensions. He observed that the animals displayed several symptoms (notably refusal to eat) in these rooms in a hierarchical fashion; that is, if an animal refused to eat in room C it also would not eat in rooms B and A. He identified the room in which an animal would eat and fed it there, moving to the next room the following day. This 'method of gradual ascent' enabled all animals to eat in room A, at which point they were fed in closer and closer proximity to the experimental cage and eventually inside it. After the cats were fed inside the cage, anxiety symptoms ceased to be observed.

Wolpe employed the same gradual approach to overcoming the animals' adverse reactions to the auditory CS. He demonstrated with two cats that sounding the CS while they ate re-established their symptoms. For the others he attenuated the CS either by sounding it at a distance or for a fraction of a second as the cats ate. By gradual increments of time or distance, the cats were able eventually to orient toward the food and eat calmly in the presence of the full-strength CS. The animals' neuroses had been eliminated!

Wolpe reported his experimental procedures and results in an illustrative, anecdotal fashion typical of an earlier era, rather than the precise, quantitative approach characteristic of Hull and later learning researchers. Consequently there were many ambiguities and apparently contradictory results within his study. Training procedures varied for different animals, and there were obvious individual differences in their responses to training, but the lack of systematic quantitative data made specification or interpretation of these differences difficult. Similarly, it was not possible to compare the 'forced' solution to the gradual approach, or to determine whether either was superior to an ordinary extinction procedure (whereby an animal is merely exposed to the CS for repeated trials with no further shock) – which Wolpe presumed to be ineffective and did not bother to include. Even his conclusion that conflict was not important for experimental neurosis was confounded by the fact that his non-conflict subjects received two to 10 times as many shocks as the conflict animals.

Nevertheless, Wolpe's experience in this study convinced him that he had found the necessary and sufficient principles to account for neurotic behavior and its amelioration. Therapy was a matter of turning these principles into techniques in the consulting room.

Neurotic Behavior

Wolpe defined neurotic behavior thus:

> Neurotic behavior is any persistent habit of unadaptive behavior acquired by learning in a physiologically normal organism. Anxiety is

usually the central component of this behavior, being invariably present in the causal situation. (1958, p. 32)

For Wolpe, neurosis was the sum of an organism's maladaptive behaviors rather than an intrapsychic state. The term 'habit' in the above definition may be taken in the Hullian sense of stimulus–response connections; thus neurosis consisted of particular responses to specific situations. 'Unadaptive' referred to the outcomes of behavior which did not promote the survival or well-being of the individual. 'Persistent' described the long-term nature of this behavior, and the fact that it did not remit in the usual course of daily living. 'Acquired by learning' emphasized the experiential foundation of such behavior, as opposed to a genetic or neurologic deficit. Wolpe recognized that there were individual differences in susceptibility to neurotogenic situations but his emphasis was on the learning experience. 'Learning' meant acquisition according to Hullian learning theory principles. By specifying a 'physiologically normal organism' he excluded maladaptive behavior due to genetic or organic factors, particularly the psychoses. 'Anxiety' was the heart of neurotic behavior. Acquisition of maladaptive anxiety started the neurotic on his/her unhappy life, and most of his/her symptoms were manifestations of or attempts to deal with anxiety.

Observations of Animals
In his review of the experimental neurosis literature (1952a; 1958, pp. 37–55), Wolpe cited the following descriptions of anxiety responses in the experimental situation: deterioration of previously learned responses, resistance to experimental participation, distressed vocalizations, micturition and defecation, refusal of food, and hyper- or hypoactive motoric behavior. Behavioral disturbances were frequently reported in subjects' living quarters, apart from the conditioning situation.

He reported similar observations in his own experiment, in which the following anxious behaviors consistently occurred in all animals: mydriasis, resistance to being put in experimental cage, muscle tension, and refusal to eat meat pellets in the cage even after starvation for up to three days. He reported the following behaviors occurring on a more intermittent or idiosyncratic basis: agitated motoric activity, immobility, ceaseless vocalizing, piloerection, rapid respiration, micturition, and 'hypersensitivity' to extraneous stimuli. Outside the experimental cage, Wolpe reported that some cats refused to eat in the experimental or other rooms, and responded with crouching and mydriasis whenever he entered their living chambers. In all, the picture was one of autonomic arousal and disrupted motoric behavior.

Like many others of this period, Wolpe defined anxiety in terms of autonomic arousal, primarily of the sympathetic branch.

> By anxiety is meant the autonomic pattern or patterns that are characteristically part of the organism's response to noxious stimulation .... The response elements that typically constitute an anxiety response are largely those associated with a widespread discharge of the autonomic nervous system, and predominantly of its sympathetic division. The usual manifestations are tachycardia, raised blood pressure, mydriasis, palmar hyperidrosis, and dryness of mouth .... Marked parasympathetic manifestations may also be observed. Extreme examples of the latter are evacuation of the bladder or bowels. Besides these somatic responses, the work of Hess ... suggests that there are other autonomic effects which may show themselves as increased irritability. It is possible that this is responsible for the diffuse rise in muscle tension that is characteristic of anxiety. (1958, pp. 34–5)

Clinical Observations

Using his autonomic theory, Wolpe (1958, p. 36) described the varied symptoms of autonomic arousal and the many ways in which such arousal undermined adaptive functioning in humans. He noted that a generalized increase in muscle tension may impair coordination, cause tremor, and produce muscle pain such as 'fibrositis' and headache. Mental effects of anxiety included impairments in concentration, recall, 'flow of associations', and 'registration of impressions'. Anxiety could interfere with sexual functions, resulting in erectile and ejaculatory problems for men and 'frigidity' for women.

Wolpe noted that anxious people could respond to their own arousal with 'secondary reactions,' causing further complications. Autonomic arousal might result in strange feelings which could cause a patient to conclude that he was losing his mind. Anxiety-produced hyperventilation could result in symptoms such as paresthesia, tremor, myalgia, and precordial pain. Furthermore, 'secondary conditioning' could occur, in which anxiety was conditioned to the endogenous stimuli which accompanied the symptoms, resulting in a vicious circle such that anxiety produced a symptom or sensation which generated more anxiety.

The idea that neurotic symptoms involved a two-stage process was implied in Wolpe's later outline of the 'consequences of neurotic anxiety' (1969, pp. 24–6). The first stage was the occurrence of the largely sympathetic autonomic reaction described above. Further symptomatic behavior then occurred as a reaction to or a consequence of the underlying anxiety response. Wolpe adapted Lang's (1968) tripartite model of anxiety to organize these 'consequences.' Lang's model proposed three response dimensions to anxiety, variously termed the physiological/autonomic, cognitive/verbal, and behavioral/motoric. According to this model, anxiety responses in each dimension could occur simultaneously or in any combination in different people or at different times in the same person, giving rise to many patterns of anxiety. In contrast, anxiety for Wolpe remained a unitary reaction which served as the core for secondary responses in these three avenues of expression. Wolpe's most recent listing of the symptoms arising from underlying anxiety is shown in Table 2.1 (Wolpe, 1990, p. 12).

Stimuli Which Evoke Anxiety

Wolpe maintained that anxiety was aroused initially by painful or otherwise harmful stimuli; it was connected to other stimuli which coincided with the harmful ones; it thereafter could be called forth by those coincidental (conditioned) stimuli; and it could spread to additional stimuli similar to the coincidental ones through the process of stimulus generalization, or to stimuli associated with the CS through the process of higher-order conditioning. Thus to understand fully the origins and maintenance of an individual's anxiety it was necessary to discern the antecedent stimuli which controlled the reaction. There were three major categories of anxiety-producing situations: unconditioned stimuli, which were inherently capable of generating the fear reaction; conditioned stimuli, present at the time of arousal, which could later elicit the reaction; and generalized stimuli, which bore varying degrees of similarity to conditioned stimuli.

Unconditioned Stimuli

In his review of the experimental neurosis literature, Wolpe identified two major categories of unconditioned stimuli (UCS) which inherently elicited the anxiety response. These he termed 'ambivalent' stimuli and 'noxious' stimuli; they were confounded in many studies and it was difficult to separate their workings. In addition, he noted that in humans it was often the case that just witnessing, being told about, or thinking about certain events was sufficient to evoke the anxiety response.

Ambivalent Stimuli. In many experiments, discrimination training was provided to teach salivation or food approach to one stimulus, and to withhold response or make a different response to a different

Table 2.1   *Consequences of neurotic anxiety*

Physiological event	Common clinical consequences
A. Autonomic event	
1. General autonomic response predominantly sympathetic	Feeling of anxiety, dread, panic, etc. Feeling of depression Feeling of threat of losing control or of insanity
2. Hyperventilation	Dizziness Fainting attacks Headaches Paresthesia Tachycardia Panic attacks
3. Autonomic discharges especially channeled into one organ system	Psychosomatic symptoms, e.g.: Neurodermatitis Asthma Vasomotor rhinitis Peptic ulceration and syndrome Irritable bowel syndrome Increased/decreased frequency of micturition Dysmenorrhea Hypertension Migraine
B. Motor event	
1. Prominent muscle tension, general or localized	Motor disturbance, e.g.: Tremor Stuttering 'Fibrositic' pain (e.g. backache) Ocular dyskinesia
2. Motor avoidance conditioning (may be conditioned to be either simultaneous with anxiety or secondary to it)	Avoidance of anxiety-evoking stimuli
3. Inhibition of complex functioning	Impaired vocational function Impaired social function Impaired sexual function
4. Complex motor behavior in combination with anxiety or related to anxiety reduction	Compulsions Character neuroses, e.g.: Promiscuity Aimlessness Sexual deviations, e.g.: Homosexuality Pedophilia Exhibitionism Voyeurism
C. Cognitive event	
1. Cognitive focus on anxiety responses	Hypomnesia due to 'nonregistration' of external events
2. Inhibition of a segment of experience by intense anxiety	Impairment of learning and performance Circumscribed amnesia

stimulus. Stimuli discriminative for making and not making the response then were made very similar, resulting in conflict between the tendencies to respond and inhibit responding. The paradigmatic example was the circle-vs.-ellipse experiment of Shenger-Krestov-nikova (Pavlov, 1927, pp. 290–1). A dog was trained to salivate to a circle projected on a screen and not to salivate to an ellipse. The axes of the ellipse were progressively changed so that it became rounder, and when the ellipse looked very much like the circle, the animal suddenly exhibited 'neurotic' behavior. Rather than the conflict between excitatory and inhibitory cortical states which Pavlov theorized, Wolpe proposed that this arrangement simply resulted in an autonomic anxiety reaction. Thus experimental neurosis was not a neurologic 'breakdown', but a persistent unadaptive anxiety response conditioned to cues incidental to insoluble problem situations. Though usually not thought of as such, the unconditioned stimulus (UCS) in such studies was the presentation of cues which controlled incompatible responses. Confronted with the conflicting stimuli, the animals responded with anxious arousal which disrupted the responses conditioned to those cues and produced other neurotic symptoms.

Noxious Stimuli. There were numerous studies employing electric shock or other noxious stimulation. Although most of these experiments were arranged to produce conflict, as in the Masserman (1943) study, Wolpe felt the use of noxious stimulation was by far the most important factor. His cat experiment supported his contention that it was the aversive stimulus, not the conflict, that resulted in neurotic behavior. In further support, Wolpe cited the classic study of Watson and Rayner (1920). These researchers made a loud noise by striking a metal bar with a hammer behind an 11-month-old infant as he reached for a white rat. 'Little Albert' responded with startle and withdrawal, and subsequently displayed aversion to the rat as well as a variety of white, furry objects. Their report of fear conditioning has assumed almost mythic proportions as the paradigm for anxiety learning (Harris, 1979). Wolpe referred to it as the only example, other than his own experiment, of fear conditioning employing strong noxious stimuli alone. He ignored the extensive research on avoidance learning which employed strong electric shock because he felt avoidance responses in and of themselves were not neurotic.

Wolpe distinguished a subset of studies employing weak shock which did not, in itself, seem to produce anxiety. The research of Liddell and his associates (Liddell, 1964) served as the exemplar. They employed a mild shock to elicit a leg flexion reflex in sheep or goats. A bewildering variety of training parameters resulted in experimental neurosis, but Wolpe noted two features common to all – repeated noxious stimulation and confinement. Wolpe (1958, pp. 63–4) proposed that the mild anxiety produced by repetitious mild aversive stimuli 'summated.' In other words, he theorized that the amount of anxiety was proportional to the strength of the noxious stimulus. Even slight aversive stimuli generated some anxious arousal, and residual arousal from each trial persisted and accumulated until a critical mass was achieved, at which point it disrupted the organism's ongoing performance and other overt symptoms were manifested. As for the confinement factor, Wolpe (1958, p. 65) proposed three ways in which it could contribute to the production of neurosis. First, it allowed the anxiety conditioned to the incidental cues to accumulate. Secondly, the anxiety was focused on a restricted number of stimuli rather than spread out over changing environmental cues. Thirdly, autonomic anxiety responses were stronger when there were no reciprocally inhibiting musculoskeletal escape responses.

Human Examples. Just like animals in experimental settings, humans developed anxiety in situations involving one or a few severe noxious stimuli, many instances of mild noxious stimuli, or difficult discriminations producing conflict between equally strong responses (1958, pp. 78–9). As an example of a severe noxious stimulus, Wolpe cited a young woman who received an accidental intravenous injection of procaine while seated in a dental chair, evoking spasms, tachycardia, nausea, hot and cold flushes, and partial blackouts. Subsequently, she had an anxiety reaction when sitting down in a hairdresser's chair, 'a conditioned response explicable by the tactile similarity between the dentist's chair and the hairdresser's.' An example of repeated exposure to weak noxious stimuli was provided by 'the case of a schoolboy who developed violent emotional reactions to classroom situations on the basis of multiple pinpricks by a teacher who viciously disliked him.' With respect to ambivalent stimuli, Wolpe proposed that simultaneous, strong, conflicting action tendencies generated anxiety. He described a hypothetical example of a young woman engaged to marry a man she disliked while fearful of social criticism for breaking the engagement, but provided no actual clinical examples of ambivalent stimuli.

Cognitive Sources. Wolpe recognized that patients might have erroneous beliefs which underlay some of their anxious reactions (1958, pp. 106, 199–200; Wolpe and Lazarus, 1966, pp. 130–2).

Examples cited ranged from simple items of misinformation, such as the idea that masturbation weakens the body or pine bark secretes a deadly poison, to complex attitudes about society or oneself, such as the notion that anxiety reactions mean that one is 'mentally abnormal.' Wolpe regarded such beliefs as stemming from the behavior of powerful figures in the patient's life, such as parents' misguided teachings or a dominating spouse's critical attitude. In effect, such actions or instructions served as unconditioned stimuli.

As 'cognitive behavior therapy' grew in popularity, Wolpe devoted more attention to 'misconceptions' and their treatment. He explicitly distinguished 'cognitively learned' from 'classically conditioned' anxiety (1981a) and devoted an entire chapter to 'cognitive therapeutic procedures' in the third edition of his textbook (1982). In this analysis, Wolpe noted that cognitively based fears may arise from misinformation provided by others, observation of other people's reactions, or erroneous inferences about one's own experience. Examples included parental injunctions against sex, observing a parent react fearfully to insects, or inferring that one is going crazy because of strange bodily sensations. The cognitive basis of anxiety could be quite simply determined by asking the patient to what extent he or she truly believed the feared event to be actually dangerous (Wolpe et al., 1985).

The manifestation of cognitive anxiety included both the patient's statement, or a verbal component, and physiological arousal, or an autonomic component, when confronted with the fearsome situation or even when thinking about it. Wolpe observed that contiguity between the cognitively produced autonomic arousal and the feared object could lead to the development of Pavlovian conditioned anxiety, requiring both cognitive correction and emotional reconditioning. He provided the case example of a woman who, after reading a magazine article, became alarmed that her skin rash indicated a terrible disease. Even though a dermatologist convinced her that she did not have a disease she continued to be so upset at the sight of the rash that she required therapy (1982, p. 32).

Fears having their basis in Pavlovian conditioning involved an initial experience of usually overwhelming autonomic arousal which was automatically elicited by the threatening stimulus and conditioned to other stimuli in the situation. Wolpe stated that no cognitive error was involved because the person did not believe that the conditioned stimuli actually portended danger. For example, a veteran suffering from war neurosis automatically reacts to a flash of light or the sound of a plane, but does not believe that such events are actually harmful (1982, p. 28). Wolpe considered the possibility that misperceptions might arise from Pavlovian conditioning only in the context of patients' fears that the bodily sensations of arousal mean they are going crazy or dying.

Wolpe (1981a) analyzed the relative frequency of cognitive and conditioned anxiety etiologies by asking an assistant to select from his files 'the first 40 cases whose central complaint was unadaptive fear.' He then analyzed these cases as to their autonomic conditioning or cognitive etiology, and further as to their origins requiring a single learning trial or repeated exposures. Almost two-thirds were found to have a Pavlovian conditioned origin, and of these, 80 percent were based on a single conditioning event. The cognitively based fears were equally likely to have single or multiple event causation. He found two cases in which both conditioning and cognitive precipitating factors were present, and two cases in which he could not determine the causal events. The preponderance of cases in the single-event Pavlovian conditioned category supported the basic importance of this model of experimental neurosis.

Conditioned Stimuli

Wolpe was far more interested in the CS than the UCS, for it was the CS that distinguished neurotic from non-neurotic fears. It was their reactions to innocuous events not portending actual danger that disrupted neurotic persons' lives and resulted in their seeking treatment.

> What differentiates normal and neurotic fears is the character of the stimulus situation to which the conditioning has occurred. If that stimulus situation is objectively either a source of danger or a sign of danger, the fear is appropriate or 'adaptive'; if it is neither the fear is neurotic. (1982, p. 27)

In his review of the experimental neurosis studies, Wolpe regarded the general apparatus cues as conditioned stimuli, triggering the animals' struggles and autonomic arousal. In his own experiment, he observed that the cats became upset when placed in the training chamber or brought into the experimental room, or when he himself appeared in their living area. He noted that the animals' symptoms were intensified when the buzzer which had originally preceded the shock was sounded, and that their symptoms were less likely to occur when the animals were placed in dissimilar rooms. His observation of a gradient of arousal as a function of various stimuli played a key role in the development of therapeutic interventions.

Out of the myriad stimuli present in a threatening situation, which are conditioned to the fear response? Wolpe considered two factors pertinent to this question: 'psychological confinement' and 'preparedness.'

Psychological confinement (1958, p. 81) was analogous to the physical confinement typical of animal experimental neurosis situations. This was described as a 'dominating presence in thought' of certain stimuli, which was not related necessarily to their 'prominence in the outside world.' Thus, whatever a person happened to be attending to or thinking about at the time of an aversive experience was likely to be connected to the fear response. Throughout his case examples and published diagnostic interviews, Wolpe focused on what the client chanced to be noticing, thinking, and feeling in the conditioning situation. These may have been exteroceptive stimuli, such as dark shapes or the interiors of automobiles, or interoceptive stimuli, such as feelings of sexual arousal or tingling in the extremities.

The second factor concerned 'prepared stimuli.' In the 1960s, research on conditioned taste aversions in animals indicated that taste as a CS and nausea as a UCS could be conditioned easily, as could auditory or visual CS with shock UCS, but that the reverse was impossible (Garcia and Koelling, 1966). These findings were expanded into a theory of 'preparedness' by M.E.P. Seligman (1971). According to this theory, events of evolutionary significance, such as darkness, insects, or snakes, could serve as conditioned aversive stimuli with special ease because of genetic predisposition, whereas modern objects often associated with pain, such as hammers or hot stoves, do not appear as phobic stimuli. This theory was contrasted to the theory of 'equipotentiality', according to which all 'neutral' stimuli serve equally well as CS in relation to any type of UCS.

Wolpe (1982, p. 26) questioned the phylogenic explanation of preparedness, suggesting that cultural history may be responsible for the predominance of certain events as the objects of fears and phobias. He also noted that some objects may be 'protected' from becoming aversive conditioned stimuli because of a history of pleasant associations. While not directly asserting the theory of equipotentiality, the case examples Wolpe presented were consistent with it.

Wolpe (1990, pp. 16, 26; 1993) briefly considered more recent conceptualizations of Pavlovian conditioning which showed that mere coincidence between the CS and UCS is inadequate to produce learning (Rescorla, 1988). There are a variety of experimental findings which indicate that the CS must predict, or 'provide information' about, the UCS occurrence rather than merely be temporally contiguous with it. Wolpe rejected the cognitive implications of these data in favor of neurological explanations.

Generalized Stimuli.   Wolpe (1958, p. 12) cited Hull's principle of 'primary stimulus generalization' to account for anxiety reactions to events not directly associated with the UCS. According to Hull, every stimulus situation is a compound made up of many dimensions. Generalization occurs to the extent that stimuli overlap or share physically similar components. Wolpe explained the anxiety reactions of his cats in rooms other than the conditioning cage on the basis of the physical similarity of the rooms (1958, pp. 50, 53). He also cited Watson and Rayner's Little Albert (1920) who, after a fear response was conditioned to a white rat, also reacted fearfully to other white or furry objects (1958, p. 48).

Although primary stimulus generalization occurs in human neurotic reactions, Wolpe was much more concerned with what he initially termed 'involvement by continuity' (1958, p. 98) and later called 'secondary generalization' (1969, pp. 9–10). According to this principle, stimuli which evoke similar 'feelings' or 'internal responses' form a dimension. His exemplar was the case of a claustrophobic woman who felt anxious along the dimension of 'feeling of enclosure', including stimuli such as a tight zipper, difficult-to-remove nail polish, or a tight ring, as well as being physically confined in closed rooms (Wolpe, 1969, p. 10; 1990, p. 160). Thus, the same interoceptive response to a variety of stimuli served to trigger anxiety.

Second-Order Conditioning.   Wolpe recognized that, in humans, conditioning based on physically traumatic stimuli is relatively uncommon (1958, p. 78). More usual are exposures to previously conditioned aversive stimuli, a process described by Pavlov as 'second-order conditioning.'

> The main *difference* between experimental and clinical neuroses is that, whereas in the former the original fear arousal is by an unconditioned stimulus such as electric shocks, in clinical neuroses it is a conditioned stimulus such as the comprehension of grave danger. Clinical neuroses originate in second-order conditioning. (Wolpe, 1982, p. 41, italics in original)

In humans, any stimulus which, based on prior learning, produced a 'comprehension of grave danger' could serve as a UCS even though it was not itself physically harmful. It was sufficient if it produced the autonomic anxiety arousal which was then conditioned to coincidental stimuli in the situation. In cases of war neurosis it was not necessary that the soldier actually be wounded or physically harmed; the *threat* of death or injury served as the UCS by which anxiety was conditioned to explosive sounds, the broad blue sky, or the desert sand (Wolpe, 1958, pp. 78–9). In other cases, the stimuli may not portend objective danger; for example, the threat of hell-fire in a restrictive religious family can result in anxiety conditioned to sexual arousal (Wolpe, 1958, p. 79). This is the process by which fear can be spread on the basis of information. That is, a person fears lightning, or contaminated food, or firearms, not because of direct pairing with painful stimuli but because the use of language allows such things to be associated with 'danger' (Wolpe, 1982, p. 27). Such a process can be maladaptive when a person has a 'misconception', a belief that certain events are harmful when in fact they are not, and responds with anxiety to those events (Wolpe, 1958, pp. 199–200). Second-order conditioning accounts for the 'cognitive sources' of anxiety, as described above.

The Persistence of Anxiety

If anxiety is learned, then it ought to follow the laws which control other learned behaviors. A basic principle of all learning theories was that of extinction, in which repeated occurrences of the response to the CS, without further pairings with the UCS, resulted in the eventual disappearance of the conditioned response. However, a defining characteristic of anxiety was persistence even though the noxious UCS no longer occurred. The precipitating conditions for human neuroses were often lost in the dim mists of the past, yet maladaptive behavior persisted in the face of benign environments.

To account for the observation that experimental neuroses in his animals could not be extinguished, Pavlov had proposed that their nervous systems had been irreversibly damaged. Wolpe rejected this hypothesis but found it necessary to develop special considerations to account for an apparent exception to the principle of extinction for the conditioned anxiety response. Wolpe (1952a) initially proposed that neurotic behavior did not extinguish because the underlying anxiety continued to be reinforced through its own reduction. He later added a second hypothesis, suggesting that anxiety was less subject to inhibition or interference than other responses (1958, p. 66).

Anxiety Drive Reduction

Wolpe (1952a; 1958, pp. 22–3) initially maintained the Hullian theory that reinforcement via drive reduction was necessary for the acquisition and maintenance of all responses, including anxiety. Thus, the anxiety response was reinforced by the reduction of the anxiety drive. Referring to his cat experiment, Wolpe (1958, p. 66) hypothesized that removing the animal from the experimental cage at the conclusion of each session resulted in anxiety drive reduction, reinforcing anxiety responses conditioned to stimuli in the cage. He suggested that the same process, though weaker, could occur throughout a session; if the animal was oriented toward a part of the cage which evoked a strong anxiety response, and then turned toward a spot evoking a lesser reaction, some drive reduction would occur, thereby strengthening the anxiety response.

Wolpe's position was similar to that of Hull's student Neal Miller (1948; 1951), who voiced concern over the inherent contradiction of a response strengthening itself through its reduction. If this were so, the response would never extinguish. Miller found that anxiety-motivated avoidance responding was resistant to extinction, but not impervious. Mowrer (1947; 1950, p. 279) challenged the drive-reduction theory. Instead, he proposed a two-factor theory in which mere temporal contiguity between the CS and UCS was sufficient for autonomic learning, while drive reduction was required for motoric learning. If drive reduction occurred at the termination of a stimulus, then a sudden offset of the UCS should be more reinforcing than a gradual decline. Mowrer's series of experiments manipulating UCS offset supported the contiguity theory of anxiety conditioning.

Citing Mowrer, Wolpe conceded that 'the argument of this book will not be affected if it should turn out that the onset of anxiety is all-important to its learning and its reduction of no moment at all' (1958, p. 23). His subsequent discussions of anxiety acquisition no longer referred to drive reduction. For example he noted that '[fear] conditioning can theoretically occur to any kind of contiguous stimulation' (1982, p. 25), implying acceptance of the contiguity theory of anxiety conditioning. On the other hand, he continued to contend that all learning, motor, perceptual, and (presumably) emotional, was based on stimulus–response neuronal connections 'cemented' by cessation of firing of 'drive neurons' in the central nervous system (1982, p. 16). Thus at the phenomenologic level of experience and observation Wolpe seemed to accept the contiguity theory of anxiety conditioning, though at a neurologic level he maintained the necessity of drive reduction.

Although Wolpe acknowledged that simple contiguity might be sufficient for anxiety acquisition, he continued to support the drive-reduction theory for its maintenance. Thus each time a CS evoked the anxiety response, that response would be strengthened when the stimulus terminated or the individual turned away (1982, p. 242). Taken to its logical conclusion this leads to a reductio ad absurdum – any response leading to pain should be repeated because it reduces the pain when it stops. To be consistent, the same process should also be true for other conditioned drives such as appetite or sexual arousal. Indeed, Wolpe (1958, p. 23) cited research which showed that rats learned to press a lever followed by a click that had been associated with food, or to run a maze followed by the sight and smell of a receptive female, in support of the idea that reinforcement occurred by arousal of the hunger or sex drive of the CS, followed by drive reduction when the stimulus was terminated. If the conditioned hunger or sex drive itself was reinforced in this manner, analogous to anxiety, this theory would predict self-perpetuating behavior which would never extinguish. However, there is much evidence that such 'secondary reinforcers' require periodic pairing with the unconditioned reinforcing stimulus in order to maintain their reinforcing properties. Without such, the behavior soon extinguishes. Wolpe did not address these problems of what may be called autonomous reinforcement in anxiety and other learned drives.

Inhibition

Several theories of extinction proposed that the extinguished response was replaced by some other response, but differed with respect to the nature of the competing response. Hull's theory proposed that internal inhibitory processes occurred which strengthened the response of 'not responding.' Guthrie's (1935) theory proposed that external responses displaced the original one. Wolpe adapted both to account for the persistence of anxiety.

Reactive Inhibition. According to Hull's theory, each occurrence of a stimulus–response sequence generated fatigue in the specific muscular effector system, which he termed *reactive inhibition.* Reactive inhibition constituted a drive which was reduced by and thus reinforced cessation of responding. Under conditions where the response was no longer reinforced, reactive inhibition accumulated and eventually response cessation overcame the tendency to respond. During a rest period, reactive inhibition dissipated and spontaneous recovery of the response occurred. In addition, the drive reduction associated with cessation of the response reinforced the response of 'not responding,' a learned inhibitory reaction termed *conditioned inhibition.* When the strength of conditioned inhibition exceeded the original habit, then total extinction of the response was observed.

Wolpe (1952e; 1958, pp. 24–9) emphasized that, although similar to fatigue, the inhibitory drive was a central neural rather than a peripheral process. In support he cited Pavlov's experiments in which the same response was conditioned to two stimuli; extinction of the response to one stimulus did not affect its occurrence to the other stimulus. According to Wolpe's neurophysiological theory, inhibitory conditioning paralleled excitatory conditioning and produced decreased conductivity of the central synapses linking the original stimulus and response, but it did not necessarily reinforce the 'response of not responding' as suggested by Hull.

Wolpe (1958, pp. 66, 71) proposed that anxiety, being primarily an autonomic response, generated very little reactive inhibition, as contrasted to musculoskeletal responses. Thus there would be little interference from conditioned inhibition, protecting anxiety from extinction. However, this explanation ignored empirical evidence which showed the ease with which autonomic conditioned responses, such as salivation, heart rate or electrodermal responses, could be extinguished. Why anxiety, as a diffuse autonomic response, should be less subject to extinction than simple autonomic reactions was not explained. Wolpe later questioned the importance of the reactive inhibition mechanism (1969, pp. 8, 17) and finally relegated it to the extinction of motor responses (1982, p. 17).

Reciprocal Inhibition. Wolpe borrowed the term *reciprocal inhibition* from the pioneering neurophysiologist Sir Charles Sherrington, who used the term to describe the finding that the spinal reflex excitation of a particular muscle group prevented the occurrence of an antagonistic group, and vice versa. Wolpe proposed that the term 'be expanded to encompass all situations in which the elicitation of one response appears to bring about a decrement in the strength of evocation of a simultaneous response' (1958, p. 29). He recognized the similarity of this concept to the interference, or *counterconditioning*, theory of Guthrie (1935, pp. 64–84), who had proposed that extinction was essentially a matter of learning new responses to old stimuli. But where Guthrie was concerned with overt response displacement, Wolpe proposed that incompatible responses had their effect at the neural level, inhibiting the original synaptic connections. Thus the competing response need not totally replace the original one; it could serve only to inhibit the response at a neural level. Wolpe emphasized that reciprocal inhibition functioned not only with respect to motor responses, but also in the realm of cognitive and verbal habits, and, most especially, in the case of autonomic reactions (1976a, pp. 12–16).

One problem for interference theory was the source of competing responses. It was suggested that, ordinarily, extinction occurred when stimuli associated with incompatible responses intruded into the situation, or momentary fluctuations in response strength made an incompatible response more likely. This was the mechanism responsible for ordinary 'forgetting' (1958, p. 30). Wolpe observed that low-level conditioned anxiety responses in laboratory experiments readily underwent extinction, and those occurring in most people were subject to reciprocal inhibition by the 'normal emotional responses of daily life,' but the neurotic anxiety response was so strong that it inhibited all other responses which might be evoked in that situation (1982, p. 46). Neurotic anxiety crowded out all other reactions and thus insured its persistence. Wolpe (1982, pp. 17, 44), citing Amsel (1962), noted that 'frustration' responses evoked by non-reward were particularly important for competing with previously positively reinforced responses. Mowrer (1960, p. 419) proposed that a parallel reaction, termed 'relief,' occurred when the aversive UCS failed to follow a CS. Wolpe did not consider this a possibility for the general extinction of anxiety, though he employed a variation of this theory in developing a therapeutic procedure.

Types of Neurotic Disorders

Wolpe did not propose a formal diagnostic or classification system and was quite critical of the most widely accepted system, the *Diagnostic and Statistical Manual (DSM)* of the American Psychiatric Association (American Psychiatric Association, 1980). He felt that this approach, based on description of common symptoms, lumped together cases of widely differing etiologies and thus ignored information vitally important for adequate treatment (Wolpe, 1990, pp. 253, 257, 268, 282). Instead, Wolpe emphasized the contribution of several etiologic variables which sometimes served to define diagnostic categories and sometimes led to individual differences within categories, but in all cases were necessary to consider in developing an appropriate intervention program. These variables included: biologic factors, the role of anxiety in the disorder, the way in which anxiety was acquired (Pavlovian conditioned or cognitive learning), the characteristics of the conditioned stimuli, and the characteristics of the maladaptive behavior.

Biologic Factors
The first and most important distinction Wolpe made was to differentiate learned from organically based disorders, asserting that

relearning procedures were appropriate primarily for the former. He regarded the following disorders as biologically based: psychopathic personality and psychoses (1958, p. 205), schizophrenia (1970), endogenous depression (1973, p. 236), and certain types of panic (1982, pp. 285–6). He rejected the psychoanalytic notion of a continuum between schizophrenia and neurosis which produced the category of 'borderline' personality disorders (1982, p. 9). The proper treatment for biologic disorders was medical, though he realized that persons suffering from some organic conditions might also have learned secondary maladaptive habits which could be overcome through relearning procedures. He was quick to recognize the usefulness of operant conditioning techniques with schizophrenic patients, but he noted that changes in particular habits did not constitute a 'cure' of the psychosis (1969, p. 221). Similarly, some maladaptive psychopathic behaviors were subject to relearning (1982, p. 8).

Wolpe held that endogenous depression, based on Eysenck's (1970) theory, was due to a 'biological insufficiency' and could be diagnosed on the basis of characteristic symptoms (such as motor retardation) and medical tests (such as sedation threshold) (1973, p. 236; 1982, pp. 270–82). It required medication therapy. Similarly, some panic disorders were due to a variety of biologic factors (1990, pp. 258–68). These included effects of certain drugs, hyperthyroidism, hypoglycemia, mitral valve prolapse, Ménière's disease, or temporal lobe epilepsy. He rejected a current theory that all panic attacks are due to abnormal lactate metabolism. Biologic-based panic could result in 'pseudoagoraphobia' (1982, p. 285).

Wolpe proposed that biologic factors also played a role in learned neurotic disorders. The conditioning experiences described for many of his patients, while unpleasant, did not seem beyond the experience of many ordinary people who did not become neurotic. Even traumatic experiences, such as combat, bereavement, or child abuse, which produce transitory disturbances and increase the probability of long-lasting disorders, are not universally neurotogenic. Wolpe held that genetic predisposition was an important factor in accounting for such individual differences (1958, pp. 76–7; 1982, pp. 33, 36–7).

Wolpe hypothesized that 'innate emotional lability,' a state of heightened reactivity and variability, was an important factor in anxiety conditioning. In support, he cited research from the 1930s that found differences between very young human infants in their reactivity to a variety of stimuli, presumably related to genetic differences in neural functioning. He concluded that 'an individual who is emotionally highly sensitive would have a greater intensity of anxiety aroused in him under given conditions than an individual who is relatively phlegmatic' (1982, p. 36). He also cited Eysenck's (1957; 1961a) personality theory which proposed two genetically determined orthogonal dimensions, 'neuroticism' and 'extraversion–introversion' (1958, p. 77). High levels of neuroticism were characterized by autonomic over-reactivity whereas low levels were characterized by normal reactivity; Eysenck did not propose a condition of under-reactivity. High levels of introversion were characterized by easily established stimulus–response connections, whereas high levels of extraversion resulted in difficulty in establishing such connections. *Dysthymia* resulted from the conjunction of high degrees of neuroticism and introversion, serving as the predisposition for learning neurotic anxiety. *Psychopathy* resulted from the conjunction of high levels of neuroticism and extraversion, leading to difficult conditioning and little anxiety. *Hysteria* resulted from the conjunction of high levels of extraversion and somewhat lower levels of neuroticism. *Normals* fell midway on the introversion–extraversion scale and were low in neuroticism.

Biologic factors were also important considerations in drug and alcohol addictions and in psychosomatic disorders. Chemical addictions were regarded as due to an acquired biologic state that Wolpe called 'craving,' which stemmed from the binding of endorphins to pain receptors as a result of prolonged drug usage (1969, p. 210; 1982, p.8). Wolpe did not address the popular notion of genetic factors in alcoholism. With respect to psychosomatic disorders, Wolpe cited the seminal work of Wolff (1950; Wolf and Wolff, 1947), noting the role of biologic predisposition in 'channeling' anxious autonomic arousal into specific organ systems (1958, p. 36; 1980; 1982, pp. 292–6). He cautioned that the relative contribution of physiological and psychological factors varied from case to case, necessitating thorough medical evaluation.

The Role of Anxiety

As given in Wolpe's definition of neurosis, anxiety played a fundamental role in all but a few neurotic disorders. Some disorders in which anxiety was not a factor were considered inappropriate for his treatment methods, while other non-anxiety-based disorders were addressed. Wolpe urged that disorders which ordinarily were not considered to be anxiety-related should be examined more closely to discern the operation of anxiety. In obvious anxiety-based disorders, an important consideration was the manner in which the anxiety response was acquired.

Non-Anxiety Disorders. The major non-anxious neurotic disorder described by Wolpe was hysteria, which received extensive analysis in his early work but subsequently was mentioned only in passing (1958, pp. 85–9, 185–92; 1969, p. 28; 1990, p. 95). The early concern probably reflected his interest in differentiating his theory from the dominant Freudian view, in which hysteria figured prominently. As mainstream psychiatry decreased its concern with this disorder, so did Wolpe. Basically, he considered hysteria to be a conditioned reaction to a disturbing situation in non-autonomic physiologic systems, primarily the sensory or motor systems. Following Eysenck, Wolpe proposed that hysterics reacted in the manner they did because, as they were predominantly extraverts, it was less likely that autonomic anxiety reactions would be aroused and conditioned. Concurrent anxiety reactions could also occur depending upon the degree of extraversion. Anxiety deconditioning techniques were indicated for anxious hysterics while other relearning procedures were indicated for non-anxious cases.

In addition, Wolpe proposed that a number of 'other "pure" learned unadaptive habits' lacked the anxiety which characterized neurosis. He included some tantrums, nailbiting, trichotillomania (hair-plucking), nocturnal enuresis, extreme stinginess, and chronic tardiness (1982, p. 8). Since anxiety was not a factor, he did not address the relearning procedures which might be relevant for these habits.

Hidden Anxiety. Many diagnostic groupings overlooked or down-played the anxiety which Wolpe felt was a key to maladaptive behavior. Hidden anxiety was seen as important in depression, sexual deviance and dysfunction, addictive disorders, psychosomatic disorders, and stuttering.

Wolpe distinguished 'neurotic' from 'normal' and 'endogenous' depression (1973, pp. 234–7; 1982, pp. 270–82). He regarded normal depression as a time-limited response to serious loss or deprivation which might be adaptive if it led to seeking substitutes for the lost object of desire. He felt that chronic stressful conditions could lead to prolonged and severe depression which could still be considered 'normal,' implying that it was not a matter for clinical intervention. Neurotic depression was based on conditioned anxiety, which at one time he regarded as acquired, following the paradigm of 'learned helplessness' (1973, p. 235; Maier et al., 1970). Later he rejected the learned helplessness model because of its time-limited effects and lack of generalization, and suggested that anxiety leading to depression was acquired in the same manner as anxiety for other disorders (1982, pp. 272–3). Some symptoms of depression, such as anorexia and motoric retardation, were seen as direct manifestations of anxiety. Other symptoms, including the depressive 'emotional tone' could result from high levels of continuous anxiety becoming neurologically 'rechanneled' from original neural pathways due to 'protective (transmarginal) inhibition' (1990, p. 279). On the basis of a review of 25 patients, Wolpe (1979) distinguished four different 'contexts' related to the source of anxiety which produced depression: direct anxiety conditioning, erroneous cognitions, interpersonal inadequacy, and excessive reaction to bereavement. An appropriate treatment program for depression thus required determination of the factors responsible for each individual's anxiety.

Wolpe proposed that anxiety played a role in sexual deviances such as fetishism, exhibitionism, pedophilia, and homosexuality, in which interpersonal anxiety inhibited arousal to appropriate sexual cues while sexual arousal was conditioned to inappropriate ones (1990, p. 311; Stevenson and Wolpe, 1960). At one time he accepted twin studies which indicated that homosexuality was genetically determined (1969, p. 258). However, an apparently spontaneous reversal of sexual preference in an early case who presented for treatment of depression (1958, p. 208; Stevenson and Wolpe, 1960), and experience with subsequent cases, led him to conclude that male homosexuality was generally based on one or more of three kinds of learned habits: anxiety conditioned to women in contexts of emotional or physical closeness; unassertiveness and submission, especially toward women; and positive erotic conditioning toward males (1973, p. 238). He felt that homosexuality might be satisfactory for many men and women, but men who found it unacceptable had a right to treatment (1990, p. 311). He presented no analysis of female homosexuality.

Sexual dysfunction of both men and women nicely fit the conditioned anxiety model (1958, pp. 130–5; 1990, pp. 298–9). Wolpe theorized that the etiology of sexual anxiety stemmed from actual or threatened punishment of childhood sexual explorations, or pain or embarrassment during adult sexual activity. Wolpe hypothesized that there was a direct physiologic basis for the inverse relationship between anxiety and sex, since preorgasmic sexual arousal is predominantly a parasympathetic function, while anxiety is predominantly related to sympathetic arousal. In males, sympathetic arousal would inhibit erection and facilitate ejaculation. Anxiety could become conditioned to a wide variety of stimuli associated with sexual activity. Once anxiety was established in the sexual situation, its inhibitory effects could cause further humiliation, causing more anxiety, and so on in an escalating fashion.

In Wolpe's view, addictive behavior originated from the patient's use of various substances to alleviate 'emotional distress.' He noted that in some cases the original stressful conditions ceased but the behavior continued under the control of the 'endogenous impulse' of craving (1969, p. 210). In such circumstances, direct attack on the cravings was indicated. In other cases, the use of substances were the patient's means of controlling neurotic anxiety which must be addressed first, otherwise attempts at removing the addictive behavior would be unsuccessful or lead to 'symptom substitution' (1969, pp. 200–1).

Wolpe noted the role of anxious autonomic arousal in many 'psychosomatic' disorders, suggesting that the anxiety aroused by various upsetting situations manifested itself in various physiologic conditions, such as hypertension, gastric disorders, and headache (1958, pp. 35–6; 1980). This was similar to concurrently developing theories of 'stress,' which addressed autonomic and hormonal reactions to the demands of living but paid less attention to their relation to conditioned stimuli (Selye, 1976). Both formulations focused on pathophysiologic arousal to various life situations, and Wolpe's methods of treatment for anxiety were easily adapted for treatment of stress (or psychosomatic) disorders (Moore, 1965; see Chapter 5).

Wolpe regarded stuttering as the product of interpersonal anxiety which was manifested as a motor disturbance (1969, p. 25; 1973, pp. 232–3). He noted that 'in some cases motor operants will keep the stutter going to some extent after the anxiety has been removed and their separate extinction will be needed' (1973, p. 233). Later, he cited evidence for a 'physiological predisposition' for stuttering (1990, p. 289). But apparently this was not sufficient for regarding the disorder as strictly biological, and he continued to recommend anxiety deconditioning as the treatment of choice.

Conditioned and Cognitive Anxiety. Wolpe emphasized the importance of determining if the patient really believed the object of his or her fears to be dangerous or harmful. The origin of such belief was to a great extent the result of the way in which the anxiety was acquired, either through Pavlovian conditioning or by cognitive means of misinformation and misperception. Cognitive-based anxiety was an important factor in many disorders, including simple and social phobias, agoraphobia, depression, and obsessional behavior.

When faulty beliefs existed, Wolpe proposed that, in general, it was necessary to address them first before proceeding to decondition anxiety (1982, p. 87). For example, in a simple phobia such as fear of snakes, the belief that all snakes are poisonous had to be corrected before the patient would be amenable to the goal of touching one. Among agoraphobics, different types of faulty beliefs were responsible for different varieties (1982, p. 284). One type resulted from the belief that the endogenous stimuli characteristic of anxious arousal portended death or collapse. Another type was characterized by the belief that the outside world was physically dangerous. A third category was comprised of unhappily married women who believed themselves to be incapable of getting by on their own. Among neurotic depression disorders, Wolpe distinguished four categories related to cognitive factors (1982, pp. 274–81). One type was characterized by their 'erroneous self-devaluation cognitions' which resulted in anxiety, as distinguished from those who experienced 'directly conditioned' anxiety and presumably did not misconstrue their experience. A third category was comprised of those who felt no control over important interpersonal situations, becoming anxious at the thought of hurting others' feelings or appearing to be pushy. This also appears to be a cognitive error, though Wolpe did not describe it as such in this context. A fourth category was comprised of 'overreactions' to loss or bereavement. The reaction to loss was termed 'distress' rather than 'anxiety,' and was made possible by endogenous susceptibility, previous conditioning of anxiety to loss, or the development of self-devaluative cognitions. Wolpe's categories emphasized the variation, particularly in cognitive anxiety, that was seen in depression, and the importance of individualized treatment plans.

With respect to interpersonal anxiety, in some instances the etiology was based on Pavlovian conditioning, as in the case of a man who as a child had been threatened with death by his mother holding a knife (1958, p. 121), or another who was frequently beaten by his mother (1969, p. 256). But interpersonal anxiety often seemed to have a cognitive origin, as in the case of a man whose parents had insisted on submissiveness (1973, p. 82), or a woman who had worried about speaking in front of her class in elementary school (1973, p. 41). In addition, many persons with interpersonal anxiety had the erroneous belief that one must always put others before oneself and that it is wrong to behave assertively. As with other cognitively based fears, Wolpe held it necessary to address first this erroneous philosophy before proceeding with methods to overcome anxiety (1973, p. 83; 1982, pp. 121–2).

Conditioned Stimuli and Responses
The remaining variables necessary to consider in diagnosing a patient concerned the identification of stimuli which controlled his

or her anxiety reactions, and the characteristics of those reactions themselves. With respect to this latter variable, there was some disagreement between Wolpe and the *DSM* categories. Most disorders were defined in terms of symptoms and, to some extent, the circumstances giving rise to them. Wolpe was most interested in the current events in the patient's life which evoked anxiety, since those were the situations which the patient would have to overcome. Information concerning the original anxiety learning situation was useful, but neither necessary nor sufficient, since anxiety often spread through generalization and second-order conditioning to encompass many stimuli beyond those comprising the primary learning experience. Wolpe's stimulus–response analyses of a number of neurotic disorders are briefly outlined below.

Phobias commonly are defined in terms of the anxiety-evoking stimuli. Wolpe felt that simple phobias were relatively rare and were over-represented in behavior therapy research (1982, p. 10; see Chapter 3). However, epidemiologic evidence indicates that 'simple' phobias meeting *DSM* criteria are very prevalent in the general population, but present for treatment relatively infrequently (Robins et al., 1984; Boyd et al., 1990). Wolpe emphasized the importance of thorough understanding of stimulus–response factors in phobia because apparently straightforward fears of objects were sometimes not the most relevant dimension (1969, p. 30). In addition, he proposed that complex disorders often could be broken down into simpler components and each treated individually.

> It must not be assumed that . . . it is only for 'simple' cases that these methods are adequate. Leaving aside the consideration that history is crowded with 'simple' phobias that nobody could cure, investigation from the present standpoint reveals that even difficult 'character neuroses' usually consist of intricate systems of phobias that can be organized and treated along the same lines as a 'simple' phobia. (1958, p. xi)

Social phobias, or interpersonal anxiety, were much more common in Wolpe's experience (1982, p. 10). People in authority comprised a frequent stimulus dimension, resulting in fears of criticism or rejection, manifested by avoidance of social gatherings or relationships, as well as inhibition of feelings such as anger or joy. Additional symptoms such as psychosomatic disorders or depression often resulted from social anxiety. Agoraphobia was cited as an example of a complex disorder in which an apparently common stimulus–response relation existed, namely a fear of separation from persons or places of safety, but which involved many additional considerations for an adequate case formulation and treatment plan to be developed (1990, p. 11).

'Free-floating anxiety' was regarded as a type of phobic reaction to omnipresent aspects of the environment, such as light and shade contrasts, amorphous noise, spatiality, bodily sensations, or the passage of time (1958, pp. 83–4). Wolpe noted that there was no sharp division between specific anxiety-evoking stimuli and those evoking free-floating anxiety, but rather a continuum of pervasiveness existed. Wolpe suggested that two factors were important in the etiology of free-floating anxiety. The first was intensity of anxiety during the initial conditioning experience; the more intense the reaction the greater number of stimuli were likely to be conditioned. The second was a lack of clearly defined stimuli during the conditioning experience, allowing vague stimuli to become conditioned. Wolpe distinguished 'free-floating' anxiety from 'generalized anxiety disorder' as defined by the *DSM*, suggesting that some patients presenting with the symptoms listed by the *DSM* might be suffering from an organic disorder for which psychotherapy would be inappropriate (1990, pp. 268–9).

Panic disorder was the result of conditioning of the panic response to cues present during an initial panic attack which could be brought on by biologic factors, described above, or psychologic factors, such as high levels of stress coupled with a precipitating event (1990, pp. 258–68). Wolpe accepted the *DSM* description of panic disorder and agreed with Ley (1985; 1987) that the symptoms of panic were often brought on by hyper-ventilation in the stressful situation. He did not agree with Ley that all such patients panicked in response to endogenous stimuli associated with hyperventilation because they misattributed the sensations to portending death or insanity. He suggested that in some cases the endogenous sensations functioned simply as a CS, because of their association with the aversive panic experience, and directly evoked the panic response with no intervening cognitive misattribution. As with agoraphobia, treatment would depend on the particular sub-group based on etiologic factors and controlling stimuli.

'War neurosis' provided a paradigmatic example of the classical conditioning of neurotic anxiety most comparable to Wolpe's cat experiment (1958, p. 78; 1982, pp. 27–8). Although he was con-fronted with such cases early in his psychiatric training, this condition played little part in the development of his theory and practice other than as an exemplar. Wolpe later took up the issue in response to the growing interest in post-traumatic stress disorder

(PTSD) as defined in the *DSM*, which described the manifestation of additional symptoms in the absence of specific conditioned stimuli (1990, pp. 270–3). He agreed that PTSD originated in a variety of violent, traumatic conditioning situations in addition to battle, but offered no explanation for the occurrence of symptoms not directly related to conditioned stimuli. He also noted the relative ineffectiveness of treatments, even those based on relearning principles, and admitted his own failure in two cases.

Obsessional behavior was Wolpe's preferred term for obsessive–compulsive disorder, noting that the conventional differentiation between obsessions (recurrent, persistent, intrusive ideas) and compulsions (predominantly motor activities) was of little practical value (1958, p. 90; 1982, p. 294). Wolpe distinguished two categories of obsessional behaviors – those which reduced anxiety and those which elevated it (1958, pp. 90–3). Anxiety-reducing obsessional behavior occurred as a reaction to conditioned anxiety-evoking stimuli and was reinforced by anxiety relief. He proposed that its etiology involved a two-stage process: first, the patient learned a well-defined escape or avoidance response which warded off a real, very strong or oft-repeated threat; then, perhaps years later, that response recurred whenever conditioned anxiety was aroused. Anxiety-elevating obsessional behavior occurred initially in the anxiety conditioning situation and thereafter appeared whenever anxiety was aroused, serving to exacerbate the arousal and the behavior. How this reaction was maintained was unclear, since reinforcement via anxiety reduction did not occur and Wolpe suggested no other mechanism. Wolpe commented that in a few cases the obsessional behavior might become conditioned to incidental stimuli independently of anxiety, but offered no further elaboration (1990, p. 294).

Individual Factors

In addition to genetic factors and other biologic variables which predispose a person to certain disorders, Wolpe hypothesized a number of other factors to account for individual differences in learning neurotic behavior (1982, pp. 33–7).

Learned Predispositions. Wolpe proposed that non-neurotic anxiety reactions which have been learned in various contexts throughout the individual's life may summate with the anxiety evoked by a particular situation, making it more severe than otherwise would have been the case (1958, p. 76). Wolpe gave the example of a woman who, as a child, forgot her lines while giving a recitation; this resulted in some discomfort but no interference in subsequent classroom speaking performances (1982, pp. 30, 36). As an adult, she experienced enormous anxiety on the occasion of being the center of attention while accompanying her prominent husband at a professional convention; thereafter she was very afraid of all public presentations as well as speaking to strangers. In this case, the woman's pre-existing sensitivity to scrutiny made the convention experience aversive enough to result in neurotic anxiety conditioning. Wolpe also cited a study of British air personnel in World War II that found a direct relationship between pre-existing 'emotional sensitivity' and the subsequent development of war neuroses.

Transient Factors. Wolpe raised the possibility that certain episodic physiologic or other conditions could heighten the reaction to an adverse event and result in neurotic conditioning (1958, p. 77; 1982, p. 17). He included fatigue, infection, hormones, drugs, and 'special conditions of consciousness such as hypnagogic states,' as such conditions. As an example Wolpe cited a case in which illness, fatigue, and alcohol impaired the groom's wedding night performance, resulting in anxiety-produced impotence which became conditioned to sexual stimuli (1958, p. 132).

Anxiety-Inhibiting Stimuli. Wolpe suggested that the effects of a stressful event might be ameliorated by surrounding events. He cited a study of children subjected to air raids who were less likely to be sensitized to such events if their parents behaved calmly. One may surmise that this factor operates in both directions, such that anxiety could be facilitated if others reacted to a situation with panic. Wolpe did not develop this possibility, nor suggest stimuli other than social events which could inhibit (or enhance) anxiety conditioning.

Information. Wolpe proposed that information, or its lack, might influence the development of neurosis. The example cited was of patients who experience bizarre sensations in an anxiety-provoking situation, from which they draw disastrous conclusions such as that they are dying or going crazy. He noted that patients who consult a physician about these sensations and fail to get an adequate explanation may become even more anxious. These secondary fears can be more disabling than the original anxiety, agoraphobia being a prime example. Lack of information is a major factor in cognitively based fears, leaving the patient open to accepting misinformation and making faulty inferences.

II. Therapy: Unlearning Neurotic Behavior

Special interventions were required to overcome the persistent, pervasive, disruptive, multi-faceted anxiety reaction. The task for the psychotherapist was to arrange the special circumstances necessary to promote the unlearning of anxiety. The title of Wolpe's first book, *Psychotherapy by Reciprocal Inhibition*, succinctly stated the theoretical mechanism by which maladaptive behavior could be treated. He stated his 'general principle' of therapy as follows:

> If a response antagonistic to anxiety can be made to occur in the presence of anxiety-evoking stimuli so that it is accompanied by a complete or partial suppression of the anxiety responses, the bond between these stimuli and the anxiety responses will be weakened. (1958, p. 71)

This statement may be compared to Freud's dictum, 'Where id was, there ego shall be,' which also suggested a kind of replacement theory. Freud's id and ego, as intrapsychic structures, remained hidden and bore only a convoluted relation to surface manifestations. The means of replacement was similarly convoluted and indirect, and outcome criteria were often unclear. In contrast, Wolpe's theory required the relatively objective specification and control of anxiety-evoking stimuli and anxiety-antagonistic responses, and success could be measured in terms of anxiety symptom reduction. Despite some resemblance to Freudian theory, this was truly new wine in new bottles. And unlike the attempts of Miller and Mowrer to rebottle old psychoanalysis in Hullian terminology, Wolpe's reciprocal inhibition model of unlearning anxiety delineated new tasks for the therapist which bore no resemblance to interpreting dream symbols or working through transference. These tasks included a stimulus–response analysis unique to each patient, determining responses antagonistic to anxiety which could be employed to inhibit anxious arousal, and finally arranging the situation for relearning to occur.

Stimulus–Response Analysis

The initial task of the therapist was to screen out patients having biologic or other disorders inappropriate for reciprocal inhibition therapy, as described above. The assessment procedures Wolpe employed are described in Chapter 3, but essentially he obtained a complete description of the problems which the patient experienced, in autonomic, motoric, and cognitive realms, by means of self-report and direct observation.

In keeping with his view of anxiety as a conditioned response, Wolpe searched for the situations which triggered or were otherwise associated with problematic behavior. He held that, for the most part, patients were aware of anxiety-provoking stimuli relevant to their condition, or could gain awareness through straightforward instructions to observe and remember events of their current and past experience. Repression, in the Freudian sense of actively resisting the recall or recognition of highly emotionally charged material, was not observed in his patients (1958, pp. 94, 216–17). Through accepting, non-judgemental listening, skillful, systematic questioning, and the patient's responses to questionnaires, Wolpe felt the therapist could determine the stimulus events controlling the patient's neurotic behavior.

Themes
Out of the collection of descriptions of anxiety-eliciting events, Wolpe looked for dimensions or thematic categories in which to group sets of stimuli (1958, p. 140; 1990, pp. 160–71). Theoretically, a theme was a family of stimuli related to the conditioned stimulus through the processes of stimulus generalization and second-order conditioning. Often, the theme concerned external situations, such as heights, enclosed spaces, sexual stimuli, or criticism. But in some cases events could be grouped because they elicited particular internal response-produced stimuli, such as feelings of losing control or feelings of being trapped. Often, patients' fears occurred along more than one dimension.

Multiple themes were presumably the result of multiple conditioning experiences. Multiple stimuli were likely to have been present when the aversive UCS occurred. Just as the cats learned to fear both the buzzer and the visual aspects of the room where shock was presented, a man suffering war neurosis might react to visual, auditory, and olfactory stimuli associated with battle. Alternatively, a person might confront successive aversive conditioning experiences during life, particularly if he or she were predisposed to anxiety arousal. If anxiety responses occurred frequently, additional stimuli could be conditioned through the process of second-order conditioning.

The Anxiety Hierarchy
In many instances, fearsome events could not be confronted directly because the anxiety they elicited overwhelmed all other responses. For such cases, Wolpe developed the idea of weakening the anxiety response by attenuating the eliciting stimuli (1958, p. 139). According to this theory, an anxiety-eliciting stimulus may be

thought of as a constellation of elements, each of which evokes a diminished anxiety response. Presentation of a small number of stimulus elements elicits a small amount of anxiety which can be successfully overcome. Because of the complexity of stimuli, it often was not possible to specify, much less quantify, the component stimulus elements or the amount of anxiety elicited by each.

In practice, Wolpe first approximated the relationship between stimuli and anxiety by the simple expedient of asking patients to rank order, according to the amount of disturbance they would experience if confronted by the situation, the items written as a list of stimulus events related to a theme (1958, p. 140). Later he employed the 'subjective unit of disturbance' (*sud*) scale (Wolpe and Lazarus, 1966, p. 73). The patient was asked to think of the very worst anxiety imaginable and to assign it the number 100, and to think of being absolutely calm and assign it the number zero. Then any event could be given a number between 0 and 100 according to the amount of anxiety the patient imagined experiencing. In this way, stimulus items could be quantified and arranged hierarchically on the basis of the amount of *sud*s elicited by each.

The use of the *sud* scale allowed hierarchies to be developed with a smooth progression from one item to the next (Wolpe and Lazarus, 1966, p. 73). If one item was given a rating of 80, and the next a rating of 40, Wolpe held that it was essential to discover intervening items, say, of 50, 60, and 70 *sud*s. The importance of a smooth hierarchy was based on Wolpe's theory of the spread of anxiety reduction (1958, p. 140). Elimination of anxiety to the lowest item on the hierarchy also reduced the anxiety elicited by the adjacent items. Wolpe presented the hypothetical example of an acrophobic individual who has one unit of anxiety looking out of a second-floor window, two units looking out of a third-floor window, and so on (1969, pp. 97–8). Reduction to zero of anxiety elicited by looking out of the second-floor window would also diminish to one the anxiety evoked by the third-floor window, and so on up the hierarchy. Wolpe hypothesized that the inhibition generalized to adjacent stimuli, bringing them into the range where they could be overcome on subsequent trials.

Implicit in this theory was the notion that the reciprocally inhibiting situation was powerful enough to overcome only a small amount of anxiety. If there were too large a gap between items on the hierarchy, the reduction of anxiety would not generalize to the next item and progress would be blocked. Furthermore, if the stimulus elicited too much anxiety to be inhibited, Wolpe proposed that anxiety could dominate the situation and spread to coincidental stimuli by the second-order conditioning process. Not only would progress be blocked, but this would result in a regression because anxiety would be conditioned to elements of the therapy situation, as had occurred in his cat experiment. Wolpe reported analogous effects in patients to whom he prematurely presented high anxiety stimuli (1958, p. 141). Thus it was important to progress in small steps up the hierarchy.

Anxiety-Inhibiting Responses

The next task of the therapist was to discover responses which could be employed to overcome anxiety. Wolpe's autonomic theory of anxiety suggested some responses which could be employed. Often he relied on empirical observation, noting what worked in his own clinical experience and combing the literature for reports of others. He then extended his theory to account for these observations, which in turn suggested additional approaches.

Therapist-Evoked Responses
First of all, Wolpe observed that the therapeutic situation itself often evoked emotional responses which were antagonistic to anxiety (1958, pp. 193–4; 1969, p. 13). Citing Frank (1961), Wolpe noted that the therapist could mobilize the patient's expectations of help and hope of relief. The arousal of these feelings at the same time that the patient presented his or her difficulties could inhibit some of the anxiety which occurred in the course of the discussion. This factor was common to most psychotherapeutic procedures and Wolpe proposed that it accounted for the similar rates of success found across a variety of traditional therapies (see Chapter 4). He recognized its occurrence in his therapeutic approach as well, but explicitly employed additional anxiety-inhibiting procedures.

Parasympathetic Arousal
One avenue followed by Wolpe was to observe which responses were suppressed by anxiety and, following the principle of reciprocal inhibition, to turn the process on its head and employ those responses to inhibit anxiety. Responses in this category included feeding, aggression, and sexual arousal. Their mechanism of action was hypothesized to be parasympathetic dominance, which reciprocally inhibited the predominant sympathetic arousal that characterized the anxiety response. Relaxation was added to this list on the basis of its parasympathetic qualities (1958, p. 72).

Feeding.   Feeding was regarded as limited in application to human clinical problems. Wolpe recognized the pioneering study of Mary Cover Jones in her use of eating to overcome a child's fear of a rabbit (1958, p. x; Jones, 1924). And he speculated that a clinical report of the effectiveness of subcoma insulin shock therapy in some neurotic patients was due to their increased hunger drive and the adventitious occurrence of anxiety stimuli at the time they were eating (1958, p. x). But he did not recommend feeding as a clinical procedure.

Assertive and Anger Responses.   Wolpe (1969, p. 94) noted that from the beginning of his clinical practice in 1947 he had employed procedures directed toward instigating behavior change in the patient's life situation, including what Salter (1949) called 'excitatory' behavior. But it was not until he developed his theory of reciprocal inhibition that he was able to put assertive behavior into a theoretical context. Wolpe included as assertive behavior not only angry or aggressive responses, but also the expression of friendly or affectionate feelings (1958, p. 114). Initially, he was most concerned with the anger aspect, but later he gave more consideration to other components. The broadness of this category of responses is reflected in his definition of assertive behavior as 'the proper expression of any emotion other than anxiety towards another person' (1973, p. 81).

Wolpe proposed two components to anger-expressing behavior which could inhibit anxiety (1958, p. 114). One component was 'parasympathetic ascendancy,' which was physiologically incompatible with anxiety as sympathetic arousal. Wolpe cited several studies and reviews to support his contention that anger and anxiety were incompatible at the autonomic, midbrain, and 'neurobiological' levels (1958, p. 72; 1990, p. 138). Thus, the arousal of anger in the presence of anxiety-evoking stimuli would function to weaken the power of those stimuli. However, it was important that such anger be expressed in a way that did not result in social sanctions that would reinforce the anxiety response (1958, p. 118).

The second component was motor activity, which also had the inherent physiologic property of inhibiting anxiety (1958, p. 114). In addition, Wolpe recognized that the motoric (and, one may presume, verbal) acts of assertion were usually followed by positive consequences, such as social control, which served to reinforce, in the operant sense, those behaviors. 'The counterconditioning of anxiety is thus intertwined on each occasion with the operant conditioning of the instrumental response, and each facilitates the other' (Wolpe and Lazarus, 1966, p. 40). This marked the first explicit differentiation by Wolpe of operant conditioning as a distinct process. Later, he also recognized that some people may not exhibit assertive behavior, not because it is inhibited by anxiety, but because they have not acquired the motor habits appropriate for certain social situations (1982, p. 119). In such cases, 'social skills training' was called for, though Wolpe cautioned against such training when anxiety was a factor (1990, p. 136; see Chapter 4).

Sexual Arousal. Wolpe referred to nineteenth-century physiology studies indicating parasympathetic innervation of sexual tissues as the mechanism for sexual arousal, and sympathetic activity as relevant for ejaculation (1958, p. 72). Thus, anxiety as sympathetic activity would inhibit arousal and facilitate ejaculation, leading to erection failure and premature ejaculation in men, and 'frigidity' in women (1958, p. 36). Later research by Masters and Johnson (1966) supported Wolpe's hypothesis (1969, p. 72). Wolpe cited a Russian study which indicated that experimental neurosis in dogs could be overcome by eliciting sexual arousal in the anxiety-generating situation, thus demonstrating the anxiety-inhibiting potential of sexual arousal (Wolpe and Lazarus, 1966, p. 104). He also cited a case in which a socially anxious young woman became free of her fears after becoming involved in a romantic relationship (1973, p. 164). But sexual arousal was primarily employed to overcome the sexual anxiety which lay at the root of sexual dysfunction.

Relaxation. Since eating responses were deemed unsuitable for human clinical use, assertive responses were limited to social anxieties, and sexual arousal was limited to sexual anxieties, a tool was needed for addressing all the other anxieties of human neuroses. Wolpe found that tool in Edmund Jacobson's (1938) method of progressive muscle relaxation. Relaxation was regarded as a state characterized by parasympathetic dominance (1958, p. 72). It was ideally suited for overcoming the sympathetic dominant anxiety arousal because it could be employed in a wide variety of situations.

Jacobson's procedure required the patient to increase and then release the tension in each of dozens of muscle groups throughout the body. Jacobson realized that patients could not spend their days in recumbent relaxation, and developed the method of 'differential relaxation,' in which patients learned to relax those muscles not directly required for daily activities (Jacobson, 1938, pp. 81–3). Wolpe rejected Jacobson's theory that 'nervous disorders' resulted from excessive muscle tension, and suggested that his positive findings came from inadvertent reciprocal inhibition during the interview process and happenstance relaxation in the presence of anxiety cues. Wolpe found that seven or fewer relaxation training sessions were sufficient for his program, whereas Jacobson needed 100 to 200, and Wolpe suggested that the reason for his success was that he systematically counterposed relaxation with anxiety stimuli as opposed to waiting for chance encounters (1958, pp. 135–6).

Wolpe later accepted other methods of relaxation training, such as yoga, transcendental meditation, or electromyographic biofeedback (1982, pp. 186–7). The mechanism of action in all cases was considered to be the parasympathetic dominant state generated by these procedures. Like progressive muscle relaxation, their effectiveness depended on counterposition of the relaxed state with anxiety stimuli.

Chemically Induced Responses
Given his medical training, it was only natural that Wolpe considered the use of drugs to counteract anxiety.

> Theoretically, a drug could exert a favourable influence either by depressing anxiety responses so that these are the more easily inhibited by antagonistic responses, or it could augment antagonistic responses, with the same result. It is not to be expected, however, that every drug that diminishes anxiety will give a therapeutic advantage to the antagonistic responses. The drug must have a locus of action that affects the anxiety in whatever part of the central nervous system the antagonistic response has its inhibitory action. (1958, p. 201)

Anxiolytic Drugs. Since his theory of anxiety and antagonistic responses did not specify central nervous system loci of action, but dealt primarily with the autonomic nervous system, Wolpe provided no further guidelines for drug selection. Rather, he noted that because of wide individual differences in response to a drug, it was a matter of trial and error to determine what would be effective for a particular patient (Wolpe and Lazarus, 1966, p. 116). Over the years, Wolpe recommended a wide variety of drugs, including codeine, Thorazine, and Valium.

Whatever the neurologic basis, according to Wolpe's reciprocal inhibition theory, an effective drug treatment program allowed the patient to experience the conditioned stimuli without the anxiety response, permitting non-anxious responses to be strengthened in that situation (Wolpe and Lazarus, 1966, pp. 119–20). It was important that the anxiolytic effects of drugs be paired with the relevant anxiety-evoking stimuli in order for reconditioning to occur. He criticized the work of Pavlov and other early investigators who employed various drugs in an attempt to overcome experimental neurosis in animals, because they did not systematically manipulate the variables of drug administration and exposure to stimuli. He suggested that whatever positive results were found in such studies were due to the inadvertent exposure of the animals to the conditioned anxiety stimuli while under the influence of drugs. In support he cited a two-by-two factorial study (Miller et al., 1957), which systematically studied the effects of drug (chlorpromazine vs. saline) and stimulus exposure (buzzer vs. home cage) on the extinction of signaled avoidance responding in rats. Animals which received both the drug and exposure to the aversive conditioned stimulus made far fewer avoidance responses than those receiving any other combination of variables.

A corollary of Wolpe's use of medication was that the dosage be sufficient to prevent the evocation of an intense anxiety response. Otherwise, anxiety could be reconditioned to the surrounding stimuli and result in a setback for the patient (Wolpe and Lazarus, 1966, pp. 117, 121). Wolpe held that the hazard of addiction was small, since the duration of administration was limited.

Once a patient no longer responded with anxiety while taking medication, Wolpe saw no problem in transferring the new learning to the non-drugged state. In several cases, Wolpe reported gradually fading the drug regimen (1958, pp. 202–3; 1969, pp. 181–2; 1982, pp. 232–3) but in others he did not. Though common sense might suggest a gradual withdrawal from medication, Wolpe presented no theoretical rationale for this practice. He noted only that 'as the neurotic reactions are deconditioned the dosages required become less, and it is often possible to dispense with drugs a good while before the conclusion of therapy' (Wolpe and Lazarus, 1966, p. 117).

Carbon Dioxide Inhalation. The chemical procedure that received most attention from Wolpe was carbon dioxide inhalation (1958, pp. 166–72). He first noted a 1947 clinical report in which neurotic patients were rendered unconscious by inhalations of carbon dioxide and oxygen in a 30/70 percent mixture. This was an era in which producing unconsciousness was a popular psychiatric treatment, and this method was probably seen as an addition to electroconvulsive shock and insulin coma. Wolpe suggested that whatever positive results were obtained were probably a result of the nonspecific effects of therapy, and noted that perhaps more favorable results were masked by the anxiety-evoking properties of the procedure. More positive reports from an investigator employing a single inhalation method, which produced 'no more than a very brief stupor,' stimulated Wolpe to begin his own trials. Wolpe recommended a mixture of 65 percent carbon dioxide and 35 percent oxygen, though other concentrations were suggested depending upon individual reactions.

Wolpe employed carbon dioxide inhalation for cases of free-floating anxiety, in which the evoking stimuli are continuously present, such as omnipresent features of the environment or bodily sensations. Wolpe was not sure of the drug's physiologic mechanism of action but proposed a counterconditioning process in which excitation from the intense respiratory stimulation or the complete muscle relaxation following this arousal could be antagonistic to anxiety and weaken its connection to the pervasive stimuli present at the time of inhalation. He found the procedure eliminated pervasive anxiety for several hours and up to several weeks, and hypothesized that the return of anxiety was due to the patient once again encountering external anxiety-evoking situations. He suggested that it might be possible to overcome the anxiety evoked by specific stimuli by presenting them in imagery as consciousness becomes clouded.

Other Anxiety-Inhibiting Responses

Wolpe was alert to the experimental and clinical literature which suggested additional approaches to the reduction of anxiety. He tried many in his own clinical practice, fitting them into the framework of reciprocal inhibition. All the procedures involved presentation of the anxiety stimuli, usually by means of imagery, in the context of the additional activity which was thought to inhibit anxiety. The procedures differed in the nature of the competing activity and the manner in which it was evoked.

Responses Controlled by Electrical Stimulation. Wolpe (1958, pp. 89, 173–4) was inspired by an experiment of Mowrer and Viek (1948), in which one group of rats was allowed to terminate electric shock by jumping in the air, while a second yoked-control group received the same number and duration of shocks, the termination of which was unrelated to the animals' activity. Shock was preceded by offering food, which animals in the first group consumed readily after a period of disruption, while those in the second group completely refused to eat, an indication of anxiety. Wolpe interpreted this finding as indicating that anxiety was inhibited by the motor activity of jumping. From this conclusion he developed a 'new therapeutic method' in which a mild electric shock was delivered to the hand and forearm of a patient, serving as a signal to flex her forearm. Unlike the Mowrer and Viek experiment, flexion in this procedure was a response to the therapist's instructions to flex when the shock occurred. The shock was presented as the patient imagined a slightly disturbing event from her anxiety hierarchy. Repeating the shock/flexions 15–25 times reportedly 'vanquished' her upset feelings regarding the event. Wolpe later questioned whether the motor activity in this procedure was necessary at all, proposing that weak electrical stimulation alone might be sufficient to inhibit anxiety (1973, pp. 147–8).

This apparently inherent property of mild shock to inhibit anxiety was suggested to Wolpe by the demonstration of a clinician and was modified in 'controlled experiments,' the details of which were not given (Wolpe and Lazarus, 1966, pp. 147–8). A shock, 'strongly felt *without being aversive*' (italics in original) was delivered to the patient's forearm in one-second pulses, at the rate of 8–10 per minute, for 20–30 minutes. In his example, the shock was sufficient to elicit wrist flexion. This procedure reduced patient reports of pervasive anxiety to almost zero. The patient was then asked to imagine scenes from his anxiety hierarchy as shock pulses were delivered two or three more times. Initially Wolpe accompanied each pulse with the word 'relax' but reported that he later found this unnecessary. Wolpe attributed the anxiety inhibition to the shock itself rather than the motor activity, terming the process 'external inhibition.' He borrowed this term from Pavlov's observation that an extraneous stimulus could elicit an 'investigatory' or 'defense' reflex and reduce the amount of salivation to a conditioned stimulus (Pavlov, 1927, pp. 43–7). However, there were differences between the two phenomena in addition to the fact that Pavlov was concerned with alimentary reflexes. First, Pavlov's external inhibition was usually temporary, with repeated stimulus presentations leading to 'habituation' – the recovery of conditioned reflexes to full strength. Permanent external inhibition could be produced by pre-feeding or by aversive stimuli which elicited negative arousal. It is difficult to see the parallel between these observations and the putative effects of mild shock on anxiety.

Wolpe was also inspired by several other experiments with rats that suggested that a stimulus which coincided with the termination of aversive shock acquired positively reinforcing and anxiety-inhibiting properties. Mowrer's critical review (1960, pp. 140–4) of research on this topic concluded that such a CS functioned as a 'secondary' positive reinforcer only when negative arousal was present. More relevantly, Mowrer (1960, p. 419) also proposed that the *relief* response to such a stimulus was antagonistic to fear. Wolpe developed a human analogue, again involving shock to the forearm, called 'anxiety-relief conditioning' (1958, pp. 180–1). In this procedure, the intensity and duration of the shock was decidedly unpleasant. The patient endured it as long as possible and then said the word 'calm,' terminating the shock. In this way, anti-anxiety relief responses were conditioned to the word, which the patient was instructed to utter in situations which evoked anxiety. Wolpe theorized that the greater the autonomic emotional arousal elicited by the shock, the greater the relief at its termination, and the more effective the procedure.

To summarize, Wolpe theorized that electric shock controlled several responses which were antagonistic to anxiety. First, it could elicit motor activity. However, in his 'conditioned motor response' procedure, the response was controlled by the therapist's instructions rather than by the shock itself. Thus the shock served only as a signal, and perhaps any other stimulus could have served as well. But Wolpe later concluded that it was the shock itself and not the motor response that affected anxiety. The second property of mild shock was 'external inhibition.' However, to be consistent with Pavlov, if the shock served only as a distracting stimulus its effects should have been temporary, or if it elicited a defense reaction then one would expect it to augment rather than inhibit anxiety. Finally, the offset of aversive shock elicited 'relief,' which Wolpe proposed could be conditioned to associated stimuli. This view was more consistent with contemporary learning theories.

Motoric Responses. From his earliest research, Wolpe had proposed that skeletal–muscular activity was reciprocally inhibitory to anxiety. Although such activity was part of the reaction to shock displayed by his cats, he felt that it inhibited the core anxiety, which was autonomic arousal (1952a). He included 'competitively conditioned motor responses' in his list of responses which inhibit anxiety (1958, p. 113). But other than the 'conditioned motor response,' described above, he developed no other procedures based on this principle. However, Wolpe recognized clinical reports of the use of various motoric activities to overcome anxiety, and explained them in terms of reciprocal inhibition. An early example was the report of Arnold Lazarus, in which a patient was instructed to rapidly hit a punching bag or strenuously pound a padded cushion in association with an anxiety-provoking thought (Wolpe and Lazarus, 1966, p. 146). Later examples included 'oriental defense exercises,' such as karate and kung fu, practiced in the presence of real or imagined anxiety stimuli (1973, pp. 154–5). Wolpe initially included yoga and transcendental meditation in the category of 'special physical maneuvers,' but on the basis of their autonomic effects he later classified them as relaxation exercises, adding autogenic training and electromyographic biofeedback (1982, pp. 186–7).

Wolpe did not address the apparent paradox that both quiescent motor activity, such as relaxation, and vigorous action, such as kung fu, reciprocally inhibited anxiety. The mechanism of action of relaxation was hypothesized to lie in its parasympathetic autonomic effects, presumably missing from more strenuous activities. Wolpe explained the effects of vigorous action as 'intraresponse reciprocal inhibition' (1982, p. 48), in which competition between the elements within a complex response occurs in circumstances in which one element is strengthened and becomes dominant while another element is weakened. In support he cited the study by Mowrer and Viek (1948) described above; a motoric component (jumping) of the complex anxiety reaction was selectively reinforced by shock termination, which then served to diminish another component of anxiety (eating inhibition). Although Wolpe did not consider it, the same process could be invoked to account for a phenomenon observed in signaled avoidance learning: animals calmly performed motor avoidance responses with no autonomic evidence of anxiety, but prevention of the avoidance response resulted in intense anxiety reactions (Solomon et al., 1953). It is consistent with Wolpe's theory to assume that motor activity that is not part of a complex anxiety response has inhibitory properties.

Responses Evoked by Imagery. Wolpe included the clinical reports of several investigators who instructed patients to imagine positive scenes which included elements of the feared situation (1973, pp. 149–54). These scenes (and the feelings they evoked) were presumed to be inhibitory to anxiety and neutralized its arousal. One procedure, termed *emotive imagery* (Lazarus and Abramovitz, 1962), involved imagination of situations which produced feelings of pleasant excitement. A second, termed *induced anger* (Goldstein et al., 1970), involved imagining anger and aggression in anxious situations, sometimes accompanied by punching a pillow. The third, termed *direct suggestion* (Rubin, 1972) required the patient to imagine being comfortable in everyday situations which contained some anxiety stimuli.

Responses Evoked by Models. A related procedure combined the anxiety and counter-anxiety stimuli using moving pictures or live presentation rather than verbal descriptions. Bandura and his associates produced a series of experiments in which people with

fears of dogs, snakes or heights observed films or live demonstrations of models fearlessly interacting with the feared situations
(Bandura, 1969, pp. 175–92). Comparison studies indicated
modeling procedures to have greater effects than those employing
imagery and relaxation. Wolpe recognized the method as a
'significant practical advance' and extended his theory to account
for the findings (1973, pp. 161–2; 1990, pp. 212–14). In essence,
Wolpe proposed that modeling addressed both cognitive and
conditioned anxiety. Observing a model provided corrective
information for an individual who, for example, might have the
mistaken belief that a non-poisonous snake was harmful. At the
same time, 'pleasant emotional responses' aroused by the experimenter and the model could reciprocally inhibit conditioned
arousal. In groups of subjects who were not differentiated according
to conditioned or cognitive anxiety, this 'double-barreled' approach
had obvious advantages.

Saccadic Eye Movements.   A recent innovation was first reported
by a clinician, Francine Shapiro (1989a; Wolpe, 1990, pp. 272–3).
Upon introspection, she observed the disappearance of recurring
disturbing thoughts accompanying repeated side-to-side eye
movements. She extended this observation to post-traumatic stress
disorder patients, whom she asked to hold a traumatic image in
memory while tracking her finger, moving side-to-side before their
eyes. She reported that distance from the patients' eyes, and the
length and speed of finger movement, were important variables.
Wolpe reported using the procedure successfully in two cases. He
speculated that the desensitization process occurred at the neural
level, citing an observation of Jacobson that 'relaxation of the
extrinsic eye muscles has extraordinary emotional potency' (1990,
p. 273).

Summary and Conclusions

Wolpe proposed that anxiety, in the first instance, was aroused by a
noxious unconditioned stimulus and was attached to coincidental
stimuli through the mechanism of Pavlovian conditioning. He
favored the view that acquisition and maintenance of the anxiety
response required reinforcement by reduction of the anxiety drive,
and was equivocal about Mowrer's theory that simple contiguity
between the UCS and CS was sufficient for emotional learning.
Although the prototype UCS was a painful stimulus, many human
neuroses stemmed from stimuli which only threatened rather than
inflicted harm. Wolpe believed the threatening nature of stimuli

from cognitive sources arose through parental and other social influences, but he did not find Freudian infant socialization theory to be useful. Ambivalent situations, in which two incompatible responses were evoked, could also serve as a noxious UCS. But perhaps in his efforts to downplay Freudian-based conflict theory, Wolpe did not accord more than a passing acknowledgment to conflict as a source of anxious arousal.

Conditioned stimuli comprised just about any event, external or internal, which coincided with anxiety arousal. Wolpe did not lend much weight to the theory of 'prepared' conditioned stimuli, nor did he consider later 'information' theories. Anxiety once evoked by a CS could be attached to additional events through the process of second-order conditioning. Anxiety could also spread to additional stimuli along various dimensions of similarity to the CS through the process of generalization. Wolpe's theory proposed that, once evoked, there were many pathways for anxiety to spread and gain control over the life of the neurotic person.

In clinical practice, Wolpe excluded those disorders which were not based on conditioning or on anxiety, primarily the psychoses, psychopathy, and 'endogenous' depression. His broad definition of conditioned anxiety led to the inclusion of a variety of disorders in which it often was not obvious, such as 'neurotic' depression, 'psychosomatic' (stress-related) disorders, sexual dysfunction, sexual deviance (including some cases of male homosexuality), many addictive disorders, and stuttering. In the case of the latter three, he also recognized that many factors in addition to anxiety were operative, so that simple attempts to decondition anxiety were likely to be insufficient. For most of the other disorders, such as various phobias, PTSD, and obsessional behaviors, the central role of anxiety was more apparent.

Therapy required unlearning the anxiety response. Two major extinction theories, fatigue and interference, were each able to account for some of the experimental data concerning extinction phenomena, but each also had difficulties. Wolpe saw them as complementary. He adapted them to make sense of the puzzling persistence of neurotic behavior and, more importantly, as a guide to develop methods of deconditioning. Psychotherapy with humans was considerably more complex than feeding cats in a series of rooms increasingly similar to the place where they had been shocked. But Wolpe's theoretical formulations to account for his success in overcoming his cats' neurotic behavior provided the direction for a new approach to neurotic patients.

The theory of conditioned anxiety led to a stimulus–response analysis of the patient's environment for the array of primary, generalized, and second-order conditioned stimuli which evoked the anxiety reaction in all its many guises. In these stimuli he found patterns of common relationships, termed themes, and a hierarchic arrangement of their ability to arouse anxiety. Themes and hierarchies formed the map by which to guide the assault on anxiety.

The weapons in this assault were the anxiety-inhibiting responses which Wolpe adapted from many sources, including Jacobson's progressive muscle relaxation and Salter's 'excitatory' responses. His theory provided some foundation for the wide range of anxiety-inhibiting responses, but by no means a consistent one. Some, like relaxation, were believed to act at a peripheral autonomic level. Others, like various drug-induced states, were hypothesized to have a more central nervous system site of action. The mechanism for still others, like electric-shock-controlled responses and saccadic eye movements, was not clear at all. Throughout, Wolpe insisted on an empirical criterion, and was willing to consider methods having supporting outcome data. The overarching hypothesis of reciprocal inhibition required only that the counter-anxiety response, from whatever source, occur in the presence of conditioned stimuli in a manner which allows the anxiety to be overcome.

An additional contribution of the experimental tradition from which Wolpe operated was the responsibility of the therapist to observe the results of his/her interventions and to adjust treatment to achieve the most favorable outcome. While theory provided guidelines for observing the relevant stimuli and responses in each case, and for formulating a specific intervention, the number and complexity of variables often precluded a complete understanding. It was incumbent upon the therapist to remain alert for new information and to guide treatments accordingly. And it was incumbent on the therapist, as an empiricist, to report the outcomes of his/her efforts.

3

Major Contributions to Practice

Wolpe began his practice as an explicit alternative to the psycho-analytic methods that dominated psychotherapy at mid-century. He developed and adapted therapeutic procedures using the learning principles described in the preceding chapter, and shared his methods and results with the larger professional community extending far beyond his isolated corner of the world. These innovative procedures and their connections to learning theory formed the foundations for the field known today as behavior therapy. This chapter is divided into two sections which reflect Wolpe's attention to the entire therapeutic process. The first section addresses his assessment procedures and preparation of the patient for therapy, and the second reviews his treatment methods.

Assessment and Preparation

In contrast to psychoanalysis, Wolpe (1958, pp. 105–13) clearly distinguished an assessment phase prior to intervention and explicitly told the patient his conclusions and their implication for the treatment methods to be pursued. He began assessment with a detailed historically-focused interview usually supplemented with one or more psychological inventories. The second step was education, in which he prepared the patient for treatment. During this phase Wolpe explained to the patient the nature of his or her disorder in terms of anxiety conditioning, and discussed the rationale for particular procedures to be implemented. Throughout the intervention phase, informal assessment continued so as to monitor the effectiveness of treatment and to make changes as needed.

Assessment Procedures

The purpose of assessment was to make treatment decisions. As described in Chapter 2, Wolpe's first task was to screen patients with organic or non-anxiety-based disorders who were not appro-priate for his methods. Individuals with psychotic or psychopathic symptomology apparently could be recognized by conventional psychiatric and psychological diagnostic methods. More difficult to discern were patients presenting anxiety symptoms due to organic illness or other biologic conditions. Such patients sometimes were accepted unknowingly for therapy, only to prove refractory to treatment. Wolpe recommended referral for careful medical evaluation in these cases. He also excluded unadaptive habits that did not involve anxiety, such as nailbiting or trichotillomania, and drug addictions which were characterized by biologically-based cravings and poor motivation for treatment (1982, pp. 8–9).

The second task of assessment was to determine the nature of the patient's anxiety reactions. Wolpe took special care to discover the operation of anxiety in presenting complaints in which its role was not immediately obvious. The final task of assessment was to determine the stimulus–response relationships that controlled the patient's anxiety reactions and the resulting symptoms.

The two major methods of assessment were the clinical interview and paper-and-pencil inventories. Where circumstances permitted, Wolpe occasionally employed informal direct observation outside the office.

The Clinical Interview. Wolpe provided detailed information on conducting the interview, including published transcripts and films (for example, 1958, pp. 105–6, 120–3; Wolpe and Lazarus, 1966, pp. 24–6, 29–37). His methods stood in marked contrast to psychodynamic procedures in which the patient reclined on a couch speaking to an unseen and mostly silent therapist. Wolpe recommended that the assessment interview be conducted in a business-like fashion with the therapist facing the client across a desk. Wolpe took written notes, or used a tape recorder for teaching purposes, assuring the patient of confidentiality and agreeing to use a code-name if the patient preferred. He was quite directive, asking specific questions and pursuing particular topics in a more-or-less predetermined order. At the same time, Wolpe sought to give the patient 'the feeling that the therapist is unreservedly on his side,' by means of accepting, noncritical listening. He assumed the patient to be a cooperative collaborator in this investigation and to report honestly his or her reactions in various situations. Relevant pathogenic learning experiences were presumed to have happened within the patient's memory, ruling out the idea of repressed infantile events which were the focus of Freudian approaches.

The first order of business was to obtain information about the patient's presenting problems, their current manifestations, and the circumstances surrounding their onset. Special attention was focused on determining the precipitating events that gave rise to the patient's problems and subsequent events that aggravated or ameliorated them. Wolpe looked for information concerning either the cognitive or conditioning origins of anxiety, and later events that may have modified its form or led to its spread to other stimuli. The conditioning history of each anxiety habit was traced. Concerning the etiology of their disorders, Wolpe noted that:

> Many patients are able to connect the onset of various reactions with specific occurrences or chronic states of affairs. Others can establish within reasonably narrow limits the time of onset of symptoms without being able to identify any relevant circumstances. A third group of patients can recall nothing of the onset of their neurotic reactions. I coax these to think back more carefully in the hope of arousing some recall; but if significant facts are not brought forth in a few minutes, I cease to press the point, telling the patient that I have no intention of devoting a great deal of time to raking up past history, because although it would be interesting and perhaps helpful it is not necessary: *for to overcome his neurotic reactions it is of greater relevance to determine what stimuli do or can evoke them at the present time.* However, the history of particular sequences of events is often sought later when the case presents new aspects. Also some patients spontaneously proffer relevant data from time to time. (1958, p. 105, italics in original)

Wolpe did not assign any special significance to a patient's inability to remember precipitating events and did not report any differences in type of disorder or outcome of treatment between patients who could and those who could not recall details concerning onset.

After inquiring into the presenting complaints, Wolpe then broadened his scope to include the patient's life history. He followed a general outline of topics, though the order and depth varied according to the natural flow of the patient's story. A 'Life History Questionnaire' was suggested for 'literate individuals' to fill out in order to shorten the assessment phase (Wolpe and Lazarus, 1966, p. 26), but this was not systematically developed. The patient was asked about his or her childhood development: methods of discipline, religious training, and the nature of relationships with parents or caregivers, siblings, and friends. An academic and work history was obtained: special problems, accomplishments, and relationships with peers and superiors. Then sexual history was reviewed: the patient's earliest sexual awareness, masturbation, early sexual experiences and later relationships, and emotions about sex. Marital issues, sexual and otherwise, were also explored. This thorough history was intended to reveal the origin and development of the patient's presenting complaints as well as additional issues which the patient may have been unaware of or hesitant to describe.

Questionnaires. Wolpe recommended supplementing the interview with three questionnaires: the Willoughby Personality Schedule (Willoughby, 1932), the Fear Survey Schedule (Wolpe and Lang, 1964; 1969), and the Bernreuter Self-Sufficiency Scale (Bernreuter, 1933a). They served both as diagnostic measures, revealing areas of maladjustment that might have been missed in the interview, and as outcome measures, providing a quantitative index of change during or after therapy.

The Willoughby Personality Schedule had its origins in an array of questionnaires developed in the 1920s to assess various personality characteristics (Thurstone and Thurstone, 1930). A large number of items related to 'neurotic' functioning were compiled and administered to the incoming freshmen at the University of Chicago. The Thurstones extracted 42 items which most clearly differentiated the high from low total scorers. Willoughby (1932) revised the Thurstone instrument to 25 items and changed the scoring from yes/no to a 0 to 4 scale of frequency, resulting in a total score range of 0 to 100. He felt the scale reflected 'hypersensitivity to interpersonal stress' and avoidance of social interactions. Willoughby (1934) reported split-half and test-retest reliabilities of around .90 in administrations to various college student samples, with women scoring significantly higher than men.

Wolpe, following Salter, revived use of the Willoughby in his clinical practice (1958, pp. 107–11). He verbally described each item to the patient, emphasizing that it referred to situations with no objective threat, and later employed a self-administered version that included this information in its instructions (1969, p. 28). Wolpe conducted his own psychometric evaluation, examining the pre-treatment scores of 295 unselected patients. He obtained an approximately normal distribution with the mean, median, and mode all falling between 40 and 49, with no differences between males and females in this sample. He compared these scores to Willoughby's normative student sample, finding significantly higher scores in his patient group. Wolpe used the Willoughby score to confirm a diagnosis of neurosis and to gauge the degree of neurotic reactivity. As a rule of thumb, Wolpe felt that scores below 20 were 'normal,' though he warned that low scores did not necessarily mean that neuroticism was low. That is, some patients may have had anxiety conditioned to stimulus situations which were not included on the inventory, such as sexual or somatic fears. Wolpe also looked at individual items as well as the patient's total score. He noted that 'it is not only the total score that matters but also how that score is made up. A score of 10 made up of two 4's and two 1's clearly indicates more important neurotic sensitivity than a score of 20 made up of 1's' (1958, p. 111). For example, a patient with a low overall score gave the maximum rating to an item having to do with hesitancy to help at the scene of an accident (1958, p. 154). Follow-up questioning revealed a sensitivity to pain and injury which turned out to be the key to the patient's sexual dysfunction.

More recent psychometric evaluations of the Willoughby have confirmed its reliability and validity. Administration to a sample of 100 college students and townspeople found a distribution of scores almost identical to that obtained by Willoughby, though the difference between sexes was not replicated (Hestand et al., 1971). In another study, the Willoughby was administered to 437 out-patients having a variety of neurotic diagnoses (Turner et al., 1980). The mean for this sample was comparable to that reported by Wolpe for his patients, and no significant differences between males and females were found. Internal consistency measure of reliability was quite high. Inter-item correlations and factor analysis supported the notion that the inventory measured a unitary construct labeled 'interpersonal anxiety.' Turner et al. (1980) emphasized the usefulness of this scale for research and treatment employing assertiveness training, in contrast to a number of specific measures of assertiveness which lack its construct validity. Given the importance of interpersonal anxiety in many neurotic disorders, the Willoughby appears to be a tool of widespread utility and well-suited for the tasks which Wolpe set for it.

The examination of individual items on the Willoughby pre-saged the development of more comprehensive surveys of situations which could evoke anxiety. The first *Fear Survey Schedule* was developed to screen college students for common fears in order to recruit research subjects. It listed 50 common fears rated on a seven-point scale (Lang and Lazovik, 1963). Impressed by this approach, Wolpe collaborated with Lang to develop a list of 72 items derived from clinical reports of patients; these were rated on a five-point scale of disturbance from 'not at all' to 'very much' (Wolpe and Lang, 1964). Wolpe noted the items fell into categories concerning animals, social situations, tissue damage (illness and death), noises, classic phobias, and miscellaneous. This list was expanded to 76 items in 1966, 87 items in 1969, and a 108-item inventory was offered for sale (Wolpe and Lang, 1969). As employed by Wolpe, no numbers were assigned to the ratings and no total or category scores were derived. Geer (1965) developed another fear survey, derived from reports by college students, consisting of 51 items rated on a seven-point scale. Some items were validated by comparing *in vivo* approach to situations by subjects reporting high, medium, or low fear. Later surveys have been constructed by extending and combining these early ones.

Following Geer (1965), many investigations of the psychometric properties of the various fear surveys were conducted (Hersen, 1973). For example, Hersen (1971) found correlations around .80 between the Wolpe–Lang and the Geer instruments in a group of psychiatric inpatients. Reliability has been fairly high, and factor analytic studies with different instruments and populations have shown fairly consistent factors related to small animals, social situations, and illness, in line with Wolpe's initial observation. A major topic of research was the degree to which self-reported fear on a survey was related to behavioral avoidance of the feared object and physiological arousal in its presence (Bellack and Hersen, 1977). A great deal of discrepancy between these measures was often found in college students (see, for example, Lang, 1968). One reason for the discrepancy may have been that the items were too general to predict specific behavior, at least in student populations (for example, Lick et al., 1977). Closer correspondence between verbal and other measures of anxiety is usually found in clinical as opposed to student samples (Sallis et al., 1980). For example, a study with phobic patients which monitored self-report, avoidance and heart rate during therapy found close correspondence between verbal and motoric behavior, though heart rate was related to neither (Leitenberg et al., 1971).

Wolpe promoted the Fear Survey Schedule as a means of gathering information about events which might have been overlooked in the interview. In this regard, Barlow (1988, p. 486) recently noted its usefulness in determining the patterning of additional specific fears in patients presenting with clinical phobia.

The *Bernreuter Self-Sufficiency Inventory*, similar in method and content to the Thurstone Inventory, originated as a 125-item personality questionnaire developed by Bernreuter (1933b), which asked college students about preferences or feelings in a variety of situations. Keys provided scores on six traits, such as 'neurotic tendency' and 'self-sufficiency.' Bernreuter (1933a) published the 60-item self-sufficiency subscale as a separate inventory. He reported that it distinguished college students in areas such as needing encouragement and desire to be alone, as rated by self and others.

Salter (1949, pp. 52–4) reported that low scores on the self-sufficiency inventory characterized patients of the 'inhibitory' type, and warned that such a person was 'a therapeutically discouraging problem.' Wolpe also noted that a low score indicated that the patient would have difficulty carrying out the active therapeutic tasks to be assigned in the course of therapy (1958, pp. 106–7). He suggested that the scale was useful for cases with serious dependency habits, low scores indicating difficulty in carrying out instructions for assertion (1969, p. 28) and characteristic of over-dependent persons presenting as agoraphobics (1973, p. 28); high scores characterized psychopaths and some normals. Wolpe did not suggest what special interventions might be indicated with patients scoring low in self-sufficiency. And he presented no data to support his observations of the relationship between self-sufficiency score and diagnostic category or difficulty in therapy.

In addition to the fear survey schedules, a host of other question-naires have been developed to assist in diagnosis and to provide quantitative measures for research on psychotherapy. These have been reviewed extensively elsewhere (for example, Bellack and Hersen, 1977; Jensen and Haynes, 1986). Most instruments focus on specific qualities such as anxiety, depression, assertiveness, irrational beliefs, marital satisfaction, or somatic complaints. Total scores are useful in placing a patient in a diagnostic group and in assessing pre-/post-therapy changes, but responses to specific items must be considered for these tests to be of use in developing individual treatment programs, as Wolpe noted in his discussion of the Willoughby. More broadly focused personality tests, such as the MMPI, are also employed widely for diagnostic and outcome research, though these are of little use in the stimulus–response assessment advocated by Wolpe. He suggested that the intro-version–extraversion scale of the Maudsley Personality Inventory (Eysenck, 1959b) was useful in screening psychopathic personalities (1969, p. 28).

Wolpe surveyed the use of 11 questionnaires among the clinical fellows of the Behavior Therapy and Research Society, a group one would suppose to be highly sympathetic to his assessment pro-cedures (Wolpe and Wright, 1988). The most frequently employed test was the Beck Depression Inventory (46 percent), followed by the Wolpe–Lang (42 percent), the MMPI (35 percent), the Willoughby (19 percent), and the Bernreuter (12 percent). Other than two depression scales, the use of inventories for specific traits such as assertiveness or anxiety was not included. Wolpe felt this study showed unfortunately deficient assessment procedures which could lead to ineffective therapy. He attributed this neglect to the 'myth of homogeneity,' in which all patients in a particular diag-nostic category were regarded as similar for purposes of treatment.

As an example of this problem, he described a woman diagnosed as agoraphobic who, after 20 years of psychoanalysis, and six years of behavior therapy with two reputable therapists, continued to have significant problems. Administration of the Willoughby and the Wolpe–Lang revealed high levels of neurotic anxiety and many maladaptive social fears. Only by attending to these was final success achieved.

Preparing the Patient

Wolpe recommended a collaborative relationship with patients, which required that they be knowledgeable about their disorders and cooperative in assessment and intervention. This was achieved by the therapist directly educating the patient in what the stimulus–response analysis revealed and its implications for the treatment phase. His approach was a marked change from contemporary psychotherapies, such as psychoanalysis or Rogerian therapy, in which discovery of the nature of the patient's disorder was the major part of therapy, a prolonged affair never explicitly directed by the therapist. Wolpe assumed the role of expert, analogous to the traditional role of the physician in making a diagnosis and prescribing a treatment, but differing in that he was careful to provide a rationale, invite questions, and discuss objections. His case presentations revealed that patients often did raise questions; many had had years of psychoanalysis and their orientation was far different from Wolpe's but he never reported a case in which the patient rejected his rationale.

Wolpe provided transcripts of the general description of neurotic anxiety he gave to patients. The details changed somewhat over time, but the explanation generally contained the following features: a distinction between normal and neurotic fear; a simple example of unadaptive fear conditioning; an example of stimulus generalization; and an assertion of the scientific foundation for the principles of learning. Experiences from the patient's history were given to illustrate the learning process. Here is a brief example of such an explanation:

> Fear is appropriate under circumstances of real danger – for example, walking alone at night in an unsafe neighborhood, learning that one's firm is about to retrench its staff, or being confronted by a poisonous snake. Fear is not appropriate when elicited by situations that contain no real threat – such as seeing somebody receive an injection, entering a crowded room, or feeling disapproved of by someone who has no importance in one's life. Inappropriate fear is called neurotic fear.
>
> How do neurotic fears begin? If a severe fear reaction occurs in particular circumstances, those circumstances become fear-connected so

that their later appearance in some form will automatically trigger fear. For example, an American lieutenant 'went through hell' in the bursting of high explosives in a pass in Vietnam. After he returned to the United States, when he and his wife were one day walking to a wedding in New York City, a truck backfired near them. He reacted with instant panic, and 'rolled up next to the parked car, cringing in the gutter.' Your own fears likewise (as your story shows) originated in unpleasant experiences. They became conditioned, or connected, to aspects of the experiences. That is why exposure to similar situations automatically arouses fear. Now, because this fear is the result of learning, the best possible way to eliminate it is by reversing the learning. (1990, p. 90)

Wolpe noted that when the presenting complaint concerned symptoms other than anxiety per se, as in cases of psychosomatic disorders, stuttering, or binge eating, he would point out the relationship between the level of anxiety and severity of the symptom. This prepared the patient for participating in anxiety–reduction procedures. In cases of cognitively based anxiety, Wolpe offered no script for explanation to the patient. In general, he held that anxiety due to misconceptions, discovered during the course of assessment, should be dealt with at once in an authoritative, corrective manner (1958, p. 106).

Sometimes the explanation of a patient's symptoms and the clarification of misconceptions could contribute to 'nonspecific' cures during the assessment phase. While Wolpe generally had a low opinion of the therapeutic value of 'insight,' he recognized that some patients experienced relief with the knowledge that their symptoms had an understandable basis or that situations they feared did not pose an objective threat (1958, pp. 106, 200). One might suppose that patients with cognitively based fears would be more likely to experience an early 'nonspecific' cure but Wolpe did not address this issue.

Therapeutic Techniques

The intervention phase consisted of training the patient to engage in responses antagonistic to anxiety in the face of anxiety-provoking stimuli. A variety of training procedures were developed, the selection of a particular one depending on the diagnostic classification of the patient and, most emphatically, his or her individual characteristics. In this section each of the techniques developed or adapted by Wolpe is described, with attention to historical precedents and changes over time in his practice. Similar approaches or adaptations by others are discussed briefly. Research concerning the efficacy of these procedures is presented in Chapter 4.

Cognitive Procedures

Wolpe initially considered 'clarification of misconceptions' as a preliminary phase of preparing the patient for therapy rather than an actual therapeutic technique (1958, p. 200). Later, in response to growing professional interest in cognitive therapies, he included this in a separate chapter on cognitive therapeutic procedures (1982, p. 89).

Correcting Misconceptions.   Misconceptions are erroneous beliefs that objectively benign situations or experiences are harmful. They arise from misinformation provided by powerful or respected people such as parents or clergy, or erroneous inferences drawn from observation of other people's reactions or the patient's own experience. Wolpe reported that misconceptions were particularly common in fears of the 'hypochondriacal' kind, in which a patient believed that his or her bodily reactions portended severe physical or mental illness (1969, p. 59).

The primary technique employed by Wolpe was authoritative instruction and counter-argument (1958, p. 106). The therapist invoked his own role as expert, or appealed to other authorities, in asserting that the upsetting situation did not in fact indicate what the patient thought it did. For example, Wolpe's status as a physician coupled with references to medical textbooks and negative results from medical tests enabled him to convince a hypochondriacal patient that the symptoms she experienced were not related to dreaded cancer (1982, p. 110).

Wolpe noted that mere reasoning with a patient was often insufficient to change beliefs (1982, p. 111). In such instances, he recommended participating in an activity related to the fear to change the patient's perception of the situation. For example, a man with an irrational fear of rabies was relieved by receiving anti-rabies vaccinations. Participating in therapeutic activities could also change a patient's misconceptions. For example, a woman with sexual difficulties related to mistrust began learning to trust others by closing her eyes for brief periods in the presence of the therapist (1982, p. 108).

Even when the inappropriate belief was changed, Wolpe observed that the 'insight' usually was insufficient to overcome the patient's anxieties. He theorized that the autonomic arousal generated by confrontation with situations which the person believed to be harmful became conditioned to stimuli connected with those situations; change in belief did not automatically change the conditioned arousal and its associated symptoms. Thus the work of therapy shifted to overcoming those 'secondary' conditioned anxiety reactions by other methods.

Thought-stopping. Wolpe credited J.G. Taylor for introducing him to this method and he cited still earlier precursors of this procedure. He employed it with patients who engaged in episodic, persistent, disturbing trains of thought (1958, pp. 200–1; 1969, pp. 224–6). The first step was a discussion of the futility and anxiety-provoking nature of the thought sequences. It was important that the patient agree that the thoughts were indeed unproductive and problematic. The next step was to ask the patient to close his or her eyes and to state the futile thoughts aloud. During the recitation the therapist suddenly shouted 'Stop!' and pointed out that the thoughts actually did stop, although they might soon return. This demonstration was repeated several times. The next step was to ask the patient to engage in the same sequence subvocally and to repeat the sequence each time the thoughts returned. The patient practiced several times with the therapist. Finally, the patient was instructed to practice the procedure in daily life whenever the disturbing thoughts arose. Later, the patient was told to stop the disturbing thought at its inception and to concentrate on something else.

Wolpe suggested variations if the original method was not successful. One was to accompany the initial 'Stop!' with an electric shock to the patient's forearm. Another was to instruct the patient to keep his or her mind on pleasant thoughts and to signal when the unwanted thought intruded, at which point the therapist shouted 'Stop!' Other investigators allowed the patient to self-administer a shock (McGuire and Vallance, 1964) or snap a rubber band on his wrist (Mahoney, 1971). Rimm (1973) employed positive 'assertive' statements after the 'Stop!' with his patients.

Wolpe provided only a few case examples, notably an occasion when he employed the procedure on himself (1969, p. 225). Numerous others have provided case reports and a few experimental studies have appeared (see review in Rimm and Masters, 1979, pp. 396–404). In addition to obsessive thinking, thought-stopping has been employed with intrusive images (Fisher and Winkler, 1975) and phobias (Rimm, 1973). A particularly impressive application of thought-stopping was with several hundred students, treated in large groups, who were panic-stricken after a grisly murder in a college dormitory (Shelton, 1973).

Wolpe's theoretical account of episodic disturbing thoughts and the effects of thought-stopping was decidedly sketchy. He indicated that such thoughts originated with an upsetting event, but did not propose that they were conditioned to associated stimuli. He hypothesized that thought-stopping had an anxiety-reducing effect which served as a reinforcing consequence for thought-inhibition. One might suppose that the procedure, especially when coupled with an aversive stimulus, fit the operant punishment paradigm, while the substitution of positive statements fits Wolpe's own counterconditioning model.

Life Guidance.   Wolpe observed that some patients had 'problems of living' which exacerbated neurotic behavior and obstructed therapy (1990, pp. 101–2). Included were unwise business operations, difficulties related to marriage or divorce, and conflict over family obligations. He proposed the tools of logic and persuasion in helping the patient to untangle such problems. Other than a brief case example, Wolpe provided no further details of this approach.

Assertiveness Training

Wolpe acknowledged several predecessors to his development of the assertiveness training procedure (1958, pp. 114–30; 1969, pp. 61–71; 1973, pp. 79–94), the foremost being Andrew Salter (1949). Salter discussed the therapeutic importance of 'excitatory' emotional expression, but there were obvious differences between his approach and assertiveness training. Salter regarded an 'inhibitory personality' as the basis for maladaptive behavior (1949, p. 47) and employed 'excitatory' exercises as a general procedure to change this state, regardless of the patient's symptoms (1949, p. 59). In contrast Wolpe was much more selective, prescribing assertiveness training only for patients with anxiety conditioned to social stimuli which inhibited their social interactions. Although some patients were generally unassertive, as Salter implied, others had problems only with certain individuals or situations. Whereas Salter relied primarily on instruction and exhortation to instigate behavior change, Wolpe added behavior rehearsal and, for very anxious patients, desensitization. And where Salter (1949, p. 153) had little regard for the immediate consequences of excitatory actions, Wolpe considered the possible negative consequences of assertive behavior. Thus Wolpe's assertiveness training, based on his theory of anxiety, was a much more refined and explicit procedure than Salter's. Wolpe also cited two psychoanalytic authors who employed what could be interpreted as assertive behavior, though couched in different terms, and he contrasted the method with Moreno's (1946) 'psychodrama.'

   Wolpe defined assertive behavior to include aggressive (anger-expressing) behavior as well as the expression of friendly, affectionate, and other non-anxious feelings. He provided a list of assertive statements in both the 'hostile' and 'commendatory' categories and cited Salter's six modes of 'excitatory' behavior as exemplars. Training was indicated for patients whose fear prevented them from responding effectively in a variety of social situations. Variations were developed to meet individual needs. The procedure was carried out in several steps.

Patient Education. Special care was often required to prepare a patient for assertiveness training. Wolpe cited many cases for which assertiveness training was appropriate but in which social anxiety was not the presenting complaint, including problems such as scholastic failure, obsessive thinking, stuttering, psychosomatic illness, secondary nonorgasmic response, depression, and homosexual pedophilia. Some patients had reservations or misconceptions about assertive behavior due to early training which emphasized social obligations and the rights of others at the expense of their own. Still others had strong conditioned anxiety reactions to some aspect of aggressive behavior.

To diagnose the need for assertiveness training Wolpe examined patient responses to items on the Willoughby dealing with shyness, hurt feelings, and sensitivity to criticism. Further information could be obtained by asking how the patient behaved in situations in which he or she received unsatisfactory merchandise or service. Wolpe and Lazarus published a questionnaire (1966, p. 41) and several assertiveness inventories have appeared since (Galassi et al., 1974; Rathus, 1973, for example); Wolpe recommended that of Gambrill and Richey (1975).

To persuade the patient to participate in assertiveness training, Wolpe discussed the relationship between the patient's symptoms and difficult interpersonal situations, pointing out the resentment, fear, or other negative emotions which the patient experienced. He suggested assertive alternatives to the patient's usual response and predicted more positive feelings and effective relationships would occur. He sometimes told of success attained by other patients. In his early practice, Wolpe seemed to rely on coaxing and pressure to overcome a patient's hesitancy. He later became more didactic in his approach, emphasizing the patient's rights with respect to others and teaching the differences between appropriate and inappropriate 'oppositional' and affectionate behaviors.

Assertiveness Training Components. Wolpe's first approach to instigating assertive behavior was to advise the patient to go out and try it. He cautioned that the therapist should make sure that the situation selected was a safe one; if the patient's first efforts at assertiveness were met with negative consequences it could increase his or her sensitivity and make subsequent therapy more difficult. For patients with a great deal of anxiety about assertion, Wolpe advised arranging a hierarchy of situations and starting with the easiest one. In subsequent sessions, the patient reported his or her experience and the therapist provided encouragement, correction, and suggestions for further performance. Wolpe urged patients to be alert for opportunities for appropriate assertion and noted that such behavior became easier with repeated success, a fact he attributed to progressively decreasing anxiety. In this way, the therapist's instructional control diminished and the patient became the instigator of assertive action.

The technique of *behavior rehearsal* gained precedence over simple instructions. It was well-suited for practicing behavior in situations graded according to a hierarchy of difficulty or the amount of anxiety evoked. Wolpe provided a concise description of behavior rehearsal:

> It consists of the acting out of short exchanges between the therapist and the patient in settings from the patient's life. The patient represents himself, and the therapist someone towards whom the patient is unadaptively anxious and inhibited. The therapist starts with a remark, usually oppositional, that the other person might make, and the patient responds as if the situation were 'real.' His initial response will usually be variously hesitant, defensive, and timid. The therapist then suggests a more appropriate response; and the exchange is run again, revised. The sequence may be repeated again and again until the therapist is satisfied that the patient's utterances have been suitably reshaped. It is necessary to take into account not only the words the patient uses, but also the loudness, firmness, and emotional expressiveness of his voice, and the appropriateness of accompanying bodily movements . . . The aim of such modeling, shaping, and rehearsing is frequently an effective preparation for the patient to deal with his real 'adversary' so that the anxiety the latter evokes may be reciprocally inhibited, and the motor assertive habit established. (1973, pp. 90–1)

Following Serber (1972), Wolpe recommended employing video feedback to teach the nonverbal components of assertiveness.

Wolpe published several case examples of assertiveness training, including both instruction and behavior rehearsal, illustrating how it emerged naturally from the patient's description of current life events; he also made available audio tapes and films of actual cases employing assertiveness training.

In some circumstances Wolpe felt that it was not feasible to express anger or other assertive behavior directly because of possible retaliation by an unreasonable superior. His example was of an employee who might be adversely affected by assertive action toward his boss. He suggested that it might be possible to gain control of such situations in more subtle ways by playing upon the adversary's sensitivities. To this end, he sometimes recommended that patients read the humorous books of Stephen Potter, titled *Lifemanship* and *Gamesmanship*, which described various gambits to discomfit one's adversaries (Potter, 1971), though he presented no case examples. Lazarus (1971) criticized this approach as disingenuous and Wolpe eventually ceased to mention it, perhaps in tacit recognition of the importance of honesty and the rights of others emphasized in later approaches to assertiveness (see Chapter 4).

Wolpe found that some patients had great difficulty in performing a minimal assertive action because of strong anxiety reactions to some aspect of assertiveness. In instances where a patient might fear behaving aggressively or the possible aggressive reactions of others, Wolpe suggested a preliminary program of *systematic desensitization* (see below). That is, the patient was taught to start by imagining him or herself behaving assertively along a hierarchy of anxiety-provoking situations. Once the patient was comfortable with imagining assertive behavior, the therapist could proceed with direct training.

Systematic Desensitization

Systematic desensitization stemmed directly from Wolpe's cat experiment and his theories of anxiety conditioning and reciprocal inhibition (1952a; 1958, pp. 139–65; 1969, pp. 91–168; 1973, pp. 95–162) while at the same time he recognized the pioneering effort of Mary Cover Jones (1924). Desensitization was indicated for patients whose anxiety was evoked by a wide variety of physical and social events. It seemed obvious for patients diagnosed with simple phobia, though Wolpe cautioned that such an apparently simple disorder could mislead the therapist into undertaking systematic desensitization when further analysis would reveal the appropriateness of an altogether different approach. He gave the example of a woman with a 'knife phobia' who, upon further analysis, felt anger toward her family and required assertiveness training (1973, p. 30; Barlow, 1988, p. 485, described a similar case). Wolpe was eager to demonstrate the utility of systematic desensitization for complex neurotic problems (1958, p. xi). He presented examples of its use in cases of obsessive thinking and compulsive washing (1973, pp. 229–35, 262–5), stuttering (1982, p. 290), reactive depression (1982, pp. 276–7), and agoraphobia (1969, pp. 146–7).

Imaginal Desensitization.   Based on the theory of reciprocal inhibition, systematic desensitization called for stimuli which evoked minimal anxiety to be associated with counter-anxiety responses (see Chapter 2). In standard practice the most convenient way to present and control anxiety-evoking stimuli was through verbal description of events, arranged on a hierarchy of aversiveness, for the patient to imagine. Relaxation provided the response antagonistic to anxiety. Thus systematic desensitization had three principal phases: construction of an anxiety hierarchy, training the patient in relaxation, and counterposing the anxiety stimuli with relaxation.

Hierarchy Construction. Information gathered in the assessment phase indicated specific stimuli which evoked anxiety. Wolpe found responses to individual items of the Willoughby and the Fear Survey Schedule to be particularly useful. He then proceeded to flesh out in detail the nuances of stimuli provoking anxiety. Often patients were given a homework assignment to list every situation they could imagine that evoked negative emotions, excluding those which were objectively dangerous. Patients were told that it was not necessary to have actually experienced a situation for it to be included as an item, but to imagine how they would feel if that event were to occur.

All these sources provided a pool of items. The therapist's task was to classify them into 'themes' (see Chapter 2) expressing the relationships between groups of stimulus items. Usually a patient had fears relating to more than one theme, so it was not simply a matter of finding a common thread linking all items; rather, items had to be sorted into various thematic categories. Wolpe presented no explicit rules for determining themes and the 'art' of this procedure lay in their derivation. Many themes were self-evident, but others required skillful interpretation and he warned against drawing obvious but incorrect conclusions:

> For example, a fear of going to movies, parties and other public situations may suggest a claustrophobia and yet really be a fear of scrutiny. Frequently, fear and avoidance of social occasions turns out to be based on fear of criticism or of rejection; or the fear may be a function of the mere physical presence of people, varying with the number to whom the patient is exposed. One patient showed a fear of social situations that was really a conditioned anxiety response to the smell of food in public places. A good example of the importance of the correct identification of relevant sources of anxiety is to be found in a previously reported case (Wolpe, 1958, p. 152) where a man's impotence turned out to be due to anxiety not related to any aspect of the sexual situation as such, but to the idea of trauma. (Wolpe and Lazarus, 1966, p. 67)

A hierarchy was constructed from the items in each thematic category. The items were presented to the patient with the instruction that he or she rank them in order according to the amount of discomfort which they would produce if the patient actually confronted the situation. To aid in ranking, a 'subjective unit of disturbance' (*sud*) scale was developed. The patient was told, 'Think of the worst anxiety you have experienced or could imagine experiencing, and assign to this the number 100. Now think of the state of being absolutely calm, and call this zero. Now you have a scale. On this scale how do you rate yourself at this moment?' The patient was instructed to assign a *sud* rating to each item on the various hierarchies.

Next, each hierarchy was examined to determine if there was a full range of items from low *sud*s to high and that there was an even progression from one item to the next with no large gap in *sud* ratings. Usually additional items had to be constructed to meet these criteria; this was accomplished by discussion between therapist and patient on the effects of adding or deleting various stimulus elements.

Each hierarchy usually contained multiple stimulus dimensions. 'Conventional' dimensions included frequency or number of stimulus elements, duration of exposure, and proximity in space or time to the feared event. 'Idiosyncratic' dimensions were specific to the past conditioning experience of each patient. For example, a hierarchy for a patient with claustrophobic reactions in social settings included conventional dimensions such as the number of people present and degree of familiarity with others, and an idiosyncratic dimension of time since her last meal which was related to a fear of vomiting. Hierarchies concerning criticism or rejection usually involved at least two dimensions – the nature of the opinion held and the identity of the person holding it. It was not necessary to include an item for each possible combination of dimensions, but rather a sampling of elements was employed. In some cases a sub-hierarchy for a particular dimension was interpolated. In the hierarchy below concerning 'scrutiny', the dimensions included the number, expertise and proximity of observers, and the nature of the work. This hierarchy illustrates the selection among combinations of dimensions and the use of a sub-hierarchy:

1 Being watched working (especially drawing) by 10 people.
2 Being watched working by six people.
3 Being watched working by three people.
4 Being watched working by one expert in the field. (Anxiety begins when the observer is 10 feet away and increases as he draws closer.)
5 Being watched working by a non-expert. (Anxiety begins at a distance of 4 feet.) (1969, p. 118)

Relaxation Training. Concurrently with hierarchy construction, Wolpe trained the patient in progressive muscle relaxation. He first provided the patient with a rationale, explaining that relaxation had emotional effects which directly opposed anxiety; it was useful both as part of therapeutic interventions and in life situations outside the consulting room. The patient was told that relaxation is a skill which improves with practice.

Training was accomplished by devoting about 20 minutes during six or seven sessions to an abbreviated version of Jacobson's (1938) technique (see Chapter 2). The goal was to teach the patient to discern the muscular sensations of tension and relaxation and to 'turn off' or 'let go' muscle activity. The patient was instructed to perform certain actions and to observe the sensations; the therapist also observed the patient and provided feedback and suggestions as to what the patient might feel.

The first lesson focused on the arms. He asked the patient to grip tightly the arm of the chair and observe the nature and location of the sensations in his or her hand and forearm. Next, the upper arm biceps were trained; the transcript of this exercise illustrates the essential features of his training method:

> I am now going to show you the essential activity that is involved in obtaining deep relaxation. I shall again ask you to resist my pull at your wrist so as to tighten your biceps. I want you to notice very carefully the sensations in that muscle. Then I shall ask you to let go gradually as I diminish the amount of force I exert against you. Notice as your forearm descends that there is decreasing sensation in the biceps muscle. Notice also that the letting go is an activity, but of a negative kind – it is an 'uncontracting' of the muscle. In due course, your forearm will come to rest on the arm of the chair, and it may then seem to you as though relaxation is complete. But although the biceps will indeed be partly and perhaps largely relaxed, a certain number of fibers will still be contracted. I shall therefore say to you, 'Go on letting go.' Try to continue the activity that went on in the biceps while your forearm was coming down. It is the act of relaxing these additional fibers that will bring about the emotional effects we want. Let's try it out and see what happens. (Wolpe and Lazarus, 1966, p. 62)

At the second lesson, the patient was told that the most important muscles from the emotional point of view were those of the head. The muscle groups of the forehead, eyes, nose, and lips were each tensed and relaxed in a stepwise fashion. The third lesson was devoted to the jaw and tongue, the fourth to the neck and shoulders, the fifth to the back, abdomen, and chest, and the sixth to the muscles of the legs. Wolpe described and sometimes modeled each tense–release exercise to be performed by the patient. After each exercise the patient was instructed to continue the 'untensing' activity, to 'try to go beyond the furthest point of relaxation,' for several minutes.

Wolpe judged the degree of relaxation based on patient reports of warmth, tingling, numbness, and the like, which were interpreted as signs of relaxation beyond the normal level of muscle tone. Wolpe suggested palpating the biceps and observing the position of the head and jaw as indicators of relaxation. Physiologic measures of relaxation such as electrodermal or electromyographic activity were acknowledged, but Wolpe regarded them as unnecessary for routine use. Patient reports of general calmness and use of the *suds* scale provided him with the most useful measures of relaxation. Later research developed an observational method for measuring the extent of relaxation based on the appearance of relaxed persons described by Wolpe, Jacobson, and others (Poppen, 1988).

Patients were instructed to practice for 10 to 15 minutes twice daily at home what they had learned in the office. With practice, the time and activity needed to achieve complete relaxation throughout the body decreased to the point where the patient could just 'switch it on' within a few minutes.

Juxtaposition of Relaxation and Hierarchy Items. Once the patient was able to achieve rapidly a state of complete relaxation, and the anxiety hierarchies had been constructed, the process of desensitization could begin. The overall strategy was to ask the patient to imagine successive scenes depicted by the hierarchy items while remaining deeply relaxed. It was important that the patient not experience anxious arousal so a signaling system was arranged and special steps were taken if the patient experienced discomfort.

In the first session the patient was carefully monitored to make sure that he or she remained calm. A deep state of relaxation was encouraged through a review of various body areas and direct suggestions to let go and feel at ease. Wolpe sometimes employed hypnosis to further deepen relaxation, but his use of this procedure decreased over the years. A monitoring procedure was developed whereby the patient was told, 'If you feel utterly calm – zero anxiety – do nothing; otherwise raise your left index finger.' If a signal occurred, the level of discomfort was determined by further probes: 'Raise the finger if more than 10 *suds*,' and so forth. If the patient reported more than 10 *suds*, additional relaxation instructions were given, and if anxiety persisted, calming images were described, such as watching clouds in the sky. If anxiety still persisted the session was terminated and special procedures (described below) were implemented. Otherwise, a neutral scene was then presented in order to determine the patient's ability to visualize material and to see if anxiety was evoked by some aspects of the procedure other than the content of the scene.

Next the therapist told the patient, 'I am now going to ask you to imagine a number of scenes. You will imagine them clearly and they will generally interfere little, if at all, with your state of relaxation.' The patient was instructed to raise his or her finger briefly when the scene was clearly imagined, and then to report the number of *sud*s aroused after the scene was terminated. The lowest item on a hierarchy was described for the patient to imagine for three to five seconds, after which the patient was told, 'Stop imagining that scene and concentrate on relaxing your muscles.' After about 15 seconds the scene was presented again for about five seconds. If no discomfort was reported, the next item was presented. Scenes which evoked discomfort were repeated; the *sud* rating allowed the therapist to determine if the patient's anxiety progressively diminished. If the rating did not decrease, despite good relaxation, this indicated a problem with the hierarchy. At this point the therapist could present an item from a different hierarchy or terminate the session. An examination of the difficult item was in order to modify the troublesome stimulus dimensions.

At the conclusion of the session the therapist said, 'Now I am going to count up to five and you will open your eyes, feeling very calm and relaxed.' The patient was allowed to adjust to the waking state, and the therapist asked him or her how vividly the scenes were imagined and what was felt while imagining them. Any difficulties in imagining scenes or relaxing were discussed with the patient and adjustments made for subsequent sessions.

Later sessions followed much the same course as the first one. Usually the patient required less time to become fully relaxed and instructions were limited to a reminder about the signaling system. The first scene presented was the item on the hierarchy following the one successfully completed the previous time. For some patients 'spontaneous recovery' occurred even though an item had been rated zero *sud*s in the previous session, requiring repetition of that item. For patients for whom such backtracking was needed, an 'overlearning' procedure was recommended in which a scene was presented two or three times more after it was rated zero.

The variables in the desensitization procedure included the duration of each scene, the duration of the relaxation interval between scenes, the number of repetitions of each item, the number of items presented from a particular hierarchy, the number of different hierarchies included in a session, the length of a session, and spacing of sessions. Wolpe provided general guidelines while acknowledging the need for adjustments for individual patients.

The duration of a scene was approximately five seconds. It was terminated immediately if the patient reported anxiety or reacted in a manner indicating discomfort. Initial presentations were generally shorter than later ones, and if Wolpe suspected that a particular scene might be difficult it would be presented initially for only one or two seconds. The content of the scene also influenced its duration; striking a match requires less time than walking six blocks (Lazarus, 1964). The duration of the interval between scenes was generally 10 to 15 seconds. More time was taken if the patient reported or displayed anxiety. The duration of a session might be about 15 minutes in early training, but take up more of the hour as therapy progressed. Sessions of 90 minutes were reported.

The number of repetitions of a scene was generally three or four if no arousal occurred, but could range up to 10 for difficult items. The number of different items presented within a session ranged from two or three in early sessions to 10 or more in later ones. The number of different hierarchies from which items were selected within a session could range up to four; patients rarely had more than four hierarchies. The number of sessions ranged from six to over 100, depending on the number and intensity of the patient's problems and the range of stimuli involved in each. As a rule sessions occurred one to three times a week, though spacing varied widely depending on the schedule of the patient and therapist.

Wolpe coded the data from each scene on a card, indicating the hierarchy and item, the number of times an item was presented, and the patient's reaction in *suds*. He found this information useful not only for treatment but for later research.

Transfer of Training. Wolpe (1963b) noted that there was almost a one-to-one relationship between what patients could imagine calmly and what they could experience in real life without anxiety. As a practical matter he often asked patients to try to expose themselves to real situations comparable to those to which they had just been desensitized in imagination. He regarded this as a 'consolidating maneuver' and a means of gaining 'feedback.' Patients' reports of adaptive behavior in situations which arose in the normal course of their daily lives were taken as an indication of the appropriateness of the desensitization regime. In a specific test, Rachman (1966a) found that patients reported little fear to actual phobic stimuli immediately after imaginal desensitization to those events. However, Agras (1967) reported that actual performance by severely agoraphobic patients lagged behind what they could imagine calmly. Analogue experimental studies with snake-avoidant college students showed that the number of hierarchy items completed was positively correlated with the reduction in avoidance behavior, though there was a gap between what could be imagined and what could actually be performed (Davison, 1968; Lang et al., 1965). It is likely that the actual experience of a situation is more intense than one's imagination of it while deeply relaxed, leading to a 'lag' between imaginal and actual performance.

Difficulties in Desensitization.   Wolpe candidly recognized that, despite his best efforts, some patients did not make progress. Either they experienced no decrement of anxiety within training sessions or there was little improvement in their reaction to real situations which corresponded to those accomplished during training. On the basis of his theory, Wolpe assumed such failure to be due to deficiencies in the reciprocally inhibiting response (relaxation) or in the anxiety-evoking stimuli (inadequate hierarchies or problems in imagining the items).

Some patients experienced difficulty in achieving a truly calm state of relaxation. Some very tense patients were unaware of internal feelings of tension or believed that even a small decrease in tension indicated sufficient relaxation. Such patients may have reported feeling calm when in fact their state of relaxation was not sufficient to overcome the anxiety aroused by hierarchy items. Wolpe suggested several measures to deal with this problem. Conscientious use of the *sud* scale could help the patient become more sensitive to degrees of relaxation. Physiologic monitoring of electrodermal or electromyographic activity could reveal the patient's state of arousal. More extensive relaxation training, hypnosis, or adjunctive use of anxiety-reducing drugs such as tranquilizers or carbon dioxide inhalation, were recommended to accomplish adequate levels of relaxation.

Another difficulty for some patients was a 'general fear of letting go;' they experienced autonomic arousal while attempting to relax. Wolpe suggested several remedies but the basis for choosing among them for a particular patient was not explained. These included telling the patient to become calm in his or her own way without attempting to 'let go,' desensitization to the fear of letting go, use of the 'anxiety-relief' method, or carbon dioxide inhalation. Heide and Borkovec (1984) explained relaxation-induced anxiety as due to a discrepancy between type of anxiety and type of relaxation training procedure. They recommended matching patients having 'cognitive' anxiety with a 'cognitive' relaxation training procedure, such as meditation, and those having 'somatic' anxiety with a 'somatic' procedure, such as Wolpe's. There is some slight but inconsistent evidence supporting such matching (Barlow, 1988, pp. 487–8).

Wolpe (1990, p. 182) preferred to deal with the problem on an individual case basis.

In some instances, the lack of progress could be due to hierarchies unrelated to the true source of the patient's anxiety. Wolpe warned that the therapist could be misled into constructing a hierarchy concerning the setting or context in which fear occurred rather than the actual conditioned stimuli. A case example of 'claustrophobia' turned out to be a fear not of constricted space but of dying. Some cases of agoraphobia in married women were not fears of being alone but reactions to aversive aspects of their marriage. Discovery of the actual basis of the patient's anxiety in these cases resulted in formulation of an appropriate hierarchy, or an entirely different mode of therapy such as assertiveness training.

A few patients could not conjure up visual or auditory images, and other patients could form images but no associated feelings of reality. In rare instances a patient could visualize adequately up to a certain point in the hierarchy and then become disengaged as a crucial element was presented. Suggestions for dealing with such problems included hypnosis, extensive verbal description of the scene by the therapist or the patient, and the use of actual stimuli as in *in vivo* desensitization.

Variations in Desensitization. Wolpe suggested various ways of altering systematic desensitization in order to overcome idiosyncratic patient difficulties as well as to make it more effective or efficient. These variants involved modes of stimulus presentation, ways of promoting counter-anxiety responses, or both. In addition, many clinicians and researchers published variations of the systematic desensitization procedure soon after his early reports.

In vivo desensitization. Imaginal stimuli were employed in conventional desensitization because of the practical difficulties in presenting graded doses of actual anxiety-eliciting stimuli. However, exposure to real stimuli or pictorial representations was useful for patients who had difficulties in imagination and it also facilitated transfer of training to daily life (1969, pp. 161–5). Wolpe credited the original work of Meyer (1957) of the Maudsley group in London, and cited several case reports of *in vivo* treatment for phobias of cats, earthworms, injections, and bridges.

Wolpe provided examples of *in vivo* desensitization in cases of obsessive–compulsive disorder, agoraphobia, and social phobia (1964a, 1969, pp. 161–5). In the first instance, a young man feared contamination by urine. Imaginal desensitization produced some progress, but a plateau was reached. Therefore an *in vivo* hierarchy

was employed, including the printed word 'urine,' closer proxi-
mations to a bottle of urine, and drops of increasing concentrations
of urine applied to the patient's hand while he 'relaxed away' the
anxiety aroused by these stimuli. In another case, an agoraphobic
woman feared separation from a 'reliable' person; Wolpe met with
her in a public park and required progressively longer separations.
Another woman feared that she would die from rapid heart rate;
she was required to experience several situations which induced
tachycardia. And a man who feared confinement by crowds sat in
front of a progressively larger professional gathering and engaged in
relaxation. In those instances in which relaxation was not
employed, Wolpe felt that the presence of the therapist, other
persons, or various 'natural' stimuli, evoked emotions which
reciprocally inhibited anxiety. However, this factor has often been
ignored or disputed by others (see Chapter 4).

Alternatives to Relaxation.   Counter-anxiety responses other than
relaxation were sought for patients who had idiosyncratic difficulties with standard relaxation or where it was not practical for
the patient to relax in the therapeutic or real-life situation. The
theoretical basis for these methods was described in Chapter 2.

Therapist presence.   Wolpe observed that emotional responses
elicited by the presence of the therapist could serve to counteract
anxiety arousal (1958, p. 163). This feature was particularly useful
for *in vivo* desensitization, in which the patient was actively
engaged in some activity rather than passively relaxing. Wolpe
spoke of the 'double role' of the therapist as a guide and anxiety
inhibitor (1969, p. 163).

Anxiolytic drugs.   Wolpe employed a variety of drugs such as
codeine, diazepam, and meprobamate (1958, p. 202; 1982, pp.
223–4). The critical feature of this practice was that patients were
systematically exposed to conditioned anxiety stimuli while in the
drugged state and then were systematically withdrawn from the
drug, rather than the common medical practice of simply prescribing tranquilizers for patients to consume indefinitely. The drug
could be taken to enhance relaxation during desensitization or to
reduce arousal *in vivo*. In addition to his own trials, Wolpe noted
scattered case reports of clinicians who prescribed various
tranquilizing drugs during imaginal or *in vivo* desensitization
(1973, pp. 186–7, 190–1).

Carbon dioxide inhalation.   Wolpe recommended CO_2 inhalation for pervasive anxiety (1958, pp. 166–72) and also employed it
in the desensitization of a few cases of phobias (1982, pp. 198–9).
For example, a case of 'phobia for certain configurations of the

opposite sex,' resistant to previous methods, yielded to pictorial stimulus presentations during inhalation. Despite Wolpe's repeated calls for systematic clinical study of CO_2 inhalation, little has been done with simple phobia. However, there are many clinical studies reporting the usefulness of CO_2 inhalation with panic disorder patients as a means of teaching them to overcome internal panic-arousing stimuli (Barlow, 1988, pp. 447–50).

Electric shock. Wolpe reported the use of mild electric shock for two agoraphobic patients for whom other methods had proven ineffective. In the first (1958, pp. 174–80; 1982, p. 188), the patient was instructed to signal when she had clearly imagined a scene from her hierarchy, an electric shock was delivered to her forearm, she flexed her arm, and the shock was switched off. After many repetitions the patient reported no further disturbance. She practiced *in vivo* many times a day each item she had accomplished in imagination and eventually achieved freedom from her fears. In the second instance (Wolpe and Lazarus, 1966, pp. 147–9), repeated shock pulses to the forearm strong enough to produce contractions were given prior to and during the patient imagining a hierarchy item concerned with driving increasing distances from home. *In vivo* tests showed that driving progress paralleled her success in imagery. From the description, it is not clear which procedures were related to the outcomes, nor is the shock's mechanism of action certain. Later work with agoraphobia has shown *in vivo* exposure to be critical, and electric shock may have served only to motivate the patients' practice. In any event, no further reports of this procedure have appeared.

The 'anxiety-relief' method was endorsed by Wolpe (1958, pp. 180–1; 1982, pp. 196–8). An unpleasant shock was administered to a patient's forearm for as long as could be endured, at which point he or she said 'calm' and the current was switched off. This was repeated 10 to 20 times a session, after which the patient was instructed to say 'calm' subvocally in distressing life situations. In a variation termed 'aversion relief,' the patient pressed a button to terminate shock, at which point a scene from the patient's hierarchy was described by the therapist (Thorpe et al., 1964). Wolpe presented no clinical examples of his own in support of these approaches, but cited the analogue experimental study of Meichenbaum (1973) and the work of Solyom and Miller (1965) with homosexuals. He also cited a 'respiratory relief' procedure, in which the patient held his breath as long as possible, with the hierarchy item given as the patient resumed breathing, but noted that his own trials of the procedure were 'not encouraging.'

Physical activity. Wolpe cited several case reports which employed physical activity in a desensitization paradigm (1982, pp. 195–6). For example, a flight-phobic patient practiced karate exercises while imagining a hierarchy of flying situations, and a claustrophobic patient practiced kung fu exercises while locked in a room for progressively longer durations (Gershman and Stedman, 1971). Wolpe also cited a report which employed reading as a counter-anxiety response. As with other alternatives to relaxation, there has been no systematic investigation of the anxiety-inhibitory properties of these physical activities.

Imagery. Several investigators developed procedures which employed counter-anxiety imagery in conjunction with hierarchy items, presented either in imagination or *in vivo*, in order to enhance or replace relaxation. Wolpe (1969, pp. 159–61; 1973, pp. 149–54) cited the originators of the procedures and described his own experience with them in brief examples, but provided no systematic analysis. Lazarus and Abramovitz (1962) developed the 'emotive imagery' technique in work with children's fears. First they determined the child's favorite fantasy and its various details. Then, in elaborate and colorful descriptions, the fantasy elements were juxtaposed with increasing amounts of feared stimuli. For example, a boy with a fear of darkness was asked to imagine himself as an agent of Superman awaiting secret messages in various dark rooms of his home. After only three sessions the boy was able to go to the bathroom alone at night. An additional and perhaps critical element of this procedure was that the children practiced emotive imagery *in vivo*. Wolpe and Lazarus (1966, p. 144) suggested that imagining calm and quiet scenes, such as a glowing log fire on a winter evening, could be used to enhance relaxation during desensitization. Indeed, the technique of *guided imagery* makes use of this principle. Calming imagery was employed *in vivo*; the example was given of a competitive swimmer who calmed himself between races by imagining walking along a sandy beach. The use of coping and calming imagery has been extensively promoted by Suinn (1990) in his 'anxiety management training' procedure.

Wolpe cited the 'direct suggestion' procedure of Rubin (1972) in which the imagined scenes were more realistic and relevant to adult patients' actual experiences. Patients were instructed to imagine focusing on the positive and pleasant stimuli and feelings in situations in which they ordinarily experienced anxiety. An example was given of a man with a fear of flying who practiced imagining those aspects of an airplane trip that he enjoyed, and then focused on those events during an actual trip. Wolpe contrasted direct suggestion with 'post-hypnotic suggestion,' emphasizing that the suggested responses counteracted anxiety rather than directly suggesting the disappearance of symptoms.

In the 'induced anger' procedure, patients were instructed to imagine feeling and expressing anger, as well as actually engaging in angry behavior (such as yelling or punching a pillow), while imagining items from their anxiety hierarchy (Goldstein et al., 1970). It was employed with patients for whom conventional desensitization with relaxation had been attempted but was unsuccessful. In most cases anger was an irrelevant emotion used only for its anxiety-inhibiting properties. The imagined expression of anger was extreme; for example a patient imagined chopping up a stranger with an ax or mowing down a theater audience with a machine gun. Patients were instructed to practice generating angry feelings and images *in vivo*. In six of 10 cases, patients achieved complete neutralization of anxiety and were able to engage in previously avoided or anxiety-provoking behavior. In no instance did hostile feelings actually replace the fearful ones; rather patients reported calm or indifference. No analysis of successful and unsuccessful cases was provided. Wolpe reported using induced anger with a young woman with agoraphobia for whom many other methods had failed (1990, pp. 200–1). In the course of following instructions to travel beyond her comfortable limits, she became extremely anxious and angry at Wolpe for subjecting her to 'torture.' He then instructed her to make increasingly distant excursions while verbally expressing her anger towards him. Within a few sessions her walking perimeter expanded considerably and she was able to make prolonged solo car trips.

Group Desensitization. For his doctoral dissertation under Wolpe's direction, Arnold Lazarus devised the method of simultaneously desensitizing several patients with the same fear, greatly economizing on the therapist's time (Wolpe and Lazarus, 1966, p. 142). This procedure required that patients all employ the same hierarchy items and tied progress to the pace of the slowest group member. Lazarus found the procedure to be effective with groups of patients presenting with claustrophobia, acrophobia, and sexual fears. Citing Paul and Shannon's (1966) study of group desensitization with college students having public speaking anxiety, Wolpe observed that patients with various social anxieties may be more effectively treated in groups because the presence of other people exposes them to *in vivo* as well as imaginal stimuli. Despite these advantages, group desensitization has not been practiced widely.

Evoking Strong Anxiety

Although systematic desensitization emphasized the importance of preventing the occurrence of anxiety reactions, Wolpe found in his own practice, and in the reports of many others, that circumstances in which the patient experienced strong anxiety could produce beneficial outcomes. This led him to develop a place for such methods in his own therapeutic program. These methods included abreaction, flooding, paradoxical intention, and eye-movement desensitization.

Abreaction.   Abreaction was a popular treatment during the Second World War, in which servicemen suffering 'war neuroses' recalled their traumatic battle experiences (Grinker and Spiegel, 1945). Wolpe first observed the procedure as a young physician working in a military hospital. Abreaction was characterized by intense emotional expression, such as terror, as if the patient actually was experiencing the traumatic event. It could be deliberately provoked by the therapist's suggestion while the patient had been sedated with drugs, hypnosis, or deep relaxation, and also could occur inadvertently while the patient was describing a significant experience. Wolpe rejected the prevailing psychodynamic theory, which held that repressed memories were ventilated, proposing instead that reciprocal inhibition was the mechanism of action. He held that the safe therapeutic environment evoked positive emotions which eventually overcame the fear that was aroused.

Positive outcomes of abreaction were uncertain in the military setting and Wolpe felt it was even less effective with civilian neuroses. He employed it only in two types of situations – when it occurred spontaneously in the course of therapy or assessment, and as a final resort when other procedures had failed. He gave only three case examples of his own use of the procedure, but discussed the reports of others (1958, pp. 195–8; 1983, pp. 237–8). He felt the most practical way to induce abreaction was by means of drugs, and presented a brief review of studies employing barbiturates, ether, amphetamine, and lysergic acid diethylamide (LSD) (Wolpe and Lazarus, 1966, pp. 126–9). The spotty record obtained with abreaction he felt was due to the weakness of the opposing emotions in the face of strong anxiety, and the possibility that the recalled events were not central to the stimulus dimensions related to the patient's anxiety.

Flooding.   Confronting patients with anxiety-provoking stimuli, either *in vivo* or in imagination, and continuing this confrontation until their anxiety subsided, was a procedure Wolpe termed 'emotional flooding' (1969, pp. 185–93). He did not claim authorship of this method although he had employed a form of it with three of his neurotic cats, forcing them by means of a moveable barrier to remain in the vicinity of the food dish where they had been shocked (see Chapter 2). In the early 1960s, a number of positive reports which appeared in the clinical and analogue research literature, particularly by the group at the Maudsley Hospital who reported it superior to desensitization, caused Wolpe to examine the procedure more closely. He concluded that flooding procedures were appropriate for some patients and were consistent with his reciprocal inhibition formulation (see Chapter 2).

Wolpe recommended that flooding stimuli evoking moderately strong rather than severe anxiety be employed, and that these be arranged in a graduated fashion – this was sometimes required by patients who simply would not face extreme stimuli. He also emphasized that stimulus presentation must continue until the anxiety reaction had subsided, otherwise sensitization could occur. He described his use of flooding with four patients (1969, pp. 190–3; 1973, pp. 193–200): a dentist who feared social ridicule and having a patient die in his dental chair, an agoraphobic woman unable to travel on her own, a bird-phobic woman, and a physician who feared 'insane' people. Desensitization had been tried and found wanting in the first three cases, and flooding was recommended in the fourth because the physician was soon leaving the area. Imaginal and *in vivo* flooding was successful for the first three patients, but not for the fourth – the physician remained in a psychiatric ward for hours at a time but only became more afraid. It should be noted there was no therapist present during his flooding, suggesting that this source of anxiety inhibition might have been crucial.

It sometimes may be difficult to distinguish flooding from *in vivo* desensitization, especially in those cases where the latter involves anxious arousal which the patient overcomes by relaxation, or where the counter-anxiety response is not specific, such as 'positive emotions' to therapist presence. Wolpe's case of an agoraphobic woman confronted with her racing heart, described above as *in vivo* desensitization, seems to fit the flooding paradigm as well. In practice, there appears to be a continuum across the methods of imaginal desensitization, *in vivo* desensitization, and flooding, in the degree to which anxiety is aroused. There is also a continuum in the explicitness of counter-anxiety responses. In all cases, the therapeutic goal was for the patient to remain calm in the presence of previously fear-evoking situations.

Paradoxical Intention.   Wolpe (1969, p. 186; 1982, p. 247) noted that this method had its origin in existential therapy (Frankl, 1960), but lent itself to a behavioral interpretation (Ascher, 1980). The essence of the procedure was that the therapist instructed patients to enter rather than avoid difficult situations and to try to bring on their symptoms rather than fight them. Wolpe gave only a brief synopsis of outcome studies and did not describe the procedures nor provide an analysis of the learning mechanisms involved, referring the reader to other sources (1982, pp. 247–8; 1990, pp. 226–7).

Eye-movement Desensitization.   Wolpe cited a treatment for anxiety symptoms in post-traumatic stress disorder, serendipitously discovered by Francine Shapiro (1989a), in his most recent textbook (1990, pp. 272–3). He did not include it as a procedure involving strong anxiety evocation, but it may be appropriate to include it here because patients were asked to imagine a traumatic scene, remember an upsetting thought, or focus on an unpleasant bodily sensation. This item was assigned a (high) *sud* rating. While the patients held the imaginal scene, thought, or sensation, they simultaneously visually tracked the therapist's finger, which was held about 12 inches from the patient's face and moved rhythmically left and right at a rate of two sweeps per second for six to 12 seconds. After each set of eye-movements, or saccades, the patient was asked for a *sud*s rating. Ratings were reported to decline with successive presentations. Other disturbing images or thoughts were similarly treated, but no hierarchy was constructed nor was there extensive discussion of scenes. The major differences between this method and imaginal flooding appear to be the shorter duration of item presentation and the inclusion of saccadic tracking.

Several case reports followed, including two cases treated by Wolpe (1990, p. 273; Wolpe and Abrams, 1991). Wolpe reported success with one woman having ruminative thoughts, and another having obsessive–compulsive guilt reactions. Shapiro (1989b) carried out a comparison study in which 17 patients and five volunteers with traumatic memories were randomly assigned to either eye-movement desensitization or placebo treatment, which consisted of imagining the traumatic scene without the eye movements. Patients in the eye-movement group rehearsed an irrational belief in addition to the visualized scene while tracking the therapist's finger. Self-reports on a *sud*s scale, an irrational belief questionnaire, and description of symptoms, indicated marked improvement in the eye-movement patients but not the placebo patients. The latter then underwent eye-movement desensitization resulting in similar improvements. A critique of this study questioned the adequacy of its dependent measures and controls for treatment bias, and suggested a number of experimental methods by which to assess the effectiveness of eye-movement desensitization (Lohr et al., 1992).

It is interesting that 40 years after Wolpe's original introduction of systematic desensitization, a related method appears ready to tread the same path – initial clinical reports of success to be followed by experimental investigations of effectiveness and the contribution of its various components. The turns and pitfalls along this path have been well marked by desensitization research, and time will tell if the eye-movement variation will progress as well. Theoretically, the procedure is an orphan, though Wolpe has suggested adopting it into the reciprocal inhibition family. He proposed that the eye movements reciprocally inhibit anxiety in a remarkably rapid but unknown fashion. He noted Jacobson's observation that relaxation of the extrinsic eye muscles had 'extraordinary emotional potency,' suggesting 'unforeshadowed neural processes.' A systematic theory will help guide research with this method as it has for systematic desensitization.

Sexual Therapy

Wolpe proposed that many sexual dysfunctions of both men and women resulted from conditioned anxiety responses to sexual stimuli, and that sexual arousal could be employed therapeutically to counteract anxiety (see Chapter 2). On the basis of this theory, Wolpe described a general approach and specific procedures for the treatment of sexual dysfunctions: correction of misconceptions about sex; instruction in sexual practices; reduction of sexual anxiety through explicit or implicit counterconditioning methods; and therapist-guided, graduated *in vivo* practice (1958, pp. 130–5; 1969, pp. 72–90; Wolpe and Lazarus, 1966, pp. 102–15). These principles have characterized subsequent sexual therapies (for example LoPiccolo, 1977; Masters and Johnson, 1970), though few acknowledged Wolpe, which suggests either independent development or inadequate scholarship. In specialized sexual therapy, as with other procedures, the trend has been to develop comprehensive treatment packages to employ with persons meeting certain diagnostic criteria. Wolpe has maintained the necessity of an individualized approach.

Male Dysfunction. At the diagnostic level, Wolpe distinguished two major problems in male sexual performance – inadequate penile erection ('impotence') and premature ejaculation; both were often found in the same patient. Both disorders were hypothesized to be the result of overactivity of the sympathetic nervous system due to anxious arousal conditioned to sexual stimuli. Individual assessment was necessary to determine specific anxiety stimuli, the importance of which was illustrated by the case of a man whose impotence was found to be related to fears of injury and suffering rather than sexual stimuli per se (1958, pp. 152–60). Later, Wolpe provided a more extensive review of biological factors and treatment in patients with erectile inadequacy, which he admitted were more difficult to treat than those with premature ejaculation (1982, pp. 211-12). He cited studies which found a high incidence of endocrine and other organic disorders in patients presenting with impotence, most of whom responded to appropriate medication. He recommended that thorough medical examination be undertaken routinely for patients with erectile problems.

In general, the sequence of events leading to coitus was seen as a naturally occurring hierarchy with anxiety increasing at each stage. Because each failure to perform adequately comprised another anxiety conditioning trial, the patient was enjoined from further attempts at sexual intercourse. Treatment took the form of *in vivo* desensitization guided by instructions from the therapist. Sexual arousal served as the anxiety-inhibiting response, though relaxation was also employed if needed. Wolpe provided instruction in sexual techniques, guidance in what steps to take next, and corrective feedback and reassurance if the patient met with failure while trying to progress too rapidly. The therapeutic interview was devoted to a review of the patient's sexual activities since the previous session, including the number, duration, and content of sexual activities. In cases where anxiety was so great that it completely inhibited sexual arousal, imaginal desensitization was carried out as a preliminary intervention.

A key feature of *in vivo* desensitization was securing the co-operation of a sexual partner. To enlist the patient's wife or girlfriend, Wolpe provided the man with a script by which to request his partner to be patient, affectionate, and noncritical. In cases where the partner was reluctant to participate because of negative emotions or lack of sexual feelings, Wolpe invited her to the therapeutic interview to explain the procedure and request her cooperation. If cooperation could not be assured, Wolpe did not hesitate to recommend that the man seek out another woman with whom to regain his sexual functioning, reasoning that this might actually improve his marriage, or at least he would be better off than being forced into lifelong chastity. If another partner could not be found, Wolpe noted that sexual surrogates were available through marital counselors in some locales, or prostitutes might be tried as a last resort. Wolpe did not address the ethical and legal ramifications which could arise from these suggestions in the United States' sexually repressive and litigious society.

The first step of treatment was to instruct the patient to engage in affectionate activities which did not arouse anxiety, such as kissing and non-genital caressing, with no thought of intercourse. These activities were to be carried out while fully clothed, and then while unclothed, with progressively greater degrees of mutual genital stimulation in successive sessions. If erection was achieved and the man felt comfortable and sexually aroused, the next steps were to allow the penis to touch the partner's clitoris or vulva without intromission. If these procedures were sufficient to secure an erection, then progressive increases in degree and duration of intromission, followed by progressive increases in movement, were allowed. Attention then was directed to maintaining the erection and prolonging the time until ejaculation. Wolpe cited the method of Semans (1956), in which the partner manipulated the penis to the point premonitory to ejaculation and then stopped, allowing the feeling to subside. Repeating this several times allowed ejaculation to be postponed at will. The 'squeeze technique' of Masters and Johnson (1970, p. 103) was cited later, in which the partner applied pressure to the penis when the premonitory point was reached. Wolpe reported that a simpler procedure that was often successful was to ask the couple to have intercourse as frequently as possible, instructing the man to enjoy it and let himself go without worrying about ejaculation. Under such a regime the latency of ejaculation was found to increase, but he gave no data or case examples of this approach. During all the steps prior to achieving complete and satisfying intercourse, Wolpe recommended that the man digitally or orally stimulate his partner to orgasm. Instruction and counseling was provided to both partners if there was objection to doing this or ignorance of how to do it.

Female Dysfunction. Wolpe recognized that there was a wide range of sexual difficulties in women, from complete absence of sexual feeling to high arousal but lack of orgasm with a particular partner (1969, pp. 84–90). Nevertheless, he distinguished two major categories – 'essential frigidity' (later termed 'general inhibition of arousal,' 1982, p. 215) referred to a lack of response to all males, and 'situational frigidity' was related to a particular male, usually the husband. In cases of general inhibition, Wolpe recommended a thorough gynecological examination for organic factors. He cited a case of a woman who underwent four years of psychoanalysis for a vaginal spasm later found to be due to a painful ulcer. He reported rare cases of women with a 'constitutional deficiency' whose 'sexual response system had failed to develop;' Wolpe could offer no solution. Most commonly, general inhibition was due to pervasive sexual fears resulting from childhood anti-sexual indoctrination or aversive sexual experiences. Religious teachings or negative parental attitudes that sex was dirty resulted in cognitively based fears. Sexual abuse or punishment for masturbation resulted in conditioned anxiety. In addition, he reported that some women developed their aversion to sex as an adult because their failure to achieve orgasm made sexual activity increasingly frustrating. Situational inhibition was often found to be related to negative feelings toward the husband over a variety of issues other than sex.

Treatment was tailored to the individual case, but some general approaches are apparent. In cases where sexual misconceptions were present, correction was necessary to educate the woman about sexual matters. While necessary, he found that such correction was rarely sufficient, and that negative feelings about sexual situations usually remained. Negative emotions about sexual themes were dealt with by imaginal desensitization. Hierarchies concerning nudity and other aspects of the sexual situation were typical. Wolpe cited Brady's (1966) use of methohexital to enhance relaxation during sexual desensitization. Once a patient could calmly imagine engaging in sexual activity, progressive *in vivo* practice was implemented with her partner, similar to the program employed with men. Finding a cooperative partner was not mentioned as a problem for women.

In instances where a patient's lack of arousal was related to inconsiderate behaviors on the part of the husband, Wolpe employed assertiveness training in which the woman learned to request changes in her husband's responses to her. As the husband became more attentive and considerate, the woman's feelings toward him became more positive and allowed her to respond sexually. He mentioned one case where he recommended that a passively compliant woman implement a reciprocal agreement, requesting time and attention from her husband in exchange for her preparation of dinner parties required by his profession. Wolpe recognized that the unilateral approach to changing marital relations was sometimes inappropriate, and that both partners needed to enter into negotiations to break the cycle of resentment and retaliation. He cited Stuart's (1969) early work on marital contracting, but did not describe a general approach to marital-couple counseling. Wolpe reported some instances in which the woman had lost her attraction to her spouse for indefinable reasons and was unable to say what she would like to change even if she could. In other instances the husband proved implacable to changing his behavior toward his wife. In such instances, Wolpe suggested the only alternatives to the status quo were separation or taking a lover.

Aversion Therapy

Wolpe did not originate aversion therapy procedures, but he used them early on and incorporated them in his theory and his compilation of behavior therapy methods (1958, pp. 182–4; 1969, pp. 200–18; 1973, pp. 216–29). Aversion therapy was indicated when patients displayed attraction toward inappropriate stimuli, as in obsessions, addictions, and sexual deviances. For Wolpe, the procedure called for an aversive stimulus, such as electric shock to the forearm, to be administered simultaneously with the occurrence of the unwanted emotional response. According to his reciprocal inhibition theory, the autonomic reaction to the shock inhibited the inappropriate arousal and became attached to the inappropriate stimuli. He eventually recognized the difference between this procedure and punishment, whereby the aversive stimulus follows the occurrence of the undesirable response (Azrin and Holz, 1966). Escape and avoidance responding were also involved, making the learning principles decidedly murky, especially when covert responses and imaginal stimuli were involved.

In his first efforts with four cases of 'obstinate obsessions', Wolpe instructed the patients to imagine the troublesome object or situation; when they signaled a clear image, an electric shock was administered to the forearm. This was repeated several times a session. He reported that only one of four patients, a woman with an obsession about unhealthy food, made 'significant improvement.' He also described the case of a high school student with poor grades whom he instructed to record his evening study time, telling him that at the end of the week he would receive a shock for each half-hour that he did not study. After two sessions with very few shocks, self-reported study time and mother-reported grades improved markedly. In another case, a physician who had developed a craving for Demerol was given a shock device and told to self-administer a shock whenever he felt an urge. After very few shocks on three occasions, the patient reported reduction in craving to a controllable level.

In an experiment (1982, p. 264; Wolpe et al., 1980), electric shock was employed to overcome withdrawal craving reactions induced in methadone-maintained heroin addicts by injection of naloxone, a narcotic antagonist. Two subjects went on to experience 'painless' withdrawal from methadone itself. Wolpe expressed puzzlement as to why more subjects did not want to continue treatment, even though they were paid to do so. He concluded that addicts 'cherish their addiction' and were not motivated to change.

Wolpe included a chapter on aversion therapy in each edition of his textbook on the practice of behavior therapy, in which he surveyed the work of others as well as his own applications. In addition to electric shock, he cited the use of emetic drugs with alcoholics by Voegtlin and Lemere (1942), and the use of imaginal aversive events in the technique called covert sensitization (Cautela, 1967). Wolpe initially gave extensive coverage to the aversion therapy program of Feldman and MacCulloch (1965) in the treatment of homosexual men, although he cautioned that this procedure ignored the interpersonal anxiety that was at the root of much homosexual behavior (1969, p. 208). For this reason, and perhaps in tacit recognition of Davison's (1976) questioning the ethics of therapy to alter homosexuality, Wolpe later mentioned their work only in passing (1983, p. 262).

Based on Azrin and Holz's (1966) review of the experimental literature on punishment, Wolpe presented several 'practical guidelines' for aversion therapy:

1   The stimulus should be as intense as necessary to block the pleasurable response entirely.
2   The aversive stimulus should be delivered contemporaneously with the response.
3   The aversive stimulus should not be increased gradually, but introduced at a previously determined high intensity.
4   The frequency of administration should be as high as possible; ideally the stimulus should be given with every evocation of the response to be eliminated.
5   An alternative emotional target should be available which will not be punished, but which will produce the same or greater reinforcement as that to which the response is being eliminated. For example, a fetishist or exhibitionist needs to achieve normal sexual relations.
6   *Aversion therapy should not be administered before seeking out the possible anxiety bases of the unadaptive behavior and treating them if found.* This course of action will frequently make it unnecessary to inflict pain on the patient. (1973, pp. 228–9, italics in original)

Aversion therapy was never a first choice for Wolpe. He stressed the priority of overcoming anxiety which may motivate the undesirable habit and the importance of training an alternative response acceptable to both the patient and society. Wolpe expressed no ethical concerns about aversive procedures per se. His main concern was effectiveness. If more benign procedures had failed and there was an empirical basis for aversion therapy in a particular case, the ethical stance was to administer it.

Selection of Treatment

Wolpe provided some guidelines for selection among this array of treatment options. Although first priority was based on the patient's symptoms, Wolpe consistently warned against a 'cookbook' approach in which the diagnostic label was the sole factor in determining treatment. The particular features of each case were taken into account in designing an individual program. Many if not most patients presented with an array of symptoms which required a sequence of interventions.

In his most recent textbook, Wolpe drew together a logical sequence for deciding upon intervention strategy (1990, pp. 92–3). The first consideration was whether the patient harbored any misconceptions which influenced the occurrence of his or her disorder. If so, correction of these was the first order of business. Next, social anxieties were addressed through training assertive behavior which was to be practiced in daily life. Wolpe observed that a wide range of presenting complaints, from stuttering to depression, were rooted in social anxiety which called for assertiveness training. In some patients, severe anxiety which precluded assertive behavior could require desensitization before beginning assertiveness training. Systematic desensitization was the treatment of choice in cases of anxiety in which autonomic arousal to identifiable conditioned stimuli was predominant. Variations of desensitization or flooding were recommended for patients who, for idiosyncratic reasons, could not participate effectively in the standard program. Flooding was generally called for in the treatment of contamination obsessions and for cases of panic and agoraphobia in which 'fear of fear' was predominant. Aversion therapy was a last resort for patients with attractions to inappropriate stimuli for whom anxiety deconditioning was not indicated or effective.

Whatever technique was selected, Wolpe provided the patient with a rationale explaining its connection to the overall goals of therapy. Every effort was made to answer questions and allay misgivings so that the patient was a cooperative collaborator in the therapeutic enterprise. Progress was continually monitored and adjustments made in the program if difficulties arose.

Summary and Conclusions

Wolpe's first assessment task was to screen non-learned biologic conditions, including psychotic and psychopathic disorders, and non-anxiety habit disorders. The next assessment task was to determine the factors related to the individual patient's initial learning experiences and, more importantly, the idiosyncratic stimulus–response relationships operating in the person's current environment. Wolpe took the patient's presenting complaints as a working hypothesis for the focus of assessment, reminiscent of Yates' dictum (1958a) that 'the symptom *is* the neurosis.' But he also recognized that there could be a complex network of problems which the patient was unaware of or was hesitant to discuss. To search out hidden areas of possible relevance Wolpe employed a life history review, delving into areas such as childhood development and sexual experiences. He recommended the Fear Survey Schedule and the Willoughby to uncover areas that might have been missed in the interview. Total scores on tests like the Willoughby and Bernreuter provided dependent measures for more formal analysis of treatment outcome and alerted the therapist to special difficulties that might be encountered with a particular patient. Wolpe recognized that the complete picture might not be revealed in the initial assessment period and remained alert throughout treatment for additional information that could facilitate understanding and therapy. The goal of assessment was not to place the patient in a diagnostic category, though he did employ conventional categorical labels based on symptomology. Rather, the goal was to achieve an understanding of the 'case dynamics' which would serve as the basis for selecting interventions. It was not just the symptoms, but the factors responsible for those symptoms, that determined the form and content of treatment.

Wolpe was careful to share the results of assessment with the patient and to provide a rationale for treatment procedures. This was accomplished by presenting a general discussion on how unadaptive anxiety was learned, with relevance to each individual provided by specific examples from the patient's history. An intervention strategy flowed from this analysis, one which addressed the patient's particular anxiety symptoms and their controlling stimuli. In this, Wolpe assumed the role of educator, an expert who shared his knowledge with the patient and then collaborated in the process of treatment.

Systematic desensitization embodied the essence of Wolpe's contribution to clinical practice. It required the specification of environmental/behavioral relationships, highlighting his thesis that anxiety was a maladaptive response to environmental cues. It provided the patient with a tool, relaxation, for overcoming arousal. The gradual 'systematic' aspect of the procedure provided a benign way for the patient to overcome fears as well as indicating a clear path to recovery. Wolpe's artful analyses showed that it was not a 'simple' method to be employed for 'simple' phobias, but was part of a palette of procedures to be selected from in the course of treating complex problems.

Assertiveness training was guided by the same principles for overcoming social anxieties, along with sexual training for problems of sexual functioning. Wolpe expanded his system to accommodate exposure procedures which evoked anxiety in the patient. Exposure methods were 'systematic,' in that they involved controlled 'doses' of anxiety under therapeutic guidance, and achieved 'desensitization,' in that the target of each therapy session was calmness in the presence of previously upsetting events. Variations in methods for evoking counter-anxiety responses and presenting stimulus items in all of these procedures provided flexibility in meeting the idiosyncratic needs of each patient.

To an unprecedented degree, Wolpe clearly described his methods, their relation to theory, and, most importantly, their relations to treatment outcome. Wolpe's assessment methods specified the patient's complaints and, in so doing, specified clearly the therapeutic goals. Therapy techniques were selected (and altered) to achieve these goals. This open manner of doing psychotherapy was a major factor in challenging the old ways and in stimulating empirical research on therapy effectiveness.

4

Criticisms and Rebuttals

This chapter reviews the controversies surrounding Wolpe's therapy program in two main sections. The first addresses his quarrel with traditional psychotherapy as behavior therapy became established. The second covers the intramural disagreements within the field of behavior therapy as Wolpe's 'traditional' role was challenged.

Critiques of Psychotherapy

Wolpe's goal was to replace psychoanalytic therapy, the dominant system when he began his practice, with his learning-based therapy. He was personally convinced of the rightness of this crusade by virtue of the many patients he had helped who had undergone years of psychoanalysis at great cost but with little benefit. The rebuffs he had received by the psychoanalytic professional communities in Johannesburg, Charlottesville, and Philadelphia reinforced his separateness and strengthened his resolve. Wolpe approached this goal by criticizing the conceptual basis of psychoanalysis and by emphasizing the superiority in outcome of his therapy. For Wolpe, the theory that underpinned therapeutic procedures was closely linked to the outcomes of those procedures; positive results supported the theory and negative outcomes indicated faulty conceptualization.

Criticisms of Wolpe, in turn, were directed at both his theory of neurosis and his claims of greater success. Although some questioned Wolpe's procedures, the great outpouring of behavior therapy research produced a general consensus that it was at least equivalent in outcome to other therapies, resulting in a search for concepts that bridged all forms of psychotherapies. Wolpe, of course, resisted such conclusions. For ease of exposition, the following sections consider separately conceptual critiques, research on therapy outcomes, and the search for elements common to all therapies, as related to Wolpe's theories and methods.

Conceptual Critiques

Since Wolpe was the protagonist, his attacks on psychotherapy are presented first, followed by criticisms of his approach, and concluding with a discussion of the status of the critical issues addressed by both sides.

Wolpe's Critiques of Psychoanalysis. Wolpe's (1963a) fundamental criticism of the psychoanalytic model was that it was not scientific. The unconscious processes of the psychoanalytic mind transpired in a metaphysical realm outside the physically determined universe (1958, pp. 15–16). In contrast, he felt that the experimentally established laws of learning, with their roots in neurophysiologic mechanisms, provided a firm foundation for understanding behavior, normal or neurotic, animal or human, and for effecting therapeutic interventions (1958, pp. 17–36). He was joined in this assertion of scientific superiority by Eysenck (for example, 1960, p. ix).

More specifically, Wolpe asserted that conditioning principles provided a more satisfactory account of neurotic behavior and its therapy than did the psychoanalytic concepts of 'conflict' and 'repression' (1961a,b,c; 1981b). He understood conflict between unconscious psychic forces to be the key psychodynamic mechanism for repression and the production of neurotic symptoms. These forces included the infantile libidinous urges of classic Freudianism, or more contemporary conflicts related to the immediate life circumstances, as emphasized by the neo-Freudians. Cure required conscious insight into neurotogenic conflicts and mature disposition of the repressed psychic forces. Wolpe began his attack on conflict with his cat experiment, in which he showed that aversive conditioning of the anxiety response was sufficient to produce experimental neurosis in the absence of conflict. By extrapolation, the same processes were at work in humans (1967, see Chapter 2). Cure required uncoupling the conditioned bonds between anxiety and its eliciting stimuli; the fact that it could be accomplished without achieving insight into unconscious drives rendered the whole psychoanalytic enterprise irrelevant.

Wolpe (1961c) cited authors such as Otto Fenichel and Ruth Monroe to the effect that psychoanalytic theory predicted that simple removal of symptoms without attending to underlying conflicts would lead to rapid relapse or the appearance of new symptoms. His own results, and reports of other non-analytic treatments, found that relapse rates were very low. He concluded that these findings 'have gravely damaging implications for the whole psychoanalytic theory of neurosis, but accord with a theory based on principles of learning.'

An extensive illustration of how the conditioning model provided a more cogent alternative to psychoanalytic theory was provided in a critique of Freud's case of 'Little Hans,' a child who displayed a fear of horses. Wolpe and Rachman (1960) cited psychoanalytic literature indicating that this case was highly regarded as fundamental evidence for the role of Oedipal wishes, castration anxiety, and repression in the development of phobias. Their review of the case showed that, in fact, interpretations of sexual and aggressive strivings were foisted on the lad by his father, an avid devotee of Freud, contravening what the child actually said and did. From material presented by Freud, they showed that the child's fear was explained more plausibly and simply as conditioning arising from aversive experiences with horses and that improvement was related to positive interactions with them. In an understated conclusion, they noted that psychoanalytic practices, as demonstrated in this case, have 'been a great encumbrance to the development of a science of psychiatry.'

Finally, Wolpe proposed that the means by which psychoanalysis and other therapies achieved positive outcomes, limited though they might be, was the inadvertent occurrence of reciprocal inhibition (1954; 1958, pp. 193–4). That is, in the course of most therapies, including his own, the patient discusses his or her difficulties with a person who is believed to have the capability to help. In some cases this could arouse positive emotions of sufficient strength to overcome the anxiety elicited by sensitive topics brought up during the interview, resulting in deconditioning of anxiety to various critical stimuli and producing symptomatic relief. He found that great relief occasionally occurred during the initial assessment phase and felt this accounted for so-called 'transference cures.' On the other hand, he noted that overwhelming anxiety might also be aroused, resulting in the patient becoming worse, accounting for the phenomenon called 'negative transference.' Wolpe recognized his obligation to demonstrate that the systematic employment of therapeutic procedures improved upon the base rates of recovery due to nonspecific factors, and challenged other therapies to do the same (1969, pp. 266–7).

Psychoanalytic Criticisms of Wolpe. Wolpe's allegiance to the 'laws of learning' derived from animal experiments was assailed. Such an approach was viewed as cold, mechanistic, and dehumanizing (Weitzman, 1967). The specters of thought and behavior control were sometimes raised (Marmor, 1971). More frequently, the scientific credentials of nascent behavior therapy were attacked. Many critics observed that there was no such thing as a 'modern learning theory' (Breger and McGaugh, 1965; Marmor, 1971; Weitzman, 1967). The golden age of learning theories had seen the systems of Hull, Guthrie, Tolman, Spence, and Skinner fail to attain overall consensus. Eysenck's (1960, p. 15) assertion of 90 percent agreement among learning theorists on basic facts and principles was rejected as patently untrue. The solid rock on which Wolpe founded his therapy appeared, on closer inspection, to be 'a nontheoretical amalgamation of pragmatic principles' (Weitzman, 1967, p. 304).

A related criticism was that the specific learning concepts which Wolpe employed did not pertain to what he actually did in therapy. That is, terms such as 'stimulus,' 'response,' and 'reinforcement' were lifted from their limited laboratory setting and stretched beyond recognition to account for what transpired in therapy. This criticism was borrowed from Chomsky's influential attack (1959) on Skinnerian theory. Thus a light may be defined as a stimulus in a Pavlovian conditioning experiment, and salivation may be defined as a response, but these are far removed from defining 'imagination of a scene' as a stimulus and 'anxiety' as a response in systematic desensitization (Breger and McGaugh, 1965). Such an analogy 'gives comfort to the behavior therapist but obscures differences of profound significance between the systematic desensitizations of cats and men' (Weitzman, 1967, p. 306).

Many critics concluded that what Wolpe and other behavior therapists did was simply psychotherapy business-as-usual. Feather and Rhoads (1972a, p. 498) observed that:

> Many of the published cases of Wolpe, Lazarus, and others are described in terms of interpersonal conflicts and complex cognitive strategies rather than in terms of stimuli and responses. Similarly, in the extensive case literature on systematic desensitization, many examples can be found for improving interpersonal relationships, supportive statements and reassurance, guilt-relieving comments, and other familiar techniques of supportive psychotherapy.

A group of psychoanalysts who observed Wolpe and Lazarus conduct therapy for one week concluded that suggestion, manipulation of patient expectancies, reassurance, provision of an explicit description of expected behaviors, and a positive therapeutic relationship were major factors (Klein et al., 1969). These observers noted that Wolpe and Lazarus were experienced clinicians who had received psychodynamic training and had excellent general clinical skills. The effects of specific techniques, such as systematic desensitization, over and above suggestion and general skills, were not obvious to these observers. Marmor (1969) reached similar conclusions based on his observation of a film of Wolpe conducting desensitization. These critics implied that psychoanalysis provided more than these general factors.

With respect to symptom substitution, Klein et al. (1969) noted that it sometimes occurred in Wolpe's therapy but was explained away as 'inadequate treatment.' Others stated that symptom substitution was not a straightforward prediction of psychoanalytic theory (Feather and Rhoads, 1972b; Marmor, 1971). Weitzman (1967) explained how psychoanalytic theory could account for either symptom substitution or improved functioning following symptomatic treatment; he cited David Rapaport to the effect that psychoanalysis was essentially a postdictive system that explained events after their occurrence but was unable to make predictions.

Some investigators translated Wolpe's procedures into psychodynamic terms. Weitzman (1967) provided separate accounts of systematic desensitization in terms of Freudian, Jungian, and Sullivanian concepts. Relaxation was seen as a means of increasing receptivity to unconscious contents, and the images which a patient created during desensitization were found to change into psychoanalytically significant fantasies. In line with this reasoning, Feather and Rhoads (1972b) carried out systematic desensitization to scenes related to psychodynamic themes. Seagraves and Smith (1976) reported that patients undergoing systematic desensitization had thoughts and dreams which provided 'rich material' for psychoanalytic therapy.

Many critics regarded behavior therapy as appropriate only for 'simple' problems such as simple phobias or specific sexual dysfunctions. Marmor (1980) characterized behavior therapy as concerned only with symptom removal while ignoring subjective feelings and thoughts. Murray (1976) proposed two categories of disorders: the first included symptoms resulting from faulty learning in persons with 'basically good ego functioning,' for whom behavior therapy might be appropriate; the second encompassed 'personality disturbances' resulting from intrapsychic conflicts, requiring depth psychotherapy. Murray suggested that behavior therapy might be a useful adjunct to dynamic psychotherapy, addressing specific symptoms which were dangerous, illegal, or promoted resistance, allowing psychotherapy to proceed with more basic and necessary personality reconstruction.

Discussion of Psychotherapy Critiques.   It is clear that neither side was convinced of the soundness of the conceptual system or usefulness of the procedures of the other. Many of Wolpe's critics had little regard for his claims of scientific foundations and were content to show that learning theory was as fractionated and contentious as psychodynamic theory. On the other hand, some psychotherapists showed interest in a learning point of view, though not of the type advocated by Pavlov or Hull. Birk and Birk (1974, p. 502) declared that 'in fact, psychoanalytic and behavioral theories are both learning theories; it follows that in effect *psychoanalysis and behavior therapy are both learning therapies.*' Such critics viewed learning as predicated on internal cognitive processes, foreshadowing the 'cognitive revolution' within behavior therapy (see below).

Psychotherapists who observed Wolpe or closely read his published cases were impressed by his warmth, empathy, and other clinical skills. This refuted their stereotypes of cold, mechanistic, conditioning therapy, but they had difficulty reconciling his clinical behavior with stimulus–response learning concepts. Wolpe, of course, found these concepts extremely useful for conducting assessment and therapy and could not understand how others could fail to see their connection to his cats or Pavlov's dogs.

Each side sought to account for successful outcomes by the other in terms of its own theory. Wolpe perceived the operation of unplanned reciprocal inhibition in traditional psychotherapy, while psychotherapists saw suggestion, expectancy, and transference at work in his approach. There was overall agreement that nonspecific factors were important in all therapies. Wolpe agreed that 'suggestion' was an important aspect of behavior therapy and employed it quite deliberately to promote new learning (Klein et al., 1969). Many psychotherapists expressed interest in adapting systematic desensitization to psychoanalytic ends, but Wolpe had no use for psychoanalytic techniques and criticized efforts to promote synthesis. He maintained that there was no evidence that psychoanalytic procedures had any effects beyond nonspecific ones, and that their use could only dilute the effectiveness of behavior therapy (1976b; 1990, p. 342).

Effectiveness Critiques

Wolpe's chief criticism of psychoanalysis (1952b; 1981b), in concert with Eysenck, was that it was not effective, at least no more so than general medical and supportive treatment. Wolpe also asserted that his therapy outcomes were greatly superior. Psychotherapy war was declared, in which psychoanalytic and other insight therapies were pitted against the upstart learning-based approaches. Wolpe, in the fashion of the time, presented his results in the format of retrospective reports of individual cases, for illustrative purposes, or compilations of groups of cases drawn from his files. Later, more sophisticated researchers conducted prospective studies, in which comparable patients were randomly assigned to different treatment and control conditions. Wolpe participated in two landmark projects of this nature, and his therapy procedures were the focus of hundreds of additional studies. As the number of outcome studies grew ever larger, statistical compilations of the prospective studies were reviewed. Wolpe's claims of superiority echoed throughout these reviews as well.

Retrospective Reports.   While there were a few early reports critical of psychoanalytic effectiveness (Boring, 1940; Landis, 1937; 1940), it was Eysenck's blast (1952) that set off the psychotherapy wars. On the basis of earlier surveys, Eysenck concluded that neurotics receiving custodial care or general medical advice recovered at a baseline rate of approximately two-thirds in two years. In comparison, 'eclectic psychotherapy' produced a recovery rate of 64 percent and psychoanalysis resulted in a recovery rate of only 44 percent when those leaving treatment were counted as unsuccessful, or 66 percent among those completing treatment. The bottom line was that psychotherapy added nothing to nonspecific care. Though not as widely noted, Wolpe (1952b) made a similar charge.

The counter-attack was swift (De Charms et al., 1954; Luborsky, 1954; Rosenzweig, 1954, for example). Critics emphasized that the 'non-psychotherapy' patients had indeed received ministrations such as attention, reassurance, or suggestion. Differences in patients, treatment procedures and outcome measures made comparisons across studies highly suspect and generalizations impossible. But Eysenck (1961b) was unmoved. Despite the difficulties with *post hoc* comparisons of diverse studies, he thought the recovery rate across types of patients, methods of treatment, or standards of recovery, to be remarkably stable, confirming that specific psychotherapy produced no greater effects than nonspecific attention or suggestion. Moreover, any difficulty in interpreting outcome data was the fault of psychotherapists, who could not agree on even the most fundamental issues like definitions of treatment and measurement of outcome.

Published the same year as Eysenck's scathing review, Wolpe's (1952b) outcome report could not have been more striking. He adapted Knight's (1941) criteria for therapy outcome, such as sexual and interpersonal adjustment, but emphasized symptomatic improvement, rated in five categories from apparently cured to unimproved. Wolpe conservatively judged those in the 'cured' and 'much improved' categories as 'successes' and the remainder as 'failures.' Of his initial 70 cases, Wolpe rated 86 percent as 'successes' and 14 percent as 'failures;' an additional 52 cases were rated 96 percent 'successes' (1954); followed by 88 cases rated as 89 percent 'successes' (1958, p. 216). Overall, he reported a success rate of 90 percent for 210 cases.

Wolpe also introduced the idea of efficiency of treatment. For the 88 patients reviewed in 1958 (pp. 217–18), he reported that two-thirds required fewer than 40 sessions over approximately 11 months – much less than the many years required by psycho-analysis. Unsuccessful patients received, on average, more sessions than successful ones, indicating that they were not simply drop-outs but that much effort had been invested. With respect to drop-outs, Wolpe included patients in his review only if they had an 'adequate' amount of therapy, which he regarded as about 40 sessions (1958, p. 205). He did not provide a count of actual drop-outs.

Wolpe also suggested using changes in test scores to measure outcome. He reported improvements on the Willoughby Personality Inventory, albeit in an unsystematic fashion (1958, p. 205). He sometimes neglected to readminister the questionnaire when the initial scores were low or when patients terminated treatment early. Both expedients inflated improvement scores simply by eliminating low pre-therapy scores and high post-therapy scores. Not surprisingly, great progress was found in the scores of the 'successful' patients. A final feature which Wolpe reported in favor of his treatment was the fact that most patients had neurotic problems of many years standing, and a large number had had previous psychotherapy. These factors argued against his results being due to spontaneous remission or the nonspecific aspects of therapy.

Lazarus (1963) presented a similar retrospective report of patients he had treated, several taken over from Wolpe's practice when he departed South Africa. Lazarus contacted referral sources and family members in order to judge outcome. According to what he felt were stringent criteria, he counted success in 62 percent of 126 'extremely neurotic' cases, in an average of 14 sessions. Out of a total of 408 cases, including his 'severe' sample, he reported a success rate of 78 percent. Thus his success rate was less than that of Wolpe, but it was accomplished in far fewer sessions.

Several of Wolpe's psychiatrist colleagues at Virginia, who had received training from Wolpe, published an account of their out-comes with systematic desensitization (Hain et al., 1966). Twenty-seven patients with severe anxiety-related problems, half of whom had been unsuccessful with previous treatments, were included in this series. An overall success rate of 78 percent was reported, including those who had dropped out of treatment or who had difficulty with desensitization. This was accomplished in a median number of 16 sessions.

Dozens of individual case reports followed as clinicians from all over the clinical spectrum tried out desensitization. Some had received training by Wolpe but most based their treatment on reading about his procedures. A wide range of phobias and sexual problems were treated successfully (see Paul, 1969).

But not all reports were positive. For example, Meyer and Crisp (1966) described procedural difficulties and limited outcomes with desensitization. Similar reports were published by the clinical researchers at the Maudsley Hospital, who compared records of patients receiving behavior therapy with those receiving insight and psychoanalytic therapies (Cooper, 1963; Cooper et al., 1965; Marks and Gelder, 1965). These researchers were familiar with Wolpe's methods from his visits and from their colleague Rachman, but were not sympathetic to the battle against psychotherapy that Wolpe and Eysenck were waging (Marks and Gelder, 1966). They found poor outcomes with both desensitization and psychotherapy for severe agoraphobic patients, while those with other phobias showed greater improvements with behavior therapy but no difference at approximately one year follow-up. Wolpe and Lazarus (1966, p. 159) criticized these reports, suggesting that the investigators' inexperience with behavior therapy precluded a fair comparison.

There is much to fault in such retrospective reports. Breger and McGaugh (1965) observed that retrospective reviews were always subject to selection problems and observer biases. Pointing to a history of new therapeutic methods being oversold by their proponents, they cautioned that Wolpe's reports could reflect his enthusiasm more than actual outcomes. His exclusion of an unspecified number of patients receiving 'insufficient therapy' further biased his results, since poor-prognosis patients were especially likely to drop out of treatment. These authors found it ironic that one identifying so closely with experimental psychology and the scientific method should employ traditional case-history methods to assess outcome.

Wolpe did not reply directly to Breger and McGaugh, dismissing their critique as a 'red herring' (1973, p. 277), but Rachman and Eysenck (1966) made a spirited response. Ignoring the problems of bias in retrospective reports, they pointed to the beginnings of what was to become a flood of controlled research.

In a half dozen years a relatively small number of behavior therapists, with little official support and often against the most hostile opposition, have succeeded in carrying out more controlled (and better controlled) studies than have hundreds of psychiatrists and psychoanalysts in 60 years, with all the financial resources and the prestige so readily available to them. (Rachman and Eysenck, 1966, p. 168)

Prospective Research. Prospective research addressed the problems of selection bias, nonspecific effects, and maturation effects, that were inherent in retrospective reports. While not sophisticated in research methodology, Wolpe was involved in several important early efforts and later saw his procedures of desensitization and assertiveness training become the focus of a veritable research industry. Wolpe's claims of therapeutic superiority were addressed directly in many clinical research projects and his methods and theories were dissected in a host of analogue studies.

The first prospective comparison of Wolpe's methods with traditional procedures was the doctoral dissertation of Arnold Lazarus (1961) under Wolpe's direction. Patients with a variety of 'phobic' problems, including sexual impotence, were matched on diagnostic and demographic criteria and randomly assigned to two treatment conditions, systematic desensitization or 'dynamic interpretation,' with Lazarus serving as therapist in both conditions. For expediency, all therapy was conducted in group sessions in which those with common diagnoses were seen together. Treatment duration was limited to the time required to complete the desensitization hierarchies, averaging 21 sessions. Outcome measures included self-report and direct observation where feasible. Lazarus reported 72 percent success for desensitization patients compared to only 12 percent of the 'dynamic' patients. Two-thirds of the unsuccessful 'dynamic' patients achieved success with subsequent desensitization. Follow-up at varying intervals indicated that 80 percent of the patients maintained their fearless behavior.

Obvious methodological deficiencies of Lazarus' study included the lack of untreated controls and blind observers, the heterogeneous measurement system, and the questionable adequacy of 'dynamic' treatment. After their rift, both Wolpe and Lazarus ceased all reference to this study. But the idea of direct comparison of therapies had wide impact and many researchers sought to overcome the methodologic problems.

The most ambitious and rigorous comparison of psychoanalytic and behavior therapy was that undertaken by R. Bruce Sloane and associates at Temple University shortly after Wolpe's arrival (Sloane et al., 1975; see Chapter 1). Because of its wide influence, disagreements over its findings, and Wolpe's intimate involvement as a participant, it is instructive to examine this study closely.

The two types of therapy were defined simply in terms of the therapists themselves, who employed the procedures they felt relevant for each individual patient. The behavior therapists were Wolpe, Lazarus, and Michael Serber. The psychotherapists were three eminent psychiatrists, trained in classical psychoanalysis. Ninety patients diagnosed as 'neurotic' or 'personality disorder' were matched on gender and severity and were randomly assigned to psychotherapy, behavior therapy, or waiting-list. Treatment consisted of weekly sessions over a four-month period. Dependent measures included structured interviews and numerous rating scales related to symptoms and life adjustment, which were completed by assessors blind to the treatment, therapists, patients, and family or friends.

The result which most surprised the researchers was the improvement shown in the waiting-list group. About half these patients improved in assessor ratings of target symptoms and global anxiety, more than three-quarters improved in overall adjustment ratings, and there was a significant improvement in social functioning on the structured interview. This substantiated Wolpe's concern for nonspecific factors and Eysenck's emphasis on base rates of improvement. The psychotherapy group had a significantly higher proportion and magnitude of symptom change ratings compared to the waiting-list, but did not differ on anxiety or life adjustment ratings. Behavior therapy was comparable to psychotherapy and superior to waiting-list in symptom improvement and comparable to both in anxiety improvement. In addition, behavior therapy patients had significantly higher overall adjustment ratings and showed improvement in both work and social scales of the structured interview, whereas psychotherapy patients showed no change. When more disturbed patients were considered (those scoring above the median on symptom and personality measures), behavior therapy was superior to psychotherapy in symptom improvement ratings. Psychotherapy was found superior to behavior therapy on only one measure – patient ratings of sexual adjustment. Process measures indicated differences between the two therapies as well. Not surprisingly, behavior therapists were more directive than psychotherapists, but they also scored significantly higher on objective and patient ratings of empathy. Psychotherapists rated their patients as less suitable for treatment than did behavior therapists, and their ratings of suitability and likeability were correlated with symptom improvement.

One-year follow-up assessments were confounded by treatment for most waiting-list patients, which was predominantly psychoanalytic, and by continuing treatment for some other patients.

Overall group mean improvements at four months were maintained at one year but additional treatment did not produce significant gains for any group. Behavior therapy remained superior to waiting-list in symptom ratings, with psychotherapy intermediate and not significantly different from either.

In their conclusions, the authors recognized that psychoanalytic therapy was effective primarily with the 'good' patient, whom the therapist regarded as 'suitable' and 'likeable,' while behavior therapy was effective with a broader range of patients, particularly those with 'acting out' or more severe symptoms (Sloane et al., 1975, pp. 223–6). They also observed greater variability in psychotherapy outcomes, with more showing greater improvement but also more showing less improvement than in behavior therapy (Sloane et al., 1975, p. 213). Despite these observations, they emphasized the essential equality of outcomes for both types of therapy.

This conclusion became the conventional wisdom. Traditional psychotherapists accepted their decision of a draw and hailed the study as a paragon of outcome research: Smith et al. (1980, p. 26) called it 'the single best outcome evaluation of psychotherapy ever accomplished;' Strupp (1978, p. 9) regarded it as one of 'the landmarks of outcome research;' and Bergin and Lambert (1978, p. 164) thought it 'probably the best comparative study of psycho-therapy yet carried out.'

Wolpe initially regarded this study as 'a splendid piece of research . . . unmatched by any other clinical study in the history of psychotherapy' (Sloane et al., 1975, p. ix), but he refused to accept the conclusion of no difference (1981b; 1982, pp. 330–3). He criticized the study on three grounds: biased assessors, an unrep-resentative subject pool, and inaccurate data reporting.

First, he suggested that the assessors, two of whom were psychoanalytic and one Skinnerian, might have provided ratings more similar to the psychotherapists than the behavior therapists, 'who often formulate their targets differently.' In fact, assessors' ratings corresponded more closely to those of the patients than to those of the therapists (but no differentiation was made between the types of therapists). The data also showed that behavior therapists consistently overestimated improvement compared to all other observers – patient, assessor, or informant. There were other possible shortcomings with the assessors: no efforts were made to train them or determine reliability of ratings (Poppen, 1976); and it was unlikely they remained blind to the subjects' treatment groups (Kazdin and Wilson, 1978, p. 54).

Secondly, Wolpe complained that the subject sample was

restricted to mild problems. In fairness, it should be recalled that the patients met clinical criteria for neurosis or personality disorder and fell in the 'moderate' range of pathology on several personality scales and rating instruments. The finding that behavior therapists did better with the more severely disturbed patients supported Wolpe's contention that greater differences might have been obtained with a more difficult patient population. On the other hand, these patients were not a walk-over for behavior therapy, by which none were judged 'fully recovered' at four months, while psychotherapy and waiting-list had three and two, respectively, so appraised.

Finally, Wolpe argued that, in effect, the trees of behavior therapy superiority had been obscured by the forest of no difference. He cited Giles' (1983b) review of the Temple project data, which reported eight statistically significant differences favoring behavior therapy and only one favoring psychotherapy. He felt that the 'equal effectiveness' conclusion was evidence of continued bias against behavior therapy.

Many other behavior therapists criticized this study and the conclusions drawn from it. The biggest limitation was the exclusive reliance on rating scales and questionnaires as the dependent measures, and the absence of direct behavioral observation (Kazdin and Wilson, 1978, pp. 52–60). As Paul (1966) discovered, patients' self-reports might not accurately reflect their own behavior change, and ratings based on their self-report would also suffer. Bandura (1978) saw no value in the study at all, largely because of the lack of specificity of both the independent and the dependent variables.

In summary, there was no overwhelming winner in this contest. Wolpe and other behavior therapists claimed small victories in spite of an uneven playing field. Psychotherapists finally had to accept behavior therapists into the clubhouse but were heartened by their own success. This study strongly reinforced the 'equivalence of therapies' hypothesis (see below).

As the Temple project exemplified, clinical research comparing therapy procedures was very difficult. Obtaining sufficient numbers of subjects was time-consuming and politically treacherous, selection criteria could be vague and complicated, specification of therapeutic procedures was perplexing, and measurement of complex outcomes was troublesome. Control for maturation effects by use of waiting periods raised ethical concerns about withholding treatment.

In contrast, analogue studies had the methodologic advantages of plentiful and relatively homogeneous subjects with more easily measured target behaviors. Since the problems were not major life disturbances, subjects could be assigned to brief, precisely specified treatments and control conditions with no ethical qualms. The discovery of large numbers of college students having fears of creepy animals or social situations, and the specificity of systematic desensitization and assertiveness training, made analogue research the gateway to countless doctoral dissertations and research programs.

The disadvantage of analogue research, of course, was that its relevance to 'real' patients and therapists could be challenged. The trade-offs between methodological rigor and real world relevance were widely debated (Bernstein and Paul, 1971; Emmelkamp et al., 1985; Kazdin and Wilson, 1978, pp. 158–66; Smith et al., 1980, pp. 56–7). Kazdin and Wilson noted that all prospective research could be considered analogue in the sense that selection, measurement, and time factors made research different from therapy as usually practiced. Thus there was not a simple dichotomy between clinical and analogue research, but rather a number of dimensions along which studies varied. However, both Wolpe and his critics felt there was a qualitative difference between 'weak fears' and true neuroses, and both used this argument to downplay findings contrary to their positions.

An outstanding example of analogue research is that of Gordon Paul (1966), who compared desensitization with 'insight' therapy, in a study of extraordinary methodologic rigor as well as real-world relevance. Ninety-six college students having severe fear of public speaking were randomly assigned to 'insight' therapy, systematic desensitization, placebo, or no-treatment. Outcome measures included direct observation of speech behavior by observers blind to treatment conditions, self-report on anxiety and personality scales, and physiologic measures of autonomic arousal. Professional psychotherapists administered all forms of treatment: insight was their preferred mode; desensitization was conducted according to a protocol for relaxation training and hierarchy construction; and placebo consisted of a 'tranquilizing' pill and a boring task to 'increase stress tolerance.'

Paul found that virtually all of the desensitization subjects scored as therapeutic successes on behavioral and physiologic measures, whereas less than half the insight and placebo subjects could be regarded as such. No improvement occurred in the no-treatment groups; in fact about one quarter of them refused to return for the second test speech, lending credence to Wolpe's hypothesis that uncontrolled contact with upsetting situations only strengthened anxiety. Interestingly, subjects' immediate self-ratings of improvement did not differ among the three treatment groups and there was little change in personality measures. However, therapists' ratings were more consistent with objective measures. A two-year follow-up (Paul, 1967a) showed that self-ratings had improved for almost all of the desensitization subjects, compared to half of the insight and less than one-quarter of the placebo and no-treatment subjects. In addition, desensitization subjects had higher grade-point averages and graduation rates (Paul, 1968; Paul and Shannon, 1966). Rather than symptom substitution, desensitization of speech anxiety appeared to result in widespread gains in adaptive behavior.

Comparative studies like Paul's were rare. Because of the difficulty in specifying psychotherapy procedures, analogue researchers focused primarily on investigating the necessary and sufficient conditions for desensitization and the relevance of Wolpe's theory of reciprocal inhibition (Lang, 1969). Hundreds of analogue studies addressing these issues appeared over the next decade. Early studies demonstrated that desensitization, as specified by Wolpe, was superior to placebo treatment or its individual components, such as hierarchy items presented without relaxation (for example, Davison, 1968). However, studies also appeared in which positive outcomes were obtained with procedures that omitted relaxation or gradual stimulus presentation, seeming to contradict reciprocal inhibition principles. Many different procedures, such as 'flooding' and 'coping skills,' were developed as alternatives to desensitization. The necessary and sufficient components of assertiveness training were also widely studied in analogue research programs.

Wolpe was supportive of the early analogue research of Paul and Lang, which confirmed his teachings, but became less accepting as later research suggested that various procedures were also effective. He was critical of analogue studies of 'weak fears' that could be overcome by 'minimal procedures.' And he felt that blanket treatments applied to groups regardless of individual differences decreased the power of desensitization and other methods (1982, pp. 178–80). These schisms and revisions are discussed in a later section. What is important to note here is that in the two decades following publication of *Psychotherapy by Reciprocal Inhibition*, more research was conducted on the effectiveness of Wolpe's methods than had been directed at psychotherapy outcome since Freud's publications at the start of the century.

Evaluative Reviews. As the number of therapy outcome studies proliferated, it became obvious that there were too many variables for any one crucial experiment to turn the tide in favor of one side or another. Even studies as ambitious and rigorous as those of

Sloane or Paul could be gainsaid for their sins of omission or commission. Thus the battleground shifted back to Eysenck's venue – reviewing the corpus of research and pronouncing a verdict based on the preponderance of evidence. Within two decades of Eysenck's and Wolpe's initial critiques, the number of studies had increased over a hundred-fold, with outcome measures much more complex than 'percent success.' A see-saw battle developed, as each side challenged the adequacy of the other's review, added a few more studies to the arsenal, and concluded that the data were on their side. For example, Bergin (1971) concluded that Eysenck's base rates of recovery were too high and that psychotherapy was demonstrably effective. Rachman (1971; 1973) disputed Bergin's conclusions, eliminating studies which favored psychotherapy as methodologically inadequate and citing those which supported the efficacy or superiority of behavior therapy. Rachman was attacked, in turn, for failing to employ consistent methodologic criteria for both behavioral and non-behavioral studies (Shapiro and Shapiro, 1977).

In an influential review, Luborsky et al. (1975) stated specific criteria for methodologic quality and rated studies accordingly. They summarized the outcomes in terms of 'box scores,' in which therapy could be categorized as a 'win,' 'loss,' or 'tie,' on the basis of statistically significant differences from comparison groups on whatever measures were employed by the researchers. Overall, they found traditional psychotherapies to be superior to no-treatment in 60 percent of the studies, with little differences between modes of therapy. Comparing psychotherapy to behavior therapy (mostly desensitization, but excluding analogue research), they reported six 'wins' and 18 'ties' in 12 studies. They awarded behavior therapy a faint compliment by observing that it might be especially suited for treating circumscribed phobias. These authors decried the lack of quantitative psychodynamic outcome studies, noting that the newcomer, behavior therapy, was the most active in generating data. They concluded by emphasizing the equality of therapies due to common elements, reiterating Rosenzweig's 'dodo bird verdict' (1936) from *Alice in Wonderland*, that 'everyone has won and all must have prizes.'

Wolpe (1982, p. 331; 1990, p. 339) endorsed the criticisms of Luborsky et al. by Giles (1983a; see also Kazdin and Wilson, 1978). These critics questioned the reliability and utility of the rating system, criticized the inclusion of methodologically poor studies and exclusion of relevant behavioral studies, and attacked the logic of the 'box score.' Giles (1983a) observed that all differences that Luborsky et al. found favored behavior therapy, and that some of the comparisons listed as a 'tie' on closer scrutiny could be decided in favor of behavior therapy. Such inaccuracies were clear evidence of bias against behavior therapy. Wolpe was assured that an unbiased reading of Luborsky's review supported the superiority of behavior therapy.

Meta-Analysis. A statistical procedure intended to meet the criticisms of evaluative reviews and reach a conclusion in the psychotherapy wars was introduced by Mary Lee Smith and Gene Glass (Smith and Glass, 1977). Selection bias was overcome by including all possible studies including therapy analogues, methodologic issues were addressed by evaluating the effects of procedural factors, and comparison of diverse measures was solved by converting them to the common measure of 'effect size' – the magnitude of difference, in standard deviation units, between treatment and comparison groups. Meta-analysis addressed Wolpe's claims of the effectiveness of his methods and the superiority of behavior therapy over traditional therapies.

Smith et al. (1980) reviewed nearly 500 studies and calculated over 1700 effect sizes in a review which served as the model and focal point for all subsequent meta-analyses. The largest contributor to their data pool was analogue studies of desensitization, even though they omitted 10 percent of such studies to reduce the skewing of results. Desensitization was one of 18 individual therapy types; Wolpe's other methods were included in other categories such as 'eclectic' and 'cognitive-behavioral' (Smith et al., 1980, pp. 70–7). The 18 types were grouped into six subclasses which in turn were grouped into three superclasses: Behavioral (including aversive and reinforcement procedures), Verbal (including psychodynamic and rational–emotive therapy), and Developmental (including vocational and school counseling). More than those of any other single person, Wolpe's techniques pervaded behavior therapy categorizations at all levels. At the individual therapy level, systematic desensitization and 'cognitive–behavioral' therapy (including assertiveness training) produced large and reliable effect sizes. The superclass groupings indicated that the overall average effect size for Behavioral therapies was superior to Verbal therapies, and that both were much greater than Developmental counseling, which had negligible effects (Smith et al., 1980, p. 98). This same pattern occurred in meta-analysis of 'same experiment' studies, such as the Temple project (Smith et al., 1980, pp. 106–8).

Although behavior therapies consistently provided greater effect sizes than verbal ones on many different measures, the authors attributed this finding to measurement bias. For example in examining the relationship between the type of therapy and various measures of functioning in 'same experiment' analyses, they grouped the majority of measures on which behavior therapies were superior into a 'psychological' category, and the few measures on which verbal therapies were superior into a 'less tractable' category. They concluded, 'On measures less susceptible to influence, reliable differences among therapies disappeared' (Smith et al., 1980, p. 107).

Further evidence of the effort to downplay the superiority of behavioral therapies was the construction of a 'reactivity' scale to rate dependent measures (Smith et al., 1980, p. 67). For example, direct observation by the therapist was rated highest in reactivity, and even blind scoring of behavioral tests was rated high. Low reactivity scores were given to blind assessor ratings of verbal reports and blind projective test scores. The authors magnified the reactivity scores by a power transformation and entered them into a statistical analysis to predict effect sizes for various therapy categories (Smith et al., 1980, pp. 101–5). In a highly selective reading of this analysis they concluded that:

> The independent variable accounting for most of the variance in effect size was reactivity in measurement. Furthermore, there were reliable differences among therapy groups with respect to average reactivity. Behavior therapy classes and subclasses used measures that were more highly reactive (more under the influence of therapist and client) than verbal therapies. (Smith et al., 1980, p. 105)

A more accurate reading of their analysis indicates that reactivity had a small correlation with effect size that was consistent across most subclasses of therapies, not only behavioral ones. Reactivity was one of several procedural factors that predicted effect size for various therapy groupings, no one of which predicted the 'most.' Finally, both Behavioral and Verbal therapy superclasses were substantially greater than Developmental on reactivity but differed very little, if at all, with respect to magnitude of *untransformed* reactivity scores.

In summary, Smith et al. (1980) presented meta-analysis as a kind of statistical Switzerland, a neutral technique above the psychotherapy war that could bring order to the partisan fray. Many advantages were found for behavioral over verbal therapies but in all instances the authors explained away these differences as resulting from measurement bias. On the one hand they stated that 'all outcome measures are more or less related to "well-being" and so at a general level are comparable,' and that it was reasonable to accept the judgments of the primary researchers about the value of their measures (Smith and Glass, 1977, p. 753). But on the other hand, they warned against therapies that 'work toward more easily measured outcomes,' and they recommended that 'the benefit of the doubt should be granted to theories that lack technologies readily applicable to outcome evaluation' (Smith et al., 1980, p. 31). In order to give the 'benefit of the doubt' to traditional psychotherapy, outcome measures that were obviously related to the goals of therapy were denigrated as biased. Discounting measures such as performance in situations addressed by a desensitization hierarchy cut at the heart of behavior therapy. In their hands, meta-analysis was just one more weapon in the psychotherapy war.

Reactions to the meta-analysis of psychotherapy outcome studies were split along partisan lines. Traditional psychotherapists hailed it as a major breakthrough, proving the effectiveness of psychotherapy and the equivalence of various types (for example, Strupp, 1982). Behavior therapists viewed it as seriously flawed (Eysenck, 1978; Kazdin and Wilson, 1978; Wilson and Rachman, 1983; Searles, 1985). Behavior therapists' criticisms centered on what could be called the 'bad apple' theory, in which the inclusion of methodologically poor studies ruined the whole meta-analytic barrel. They rejected the denigration of direct behavioral observation as 'reactive,' but did not address the way this variable was manipulated by Smith et al. (1980; see above). Another criticism was that selective inclusion and exclusion of studies in a meta-analysis biased the findings, and that even the wide net cast by Smith et al. (1980) left many gaps.

Subsequent meta-analyses addressed these criticisms, making special efforts to include only methodologically sound studies. Most of these analyses examined the issue of behavior therapy superiority but often downplayed differences that were found. For example, Andrews and Harvey (1981) selected studies from Smith et al. (1980) that employed only 'truly neurotic' or 'emotional somatic' patients, excluding analogue research. They found an overall effect size for behavior therapy significantly greater than for verbal therapy, which in turn was much greater than for developmental counseling. However they disregarded the difference between behavior and verbal therapies in their conclusions. Landman and Dawes (1981) also selected methodologically sound studies from Smith et al. (1980). They did not compare therapy types but noted that larger effect sizes were found for 'less severe' problems, such as snake phobia or test anxiety, compared to more severe problems, such as schizophrenia or alcoholism, implying that behavior therapy was limited to simple problems. Searles (1985) reanalyzed the data sets of Landman and Dawes (1981) and of Andrews and

Harvey (1981), using even stricter methodologic criteria, and found effect sizes for behavior therapy much larger than for psychodynamic treatment.

Shapiro and Shapiro (1982) employed a later data base than Smith et al. (1980), separating 'cognitive' therapies from psychodynamic and humanistic ones, reflecting the realignment of these approaches. They found that both behavioral and cognitive therapies were much superior to verbal/humanistic ones. In 'same experiment' studies, they found 'mixed behavioral' and cognitive procedures superior to desensitization. But they concluded that their findings had little relevance for clinical practice since methodologically sound studies were almost exclusively analogues conducted by behavior and cognitive therapists, and that the dynamic and humanist therapies were 'straw men' set up to enhance favorable comparisons. Bowers and Clum (1988) employed an even later data base to compare behavior therapy to nonspecific factors. They noted a decline in the number of analogue studies of desensitization, an increased number of cognitive–behavioral and operant procedures, and a paucity of non-behavioral research. They found a sizeable effect of behavior therapy compared to placebo treatment and concluded that the specific features of therapy accounted for twice as much of treatment effects as did nonspecific factors.

With respect to the 'reactivity' criticism, that behavior therapy employed dependent measures which were easily influenced, the findings of subsequent meta-analyses were mixed. Andrews and Harvey (1981) found no significant correlation between effect size and reactivity or observer blindedness, though effects tended to be larger when outcomes were measured by the therapist. Shapiro and Shapiro (1982) found a small but significant correlation between reactivity and effect size. Bowers and Clum (1988) found no significant correlation between reactivity and effect size, although the studies they reviewed were exclusively behavioral. Traditional psychotherapy researchers eventually regarded many of the 'low reactivity' personality measures favored by Smith et al. (1980) as insensitive to change and of little use in gauging outcome (Lambert and Bergin, 1992).

With respect to the methodologic rigor issue, it is apparent that behavioral researchers became increasingly dominant in conducting sound research while dynamic and humanist therapists made no progress in this respect. This did not represent a capitulation on the part of traditional therapists, however. Rather, it reflected the 'equivalent effectiveness' conclusion by those who accepted the importance of psychotherapy research (such as Koss and Butcher,

1986). On the other hand, many traditional psychotherapists viewed controlled research as inimical to what transpired in therapy, and excused themselves from demonstrating outcomes in this fashion (Shapiro and Shapiro, 1982).

Wolpe (1982, pp. 329–31; 1990, pp. 336–9) had mixed reactions to meta-analysis. Certainly, desensitization stood alone as the one single technique of unquestionably demonstrated effectiveness, although his therapy involved much more than this. On the one hand, he approved of the criticisms which regarded meta-analysis as a fatally flawed evaluative procedure. On the other hand, he was heartened by the report of Andrews and Harvey (1981) who focused on patient samples of the type with which he was concerned. Wolpe emphasized the superiority of behavior therapy which these authors had found (but had glossed over in their conclusions) and reproduced some of their data in his textbooks to show the greater effect sizes obtained by behavior therapy regardless of severity of disorder, amount of therapy, and length of follow-up. Wolpe concluded that even in the hands of the enemy camp, meta-analysis revealed the superiority of behavior therapy, and that only the continuing bias of vested interests obscured these findings.

Equal Effectiveness.   Wolpe had proclaimed the revolutionary idea that psychotherapy was no more effective than nonspecific care and that the new learning-based methods produced superior outcomes. Yet four decades of research evaluating therapy outcomes had produced a consensus among mainstream psychotherapists, and even some behavior therapists, that rebuffed his challenge. There was widespread agreement that a large variety of traditional psychotherapies were more effective than natural healing or 'placebo' processes, whatever that term might mean for psychotherapy (Lambert and Bergin, 1992). This consensus accepted Wolpe's methods, and other behavioral and cognitive procedures, as equally effective with traditional ones, but accorded them no special stature. The 'dodo bird verdict,' enunciated before the appearance of Wolpe or behavior therapy (Rosenzweig, 1936), was expanded to include behavioral procedures as well (Luborsky et al., 1975; Lambert et al., 1986). Inasmuch as Wolpe had striven to create an approach that rose above psychotherapy business-as-usual, this verdict represented a direct repudiation of his efforts. Shared victory was not the goal of one who had declared war on traditional psychotherapy.

What is more, the equal effectiveness conclusion supported the hypothesis that the diverse methods employed in the various therapies were not the critical elements; rather, all therapies were characterized by common factors which accounted for the uniform outcomes (Lambert et al., 1986; Stiles et al., 1986). According to this hypothesis, systematic desensitization, assertiveness training, dream interpretation, or empathetic listening – all were iterations of some more basic therapeutic principles, as yet only dimly discerned. The common factors hypothesis was not a criticism specifically directed at Wolpe, but it suggested that he, like most psycho-therapists, engaged in practices that effected therapeutic outcomes for reasons beyond his ken.

This hypothesis led to efforts to uncover the common factors, with an eye toward isolating and refining them so as to produce a more effective psychotherapy (Arkowitz, 1992). Broad domains of common factors were proposed, including patient and therapist characteristics, features of the therapeutic relationship, and 'change processes' that transcended theoretical formulations (Grencavage and Norcross, 1990; Lambert and Bergin, 1992). As yet, there is no consensus on what the specific common factors may be, much less the development of a meta-theory by which to organize them. Those concerned with common factors continue to parse them in the grammar of their own favored system (for example Goldfried, 1980).

Wolpe rejected the premises upon which this enterprise was built. His reading of the research data verified his own clinical experience, that behavioral approaches were superior to psychoanalytic and other insight therapies. In his view, the equal effectiveness con-clusion was based on several errors which may be summarized as follows. First was the bias against behavior therapy, which downplayed or distorted data that showed its greater effectiveness. Second was the research on 'weak fears,' which allowed the nonspecific features of many therapies to equal that of his methods. Third was the use of inadequate measures, namely self-report or ratings based on self-report, which tended to be unrelated to behavior change. Fourth was the conduct of inadequate behavior therapy, either by poorly trained therapists or by the use of packaged treatments, which produced less than optimal results. As for common factors, Wolpe readily admitted that such features as a warm, accepting manner by the therapist, expectancy on the part of the patient, and suggestions to think, feel or act differently, played an important role in his and other therapies. Furthermore, he incorporated these factors within the framework of reciprocal inhibition. What set his therapy apart was the deliberate use of these elements, plus specific manipulations to enhance the removal of unadaptive emotional responses and the acquisition of new behavior. In his view, this is what gave behavior therapy the edge in outcome comparisons, when properly conducted and evaluated.

Support for Wolpe's position may be found in recent con-siderations of outcome research by eminent reviewers who are by no means behavior therapy partisans (Lambert et al., 1986; Lambert and Bergin, 1992). These reviewers agreed that the meta-analysis of Smith et al. (1980) might have unfairly used 'reactivity' to downgrade the effects of behavior therapy. They noted that commonly occurring outpatient neuroses, such as those studied by Sloane et al. (1975), might be amenable to common therapy factors and not provide an adequate test of specific therapeutic features. They also observed that reporting outcomes as group averages might obscure the superior results obtained in particular cases. Finally, they noted that there were 'powerful and superior effects of some behavior therapies' for difficult problems where there is a specific symptom, such as phobic, obsessive–compulsive and sexual disorders, which can be targeted by particular procedures, such as desensitization, flooding, and modeling. However, this did not represent a total vindication of Wolpe, as they also endorsed a trend away from the 'rigid' orientations of psychodynamic or behavioral theories toward a more eclectic point of view. But it should be noted that these methods did not arise from bland eclecticism, but from particular views of human neuroses and the efforts they inspired to prove or disprove them.

Revisions and Schisms

Just as Wolpe had challenged traditional psychoanalysis, others within behavior therapy soon questioned Wolpe's authority. As the previous section revealed, those most concerned with the empirical analysis of therapy procedures and outcomes were behavior therapists, and it was natural that they turned their attention to their own domain rather than the amorphous formulations of psychodynamic and other insight therapies. In addition, within the field of academic clinical psychology, where much of this research and development transpired, there was a premium on innovation and revolution rather than replication and evolution. Thus it was that new methods and theories proliferated, and investigators emphasized their differences with Wolpe in an effort to put their own stamp on a theory or therapeutic program. In response, Wolpe sometimes modified his own position in the face of new data, sometimes pointed out similarities of a 'new' approach with his own, but in general he steadfastly held his ground and rebutted the challenges posed by the revisionists. This section reviews some of the major challenges to Wolpe within the field of behavior therapy and his replies to these developments.

The Autonomic Theory of Anxiety

Like other theorists of his era, Wolpe identified anxiety with arousal of the autonomic nervous system, predominantly the sympathetic branch, that served as the source of most neurotic symptoms (1958, pp. 34–5). Wolpe (1978a) accepted 'dual process' theory, in which conditioned autonomic arousal served as a drive which motivated motoric avoidance behavior, although he did not accept simple avoidance as equivalent to neurosis (see Chapter 2). Data which showed discontinuity between autonomic activity and avoidance responses were taken as evidence against the peripheral autonomic theory of anxiety (Bandura, 1969, pp. 426–8; 1978; Poppen, 1970). Briefly, this evidence included the findings that avoidance latencies were much shorter than autonomic recruitment times (Solomon and Wynne, 1954), autonomic responses disappeared as avoidance learning progressed (Grings and Lockhart, 1966; Notterman et al., 1952), extinction of conditioned cardiac activity and avoidance were unrelated (Bersh et al., 1956; Carlson and Black, 1959), and surgical and chemical disruptions of the autonomic nervous system did not eliminate avoidance (Wynne and Solomon, 1955). In view of these data, alternatives to the peripheral autonomic theory of anxiety were proposed.

Triple Response Theory.   Analogue investigations of desensitization routinely involved autonomic, motoric, and verbal assessment of anxiety (see Lang, 1964; Paul, 1966). Out of this assessment protocol, Lang developed a tripartite theory which held that anxiety was a complex response having components in each of these three domains (Lang, 1968; 1969). In human analogue research, as in animal studies, the relationships between autonomic activity and avoidance behavior were sometimes found to be inconsistent with each other, and verbal measures provided additional discrepancies. Within groups of subjects, correlations between the measures were often found to be very low (Lang, 1968; Leitenberg et al., 1971). Such discordance was termed 'desynchrony' (Rachman and Hodgson, 1974). According to triple-response theory, anxiety was fractionated into three separate modalities, each responsive to different factors. For example, under low 'therapist demand' conditions, a subject might report great fear and refuse to touch a snake, but show low heart rate.

Wolpe found Lang's triple-response system useful for organizing the symptomatic 'consequences' of anxiety (see Table 2.1). Thus, a patient might display tachycardia (autonomic response), avoidance of social situations (motoric response), or amnesia of an experience (cognitive response) (Wolpe, 1973, p. 24). But the basic anxiety reaction remained peripheral autonomic (predominantly sympathetic) arousal; Wolpe rejected the 'shifting sands' approaches of Lang and Rachman (Wolpe, 1990, pp. 23–5). He held that 'desynchrony' between autonomic and other measures of anxiety might occur with 'weak fears' displayed in analogue research, but not with true neurotic anxiety. Discrepancies between autonomic and avoidance responses could be related to the reciprocally inhibiting effect of motoric behavior on autonomic activity. He pointed out that anxiety involved a much broader constellation of autonomic activity than was conventionally measured in experimental studies, citing Lacey's classic finding that people display idiosyncratic autonomic profiles rather than a particular reaction common to all (Lacey et al., 1953; Lacey and Lacey, 1958). He asserted that 'there are probably subjects who respond in none of the standard modalities, but it is not plausible to suppose that feelings of anxiety can ever be totally without physiologic correlates' (1990, p. 24). He thus arrived at the irrefutable position that some autonomic activity was always at the heart of anxious arousal, and in instances of experimentally observed 'desynchrony,' the proper autonomic modalities happened not to have been monitored.

Counterconditioning. The sympathetic autonomic theory of anxiety provided Wolpe with the heuristic for overcoming anxiety by parasympathetic arousal, according to the principle of reciprocal inhibition. The anxiolytic effects of muscular relaxation, eating, anger, and sex were attributed to reciprocally inhibitory parasympathetic connections. However, it was widely recognized that anxiety reactions could also involve parasympathetic components, as when a frightened animal defecated, and that anxiety antagonists could involve sympathetic components, as in bronchial dilation during calm breathing. Such exceptions, coupled with criticisms of the peripheral autonomic theory of anxiety, prompted the adoption of the term *counterconditioning* rather than reciprocal inhibition (Bandura, 1969, pp. 430–1; Davison, 1968; Poppen, 1970; 1988). This was a concept employed by E.R. Guthrie (1935) in his interference theory of extinction, which essentially stated that the elimination of a response involved its *replacement* by some other response. Counterconditioning referred to behavior rather than inferred neural activity. For example, systematic desensitization as a counterconditioning technique replaced avoidance and physiologic arousal with approach and relaxation, without regard to unobservable neural mechanisms.

Wolpe (1958, p. 29) thought Guthrie's counterconditioning theory lacking as an overall theory of extinction. He sometimes employed the term counterconditioning as synonymous with reciprocal inhibition (for example, 1969, pp. 14–15), but nowhere elaborated a clear distinction between the two concepts. Wolpe hypothesized that reciprocal inhibition referred to neural mechanisms which underlay the overt phenomena of replacement or competition between responses of *all types*, motoric and cognitive as well as autonomic (1976c, pp. 11–18). In this context, he described the 'habit reversal' procedures of Azrin and colleagues for tics and nervous habits (Azrin and Nunn, 1973) as instances of motoric reciprocal inhibition. Counterconditioning and habit reversal were surface phenomena, while reciprocal inhibition referred to the integrative action of the nervous system.

Exposure

Exposure therapy, wherein patients were confronted with upsetting situations that provoked anxious arousal, stood in marked contrast to systematic desensitization. Exposure had its foundation in animal experiments on avoidance conditioning, in human clinical analogue research, and in clinical practice. Theoretical accounts of exposure were incompatible with reciprocal inhibition theory and provided an alternative for explaining desensitization itself. Wolpe was cognizant of exposure procedures, employed them in his practice, and sought to account for them within his theoretical system. But the practice and theory of exposure methods was widely regarded as contradicting Wolpe's approach.

Analogue Exposure Research. Flooding and response prevention procedures were adapted from animal experimentation and analogue studies with humans. 'Response prevention' referred to preventing animals from making an avoidance response (for example, Carlson and Black, 1959), and 'flooding' was a procedure in which a conditioned aversive stimulus persisted despite the animal's response (Polin, 1959). Such procedures were generally more effective than ordinary extinction trials. However, there was some evidence that anxiety remained even after avoidance responding was eliminated by flooding (Page, 1955). Poppen (1970) reported that flooding, while more effective than extinction in the reduction of eating inhibition in rats, was inferior to 'graduated counterconditioning,' a procedure analogous to desensitization. In a human study of flooding, Wolpin and Raines (1966) found that imaginal presentation of the most feared items on a hierarchy for several minutes was effective in alleviating fear of snakes, while Rachman (1966b) found briefer presentations to be ineffective.

A major variation of exposure was the development of 'implosive therapy' by Thomas Stampfl and Donald Levis (1967; 1968). Like Wolpe, they proposed that neurotic anxiety was a conditioned response resulting from aversive conditioning. Unlike Wolpe, they extended Mowrer's (1947) two-factor theory, and Solomon and Wynne's (1954) theory of 'anxiety conservation,' proposing that patients avoided remembering the primary conditioned stimuli, leaving the original anxiety cues protected from extinction, repressed and inaccessible. Furthermore, they drew upon psycho-analytic theory for 'core' stimulus themes which evoked anxiety, such as orality, anality, and aggression. Implosive therapy required exposure to stimuli related to these core areas. In practice, descriptions of anxiety stimuli were loosely arranged in a 'serial cue hierarchy,' which, compared to desensitization, began with the most anxiety-provoking items and increased from there. The therapist dramatically described horrific scenes related to unconscious and psychodynamic themes, often beyond all possibility of actual experience (Levis, 1980). Elements were added to the description to maintain maximum anxiety arousal until it was exhausted within a single lengthy session. Additional sessions addressed additional themes.

Evaluation of implosive therapy was impeded by the inter-changeable use of the terms 'flooding' and 'implosion' (Levis and Hare, 1977; Levis and Boyd, 1985) which made it difficult to determine the role of psychodynamic themes. Several analogue investigations of implosion/flooding therapy compared it with systematic desensitization. A summary of this research concluded that 'these studies have produced conflicting results, and are unanimous only in that none of them showed implosive therapy to be superior to systematic desensitization' (Rimm and Masters, 1979, p. 303). The few studies that addressed the inclusion of psychodynamic or exaggerated stimulus elements reported such procedures to be either ineffective or unnecessary (Foa et al., 1977; Marshall et al., 1977). The best that even a proponent of the procedure could conclude was that inclusion of such themes was not dangerous to the patient (Levis and Boyd, 1985).

Although Wolpe had success using Masserman's 'forced solution' with several of his neurotic cats, he did not regard other animal experiments on flooding as relevant since simple avoidance did not qualify as neurotic behavior. He observed that 'nobody has cured an experimental neurosis simply by exposing the animal for long periods (hours or days) to the stimuli to which anxiety has been maximally conditioned' (Wolpe, 1973, p. 195). He also had no use for the psychodynamic and extinction theories of implosion (1969, pp. 188–9). He rejected the notion that Stampfl and Levis' reports of success supported their psychoanalytic theory, asserting that 'a variety of other stimulus materials would also evoke anxiety that diminishes' (1990, p. 221). Analogue research showing the effectiveness of flooding or implosion could be dismissed as dealing with 'weak fears' that were easily overcome by nonspecific factors.

Clinical Exposure Research. Despite the tenuous support in the analogue research literature, exposure methods found increasing use in clinical practice. This began with early reports by the group at the Maudsley Hospital that desensitization was ineffective for patients having obsessive–compulsive disorders or agoraphobia, whereas direct exposure to upsetting situations produced great improvements (Cooper et al., 1965; Gelder and Marks, 1966; Gelder et al., 1967; Hodgson et al., 1972; Stern and Marks, 1973). Marks (1978) championed the view that exposure was the key factor in all behavioral treatments of anxiety disorders, including systematic desensitization, modeling, behavioral rehearsal, and flooding – 'all appear to be ways of exposing the patient to the frightening situation until he or she gets used to it' (Marks, 1978, p. 498). Marks was unconcerned about the process of 'getting used to it,' noting that the terms extinction, habituation or adaptation served equally well. He felt that relaxation training, as employed in desensitization, added nothing to exposure and was a waste of time better spent in straightforward contact with anxiety-evoking stimuli. He noted that a very small proportion of patients became worse (sensitization) through exposure, and called for research into such anomalous individual differences.

Several large-scale clinical research programs using exposure therapy were developed for obsessive–compulsive, agoraphobic and panic disorders in many countries (Chambless and Goldstein, 1980; Rachman and Hodgson, 1980; Emmelkamp, 1982; Steketee et al., 1982; Jansson et al., 1986; Barlow, 1988). These programs explored many treatment factors, including duration and spacing of exposure trials, actual (*in vivo*) or imaginal stimulus presentations, graduated or high-intensity (though not 'implosive') stimuli, the presence of therapists, other patients, or spouses, and the inclusion of additional therapies such as modeling, assertiveness training, cognitive restructuring, marital counseling, or drugs. Sub-groups and individual differences within these broad diagnostic categories were recognized and efforts were made to relate them to treatment variables. Exposure researchers generally favored cognitive explanations for anxiety reduction during exposure.

A discussion of exposure outcomes and their relation to treatment factors is not possible here. In very general terms, approximately two-thirds of those completing an exposure program obtained clinically significant relief, if not complete cure, with a slight decline at follow-ups at one to two years (see Foa et al., 1983). A significant problem with exposure programs was the dropout rate, with one-tenth to one-third of the patients refusing treatment or withdrawing from the program because of their discomfort. For the clinician as well, treatment could be arduous, sometimes requiring inpatient hospitalization and 24-hour daily supervision for weeks or months (Barlow, 1988, pp. 622–8). While exposure continued to be regarded as the treatment of choice for such disorders, all investigators recognized that there was much room for improvement.

It is interesting that Wolpe's early clinical reports of obsessive–compulsive and agoraphobic disorders often noted that desensitization was difficult or unsuccessful and that he then resorted to methods which included some form of stimulus confrontation (1958, pp. 160–5, 176–9). However, he did not pursue this lead and only hesitantly incorporated flooding in his clinical practice based on clinical reports of others. This stemmed from the apparent incompatibility of flooding with reciprocal inhibition theory and his concern about making patients worse (1969, pp. 192–3). With increased experience and positive clinical reports, he accepted exposure procedures, employing both *in vivo* and imaginal flooding for patients with obsessive–compulsive disorder, agoraphobia, social phobia, and simple phobia (1973, pp. 242–3; 1982, pp. 294–8; Wolpe and Ascher, 1976; see Chapter 3). But Wolpe criticized the blanket use of exposure procedures with patients placed in obsessive–compulsive or agoraphobic diagnostic categories and emphasized the necessity of determining the needs of each patient. He maintained that outcome rates could be improved if patients' social and other anxieties were addressed as well as their obsessive–compulsive behaviors, providing a case example in which limited improvement after response prevention was followed by complete remission after assertiveness training and desensitization for social anxiety (1990, pp. 296–8). In a similar fashion, Wolpe noted that agoraphobia was not a unitary disorder to be treated simply with exposure; 'more than any other category of neurosis, agoraphobia requires the therapist to have the widest possible repertoire of behavioral techniques' (1983, p. 289). He was critical of research programs in which patients meeting psychiatric diagnostic criteria were randomly assigned to variations of exposure treatment without attention to individual differences. Even the multi-faceted treatment program of his colleague Goldstein, which reported higher success rates, was criticized for failing to tailor the treatment to each individual (1990, pp. 257-8).

Wolpe (1976c; 1990, pp. 51-3) was also critical of various theoretical accounts of exposure. He dismissed Marks' 'getting used to it' hypothesis as no theory at all; since both acquisition and elimination of habits involve exposure to the conditioned stimulus, something in addition to exposure is obviously involved. The observations that patients often were exposed repeatedly to anxiety-evoking situations in the course of daily living with no beneficial result, and that sensitization sometimes occurred, also indicated that 'getting used to it' was insufficient. Other researchers made similar criticisms of Marks' reasoning (Barlow, 1988, p. 286; Rosenthal and Bandura, 1978). Wolpe criticized cognitive theories of exposure, such as expectancy and self-efficacy, as well. Patients might well change their expectation of harm or belief in their ability to perform in certain situations, but such changes followed fear reduction rather than causing it.

Still, the learning mechanisms by which exposure produced its effects presented a puzzle to Wolpe (1969, pp. 192-3; 1976c; 1990, pp. 224-5). Exposure techniques contradicted his basic premise that neurotic anxiety simply did not extinguish with repeated non-reinforced evocations but had to be overcome by some inhibitory process. He speculated that an obscure Pavlovian process of 'transmarginal inhibition' might be involved, in which the prolonged evocation of a conditioned response supposedly led to a protective inhibitory reaction. And he noted that certain features of flooding situations could evoke responses inhibitory to anxiety; these included the presence of the therapist and various distractive, cognitive, and relaxation coping strategies that were often employed. His inhibition hypothesis produced some procedural suggestions: duration of exposure had to be sufficient to allow the inhibitory process to occur; degree of anxiety was also important, in that 'moderately strong' levels should be more readily inhibited than 'maximal' levels. However, Wolpe was never clear as to why certain disorders or individuals responded better to exposure procedures than to systematic desensitization. His inhibition theory has been rejected (Rachman and Hodgson, 1980) or ignored (Barlow, 1988, pp. 285-318). Hypotheses that could be drawn from his theory concerning the duration of stimulus presentation, level of anxiety arousal, the nature of anxiety-inhibiting stimuli and responses, or the mechanism of 'transmarginal inhibition,' remain to be investigated.

Coping Skills

Those favoring operant conditioning viewed Wolpe's approach to therapy as 'eliminative,' presuming that adaptive behavior would emerge as the anxiety responsible for neurotic symptoms was removed (Goldiamond, 1975). In contrast, a 'constructional' approach proposed that patients experienced anxiety and engaged in symptomatic behavior in certain situations because they had not learned the requisite skills to respond effectively. For example, the widely studied phenomenon of snake phobia was not the result of aversive experiences with snakes but stemmed from people having little factual knowledge of snakes or skill in handling them. Desensitization from this perspective was a procedure in which people imagined appropriate ways of interacting with feared situations and practiced relaxation as a means of coping with anxiety (Goldfried, 1971; Goldfried and Trier, 1974). In a similar fashion, assertiveness training was seen as a means of learning new social skills rather than inhibiting negative emotions. The learning mechanisms proposed included operant reinforcement, vicarious learning, and cognitive restructuring, instead of Wolpe's deconditioning theory.

Modeling. A major impetus to the coping skill approach was Albert Bandura's work on 'vicarious learning.' Bandura (1971) noted that anxiety often resulted from witnessing or being instructed about negative experiences of others, not from direct aversive conditioning. Moreover, anxiety could arise when people were confronted with a situation for which they had, or believed they had, insufficient skills. According to this view, providing an anxious person with a model who demonstrated positive emotions and appropriate behavior in a troublesome situation would be doubly effective in overcoming fear – the model could teach appropriate behavior to cope with the situation as well as 'disinhibit' previously learned behavior suppressed by fear. Bandura proposed a cognitive theory to account for vicarious learning, which he felt could not be explained by conditioning models.

An influential analogue study (Bandura et al., 1969) found that desensitization and 'symbolic modeling' (watching films of a person handling a snake in a hierarchy of feared situations) were equally effective in reducing fear of snakes, while 'participant modeling' (supervised practice in the feared situations) was superior to both. Moreover, the subjects' negative attitude toward snakes and reptiles were improved most markedly by participant modeling, to a lesser degree by symbolic modeling and desensitization, and not at all by factual information and intermittent exposure during assessment.

Bandura followed with a host of analogue studies which investigated modeling factors such as mode of presentation, model competency, similarity to the subject, physical contact, and opportunities to practice. Modeling procedures were found to be very effective in reducing avoidance behavior and negative verbal appraisals, and often were superior to desensitization in comparative studies (see reviews in Rimm and Masters, 1979, pp. 103–51; Spiegler and Guevremont, 1992, pp. 251–90).

Wolpe quickly recognized Bandura's early modeling research as 'a significant practical advance,' but rejected his cognitive theory (1973, pp. 161–2). Bandura's critique of the conditioning model of fear acquisition was based on a narrow reading of Wolpe, who had always recognized erroneous beliefs as a source of anxiety (1958, p. 199). Later, Wolpe provided 'a new analysis' of modeling methods (1990, pp. 212–14), which expanded the role of beliefs in the etiology of anxiety. Wolpe suggested that participant modeling was a form of *in vivo* desensitization in which interaction with the therapist served to reciprocally inhibit anxiety. Modeling and guided participation could provide 'corrective information' for those with cognitive-based anxiety, while the therapist–model could arouse 'pleasant emotional responses' and serve as a reciprocally inhibitory agent for those with conditioning-based fears as well. Wolpe acknowledged the 'great therapeutic value' of guided participation because it addressed both etiologies of fear.

Social Skills. Wolpe initially conceived of assertiveness training in terms of anger or pleasant emotions reciprocally inhibiting anxiety conditioned to interpersonal situations. In contrast, several researchers pointed out that social anxiety could be due to three etiologic factors – deficient social skills, faulty cognitive appraisal, or aversive conditioning (for example Curran, 1975; 1977). Assertiveness training could be seen as addressing all three: the first by directly teaching appropriate social and verbal responses; the second by providing a rationale for assertiveness and supportive verbal feedback; and the third, as Wolpe suggested, by promoting positive emotional experiences in social situations. Research on assertiveness training adopted a social skills framework and focused on aspects of teaching, such as modeling, coaching, rehearsal, and feedback (Fodor, 1980). A host of analogue studies were conducted, mostly with college students having dating anxiety or other interpersonal concerns (for example McFall and Twentyman, 1973). Such research found that rehearsal of assertive behavior was superior to placebo or no-treatment, and that the addition of modeling and feedback was superior to rehearsal alone, especially for behavior more complex than simple refusal (Rimm and Masters, 1979, pp. 94–8).

A major technical and conceptual innovation in assertiveness training was an emphasis on cognitive factors. In the context of the civil rights revolution in the United States, the philosophical basis of an individual's 'right' to express his or her feelings honestly and to stand up for his or her own best interests was developed (Alberti and Emmons, 1970). A review of rights served as an educational preamble in assertiveness training programs, and patients' beliefs and attitudes about themselves and others, in the context of such rights, were addressed in the course of training. Some clinical researchers (such as Lange and Jakubowski, 1976) incorporated Ellis's RET model, in which patients' anxiety was seen as resulting from their irrational thinking. The goal of cognitive-based programs was to give the patient a general assertive outlook rather than to overcome specific interpersonal anxieties. Another technical advance, making efficient use of therapist time, was group training carried out with persons having similar concerns. This was adopted particularly for groups who felt disenfranchised by the larger culture, such as African–Americans and women (Cheek, 1976; Phelps and Austin, 1975).

The addition of cognitive and skill training components to assertiveness training may be seen as formal elaborations of what Wolpe informally practiced (see Chapter 3). He certainly dealt with patients' misconceptions about assertiveness on an individual basis, and he found the concept of 'rights' to be useful (1973, p. 89), but he did not agree that all social anxiety was due to irrational thinking. In his early collaboration with Lazarus, Wolpe recognized that assertiveness included an 'operant' component in which new motoric and verbal skills were taught, and that successful perform-ance contributed to anxiety reduction. He felt these processes were 'inextricably intertwined,' noting that 'pure social skills training' may be called for in cases where a non-anxious individual simply lacks appropriate habits (1990, p. 136), but in most cases con-ditioned anxiety was a major factor. Standardized assertiveness training packages, developed for research or workshop purposes, necessarily included cognitive, skill training, and anxiety reduction components to meet the varied needs of their participants. Wolpe's preference, as always, was to develop a treatment program tailored to the individual patient.

The Cognitive Revolution

An early critique by Breger and McGaugh (1965) presaged a major shift in behavior therapy, namely that 'peripheral S–R learning theory' was inadequate to account for complex clinical phenomena, and that a cognitive 'reformulation' was required. A decade later, a 'cognitive revolution' in behavior therapy was proclaimed (for example Mahoney, 1977), which purported to overthrow conditioning theories and methods for changing maladaptive human behavior. The effectiveness of Wolpe's procedures was either questioned or attributed to inadvertent involvement of cognitive procedures, and specific cognitive methods were claimed to produce outcomes superior to conditioning-based therapy, particularly systematic desensitization. This section reviews several cognitive 'reformulations' and Wolpe's rebuttals.

Expectancy. One of Wolpe's earliest criticisms of conventional psychotherapy was that positive outcomes could simply be the result of the patient's belief that the therapy would be helpful (1958, p. 193). Thus it was ironic that systematic desensitization should be criticized as nothing but a means of raising the patient's expectancy of benefit (Kazdin and Wilcoxon, 1976; Wilkins, 1971). Analogue research on desensitization routinely included controls for expectancy effects, such as placebo therapy or a component of desensitization minus a critical element. In most instances, desensitization proved more effective, but these efforts were criticized because the credibility of the control procedures, as rated on questionnaires, was often found to be less than that of desensitization (see, for example, Borkovec and Nau, 1972). According to this line of reasoning, the more credible-sounding therapy raised greater expectancy of benefit, which resulted in a self-fulfilling prophecy.

Analogue studies were conducted which manipulated the expectancy factor by means of instructions or bogus physiologic feedback (for example Valins and Ray, 1967). High-expectancy placebo treatments usually were found to be superior to low-expectancy placebos, but the findings were inconsistent when comparisons with desensitization were conducted. For example, high-expectancy placebo treatments were found to be superior (Tori and Worell, 1973), equivalent (Donovan and Gershman, 1979), or inferior (Miller, 1972) to desensitization. Further complicating the picture was desynchrony among outcome measures; treatment differences were variously demonstrated on verbal, motoric, or physiologic measures, but seldom on all three. Attempts to manipulate expectancy about desensitization by means of instructions also led to inconsistent results, with some studies reporting low-expectancy desensitization to be ineffective (Borkovec, 1972), while others found it effective regardless of expectancy factors (McGlynn, 1971).

In this regard, desensitization was observed to be so credible that instructions to the contrary were often ineffective (Kazdin and Wilcoxon, 1976). The basis for this inherent credibility was not considered, but the fact that analogue desensitization was not unequivocally immune to expectancy manipulations led to the conclusion that its effectiveness was due only to its ability to arouse therapeutic expectations (Emmelkamp, 1982, p. 55; Kazdin and Wilcoxon, 1976).

Wolpe (1983, p. 53; 1990, pp. 52–3, 191–2) dismissed the expectancy hypothesis, concluding that the studies which examined the role of expectancy in desensitization did not show it to be a very strong factor. That is, he interpreted the inconsistent findings as evidence against the robustness of expectancy rather than of desensitization. He also argued that expectancy manipulations were likely to be effective only in the treatment of weak fears, as in analogue research. In line with this argument, Borkovec (1973) reviewed studies which indicated that expectancy effects were found in low-fear but not in high-fear subjects, although other research found that expectancy manipulations were effective across a range of fearfulness (Sullivan and Denny, 1977). It should be added that a meta-analysis of behavior therapy research, which specifically addressed nonspecific factors, found no relationship between placebo credibility ratings and effect size, and that behavior therapy was consistently more effective than placebo (Bowers and Clum, 1988).

More fundamentally, Wolpe objected that expectancy was not a 'learning mechanism,' but only a 'behavioral event.' That is, expectancy was a therapeutic phenomenon but it did not provide an explanation. The relevant mechanism for Wolpe was reciprocal inhibition, in which expectancy, like other positive thoughts and emotions aroused by therapy, competed with anxiety. In instances of weak fears or very strong positive belief in the treatment or therapist, expectancy might be sufficient, but in most cases of clinical neurotic anxiety, faith was not enough. Rather than a replacement for reciprocal inhibition theory, Wolpe saw expectancy as another illustration of its operation. This aspect of expectancy was overlooked by the 'nothing but' critics.

Self-Efficacy.   Albert Bandura was in the vanguard of the cognitive revolution with his theory of vicarious learning, which he regarded as a mode of learning commensurate with classical and instrumental conditioning (Bandura, 1969, pp. 133–43). Borrowing a phrase from Breger and McGaugh (1965), Bandura dismissed learning theories as 'peripheral S–R connectionism' and proposed a four-stage model of mediating cognitive mechanisms. Although Bandura did not identify 'peripheral S–R' theory, it is apparent that, like Breger and McGaugh, he was referring to learning theories such as those of Hull and Wolpe. Hull had proposed a variety of mediating mechanisms between environmental stimuli and overt responding, expressed as a series of stimulus–response links, which Wolpe had sought to translate into a series of neural connections. Vicarious learning rendered these theories untenable, according to Bandura, because no responding occurred during acquisition, hence there was no 'R' to link to the 'S.'

Bandura's work on vicarious learning served as a prologue to his more ambitious self-efficacy theory (Bandura, 1977). With respect to anxiety, Bandura proposed that negative emotions arose from a discrepancy between two types of beliefs – 'self-efficacy beliefs' and 'outcome expectations' – rather than from conditioning in aversive situations as Wolpe had proposed. For example, a person who faced a social situation involving important consequences, but believing him or herself inadequate or unattractive, would experience upsetting emotion and engage in maladaptive behavior. Similarly, therapy was not a matter of deconditioning anxiety but of providing 'information' which enhanced self-efficacy beliefs. Therapy provided information through four channels which Bandura ranked in order of effectiveness. The premier channel was termed *performance accomplishments* or *enactive attainments*. Procedures which encouraged effective behavior, such as participant modeling, *in vivo* desensitization, behavior rehearsal, and some exposure therapies, were deemed effective because people who performed successfully strengthened their belief that they could continue to do so. Second was *vicarious experience*, which included modeling and some forms of systematic desensitization. Third was *verbal persuasion*, which included logical argument, factual presentation, or therapist's instructions, such as employed in rational–emotive therapy. Last was *emotional arousal*, in which low levels of physiologic arousal in usually upsetting circumstances promoted a feeling of self-efficacy. Relaxation, by itself or in the context of systematic desensitization, was placed in this category.

Bandura's self-efficacy theory added no new therapy techniques beyond the modeling procedures developed earlier, but it provided a popular framework for organizing behavioral and cognitive procedures, including those of Wolpe. It also provided a new variable to assess, self-efficacy, which mediated between the independent variable (treatment) and the dependent variable (outcome). Measures of self-efficacy took the form of performance predictions or ratings of problematic situations. A number of analogue studies found self-efficacy measures to be more closely related to outcome than were treatment parameters, such as type of treatment, number of sessions, or performance criteria (Bandura, 1982; Bandura et al., 1982). For example, Bandura and Adams (1977) found that a group of snake-phobic subjects who successfully completed systematic desensitization varied widely in their self-efficacy statements, which, in turn, more accurately predicted their actual performance with a snake than did items completed on the hierarchy. They concluded that changes in self-efficacy beliefs, rather than anxiety deconditioning, were the effective mechanism of behavior change.

Wolpe (1978b) declared self-efficacy theory a 'square peg for a round hole.' He accepted self-efficacy beliefs as an important antecedent for some complex motor acts but not relevant to emotional (autonomic) responses. He pointed out that phobics 'know' they have the motor skills to grasp a snake or leave a place of safety; the reason they do not do so is fear. Wolpe suggested that self-efficacy beliefs might improve *after* anxiety was reduced, but had no causal role in its reduction. He dismissed the Bandura and Adams (1977) study for failing to recognize that some individuals can imagine phobic stimuli but experience no fear arousal, enabling them to progress through a hierarchy but achieve no actual anxiety deconditioning, resulting in wide individual differences after desensitization.

Wolpe (1990, pp. 55, 347) also endorsed the 'trenchant analysis' of Lee (1989), who summarized self-efficacy theory as a 'metaphorical description of a hypothetical process.' She argued that Bandura's theoretical constructs were vaguely defined and pointed out discrepant interpretations among self-efficacy researchers. She observed that a major weakness was that the putative cognitive processes which synthesized the various 'channels of information' were not specified, making it impossible to relate channel inputs to efficacy outcomes. In this same vein, Hawkins (1992) inveighed against the assumption that self-efficacy beliefs were an independent variable causally related to behavior. To the extent that enactive attainments, vicarious experience and so forth could alter self-efficacy, these were the true independent variables affecting behavior. Self-efficacy, at best, served as an index of an individual's learning history, and this accounted for its success as a predictor.

Multimodal Therapy. Arnold Lazarus, Wolpe's early protégé, soon became dissatisfied with the adequacy of Wolpe's theoretical account of his therapeutic procedures (Lazarus, 1967). Lazarus developed some new twists on Wolpe's procedures, such as 'behavior rehearsal' and 'emotive imagery,' which Wolpe adopted with credit to Lazarus. After their calumnious falling-out, Lazarus wrote a series of articles and books in which he attacked Wolpe's therapy as woefully narrow, both conceptually and procedurally (Lazarus, 1971; 1973; 1974; 1976; 1977; 1980). In line with other cognitive critics, he maintained that Wolpe's traumatic conditioning model was irrelevant for the etiology of the vast majority of 'phobic-like sensitivities,' noting that less than three percent of his patients could recall such an experience. In its stead, he cited 'verbal communication' and Bandura's vicarious learning as the means by which the vast majority of fears were acquired. He rejected Wolpe's autonomic theory of anxiety, citing Bandura and Ellis in support of the view that emotional reactions were the product of cognitive processes. He termed Wolpe's use of conditioning concepts to account for complex behavior 'theory begging.' He accused Wolpe of regarding phobias simply as overt avoidance responses and of ignoring covert processes. He indicted Wolpe's use of systematic desensitization as misguided for social anxieties and ineffective for obsessive–compulsive disorders, and he recanted some of his publications favorable to reciprocal inhibition made during his earlier association with Wolpe. Without naming names, Lazarus accused 'some influential psychotherapists' of religious dogma and a messianic, cult-like insistence on adherence to doctrine, and claimed that they impeded the development of effective psychotherapy.

Lazarus' theoretical alternative included the notion that patients could manifest problems in any of seven 'modalities' (behavior, affect, sensation, imagery, cognition, interpersonal relationships, and drugs/biology or BASIC/ID), and that therapeutic procedures were required to address each relevant category. He termed this 'multimodal behavior therapy,' later dropping the adjective 'behavior.' Procedurally, he advocated 'technical eclecticism,' adopting techniques from the entire spectrum of psychotherapy based on their empirically demonstrated effectiveness rather than any theoretical derivation, and he developed several techniques involving imagery instructions, such as 'the desert island fantasy.' Like Wolpe, Lazarus was not a researcher and relied on anecdotal case reports and selective literature citation to buttress his claims.

Wolpe (1976c) designated Lazarus a 'malcontent,' a person who did not fully understand the field he was criticizing. He felt that the narrow, mechanistic, impersonal therapy that Lazarus attacked was an inaccurate perception, and he regarded most of Lazarus' 'expansions' as superfluous advocacy of features already present in his therapy. The multiple 'modalities' which Lazarus listed were routinely covered by his stimulus–response analysis. As for 'technical eclecticism,' Wolpe noted that he already included procedures that were not direct offshoots of basic research but for which there was empirical support, citing carbon dioxide inhalation as an example. (One might include 'eye-movement desensitization' as a more recent instance of such empirical eclecticism.) In this regard, he criticized Lazarus' 'desert island fantasy' and 'blow-up technique' as having inadequate empirical foundation, but he continued to give him credit for the 'emotive imagery' procedure. Wolpe commented that Lazarus' published outcomes of multimodal therapy had a relapse rate 10 times that of his own. Wolpe also criticized the total eclecticism advocated by Perry London (1972), with whom Lazarus had aligned himself, as typical of pre-scientific medicine. Lazarus' cognitive critiques were no different than those of other cognitive advocates and Wolpe did not address them specifically.

One wonders at Wolpe's characterization of Lazarus' criticisms as 'misperceptions' due to lack of understanding. Surely Lazarus had a thorough knowledge of Wolpe's system but chose to present a caricature of it. If one takes Lazarus' religious metaphor as directed at Wolpe, it provides a revealing clue. Certainly Wolpe had a mission, to overthrow psychoanalysis and other ineffective therapies, and he had a personal and professional certitude, a 'righteousness,' that aided him in this quest. However, he also maintained amicable relations with many who had theoretical and procedural differences with him. The stridency of Lazarus' criticisms probably had more to do with his own need to remove himself from the shadow of his mentor and show that he was nobody's 'disciple.'

Cognitive Therapy. Lazarus was one of many therapists interested in cognitive factors who incorporated the cognitive therapies of Albert Ellis and Aaron Beck into broad 'cognitive behavior therapy' programs. The basic premise of cognitive therapy was that most – if not all – negative emotions and maladaptive behavior stemmed from patients' mistaken beliefs about the world and themselves rather than being automatic conditioned emotional responses to stimuli associated with painful experiences. The focus of cognitive therapy was to identify and change the cognitive processes which produced dysfunctional thoughts.

Albert Ellis (1962; Ellis and Harper, 1965) identified various types of colorfully named 'irrational thinking' processes, such as 'musturbation' and 'catastrophizing,' of which patients were usually unaware. Rational–emotive therapy (RET) pointed out such thinking, emphasized its illogical nature, substituted more logical appraisals, and encouraged patients to examine their daily experiences in this fashion. In a manner reminiscent of Salter (1949), patients were often assigned 'homework' in which they were to seek out difficult situations and dispute the irrational beliefs which arose therein. Over time, Ellis explicitly incorporated more behavioral procedures into RET but he continued to employ his own terminology. (Recall Eysenck's early observation (1961b) that Ellis' procedures lent themselves to a behavioral description.)

Ellis (1979) noted many commonalities between his and Wolpe's approach. He acknowledged that RET entailed much more than disputing irrational thoughts; it employed procedures which involved role-playing, skill training, modeling, *in vivo* desensitization, and reciprocal inhibition methods, which he preferred to call 'cognitive distraction.' But he warned of problems arising from 'pure' behavior therapy as well as its cognitive derivatives (Ellis, 1980; 1983). He asserted that certain methods were 'especially likely to lead many clients into pathways of crooked thinking,' producing harm in the long run despite immediate improvements. In particular, 'gradual desensitization,' in which patients slowly and painlessly changed their feelings and behavior, only helped patients feel better rather than get better, and strengthened their self-defeating beliefs that one must never suffer discomfort. Similarly, he criticized the use of relaxation, thought-stopping, and assertiveness skills as forms of 'cognitive distraction,' which had palliative effects in the situations in which they were employed, but interfered with patients actually overcoming the bases of their anxieties, namely their irrational thinking. Ellis (1979) regarded Wolpe's attention to patients' misperceptions as inadequate because it only addressed their particular thoughts but failed to change their modes of irrational thinking.

Aaron Beck (1963; 1976) also proposed that patients initially responded to certain situations with cognitions of which they were unaware. These 'automatic thoughts' were characterized by 'cognitive errors,' such as 'overgeneralization' or 'dichotomous thinking,' which distorted the patient's perceptions and recall, resulting in negative emotions and behavior. Thought patterns were said to be organized into schemata which were laid down early in life, predisposing the individual to think maladaptively during later stressful events. Beck employed a collaborative, 'Socratic' method with patients, teaching them to weigh the evidence for their beliefs and generate alternative hypotheses. A progression was followed from identifying specific distorted perceptions to changing supraordinate schemata. Beck explicitly incorporated behavioral procedures into his treatment program, such as behavior rehearsal and graded task assignments, but with a focus on the patients' thoughts during and after practicing the behaviors. Beck and his colleagues remained receptive to behavioral methods, particularly reinforcement and skill-training approaches, and these formed an important component of his well-researched programs to treat depression (Beck et al., 1979; Hollon and Carter, 1994).

Beck (1976, p. 320; Beck and Mahoney, 1979) criticized Wolpe for neglecting the importance of cognitions. Wolpe's correction of patients' misperceptions was dismissed as a 'supportive' procedure common to all psychotherapy and of minimal effectiveness by itself. The critical cognitive factors were 'automatic thoughts' and the underlying schemata, which Wolpe failed to address. Whereas Wolpe found cognitive factors important in a 'minority' of his patients, Beck and colleagues found that virtually all patients had thoughts and images which maintained their anxiety or depressed feelings. Beck also questioned the effectiveness of Wolpe's procedures, concluding from the Sloane et al. (1975) study that psychodynamic therapy produced equivalent outcomes, and from the Kazdin and Wilcoxon (1976) review that expectancy accounted for the effectiveness of desensitization.

Philosophically, Wolpe (1978a) was opposed to the anti-materialist and anti-determinist implications of cognitive theory, epitomized by Bandura's (1974) statement of 'reciprocal determinism,' but applying equally to Ellis, Beck, and Lazarus. Citing J.G. Taylor's (1962; Wolpe and Taylor, 1963) work on the role of learning in perception, Wolpe saw cognitive processes as ultimately reducible to neuronal connections in the brain arising from the biology and experience of the individual. Citing Skinner's theory of 'private events,' and Cautela's theory of 'covert conditioning,' Wolpe regarded cognitions as a type of behavior that were subject to the same principles of learning that applied to all behavior. Citing the philosopher Ryle (1949), Wolpe noted that cognitive theory was akin to metaphysical mentalism, whereby the mind existed in some nonmaterial dimension and exerted its force on the physical body in a mysterious way outside the natural laws of cause and effect. In this respect, the cognitivist's appeal to conscious processes as the cause of emotion and action was no different than the psychoanalyst's appeal to unconscious ones; they were both based on metaphysics.

As a practical matter, Wolpe noted that cognitive features had always been present in his methods, such as his use of imagery, thought-stopping, and dealing with patients' erroneous beliefs (1978a; 1982, p. 86). He felt that cognitive therapists were making a big deal out of something that he had always handled as a matter of course, namely correcting patients' 'misconceptions' about themselves, their disorders, or the world around them. What he initially had regarded as preliminary to therapy (1958, pp. 199-200) he later labeled 'cognitive therapeutic procedures' (1982, pp. 86–114). These included education, persuasion, demonstration, and disputation, which he illustrated in case examples but did not elaborate in a systematic fashion. Both Beck and Ellis pointed out that they were concerned not simply with the content of a patient's misperception, but with the processes which gave rise to the distortion, such as 'overgeneralization' or 'musturbation.' For his part, Wolpe felt that formulations based on thoughts of which patients were unaware were projections by the therapist, similar to a psychoanalyst convincing a patient of Oedipal wishes.

By 1981, Wolpe explicitly dichotomized 'cognitively based' from 'classically conditioned' anxiety (see Chapter 2). He stated that most non-neurotic fears were of the former kind, originating in misinformation, but that most neurotic fears were due to conditioning. Rather than all neurotic problems resulting from cognitive errors, as implied by cognitive therapists, Wolpe found that only about one-third of a sample of patients had cognitively based fears. However, given their different focus on cognitive content or process, it is likely that Wolpe and cognitive therapists would disagree in their classification of patients. In a case example provided by Wolpe (1981a), a man in a minor automobile accident feared that he was going to die and subsequently was afraid to sit in a stationary car, although he 'knew' it was perfectly safe. For Wolpe, this was a clear example of autonomic anxiety conditioning, whereas a cognitive therapist might attribute anxiety to the man's 'catastrophizing' thoughts during a minor incident in which he experienced no actual harm.

Wolpe noted that cognitively based fears could generate autonomic arousal which could then be conditioned to extraneous cues, leading to a mixed etiology. Ellis (1979) suggested an opposite sequence, in which fears originating in conditioning could be maintained and perpetuated by 'cognitive reindoctrination.' Wolpe (1990, p. 126) allowed that 'hypochondriacal anxieties,' in which patients wrongly believed they had a severe disease, could arise from physical symptoms due to anxiety or other causes, but he did not consider other instances of faulty beliefs arising out of a conditioning experience.

Based on the conditioning/cognitive dichotomy, Wolpe proposed that cognitive anxiety required cognitive intervention while the more prevalent conditioned anxiety required conditioning procedures. Wolpe noted that some cognitive procedures inadvertently counteracted anxiety to the extent that the verbalizations encouraged by the therapists evoked autonomic responses incompatible with anxiety (1976a, p. 29; 1978a). He also observed that many procedures employed in cognitive therapy were analogous to *in vivo* desensitization and assertiveness training (1982, p. 114). Positive outcomes of cognitive therapy with patients having conditioned anxiety could thus be due to reciprocal inhibition.

Wolpe's bottom line, as usual, was treatment effectiveness, and he found cognitive therapies seriously lacking in this regard. The large-scale clinical trial for treatment of depression (Elkin et al., 1985), in which little differences were found between Beck's cognitive–behavior therapy, anti-depressant medication, and short-term psychodynamic therapy, he regarded as a case in point (Wolpe, 1990, pp. 281–4; 1993). The success rates that were obtained he attributed mainly to nonspecific effects and spontaneous recovery. Wolpe asserted that much higher rates would have obtained for behavior therapy had 'endogenous' and 'neurotic' depressions been differentiated, and, among the latter, appropriate separate treatments provided for cognitive and conditioned anxiety. Wolpe regarded this study as a prime example of the danger of treating all patients in a diagnostic category with the same packaged intervention and disregarding the difference between the two etiologies of anxiety.

Summary and Conclusions

The discipline known as behavior therapy was born in conflict as Wolpe sought to play David to Freud's Goliath. Wolpe's theories and methods were major protagonists in the psychotherapy war, inflamed by Eysenck's rhetoric, that raged in the research literature over four decades. Although Wolpe could not drive psychoanalysis from the field, he was able to wrest the grudging admission that his methods were legitimate and effective. Traditional psychotherapy researchers would not admit defeat but at least allowed that behavior therapy's results were 'equally effective.' This conclusion suggested that 'narrow' behavioral or psychodynamic formulations were inadequate but, to date, no overarching conceptualization has found acceptance. Wolpe refused the offer of equivalency and continued to press for victory. A major point for his side was increased acceptance (and sophistication) of outcome research as behavior therapists forged far ahead on the empirical front. The revolutionary notion that psychotherapy should have measurable outcomes became widely accepted, though some continued to plead special consideration for esoteric therapies.

Contentiousness continued within the behavior therapy camp as Wolpe's theories and methods were subjected to rigorous empirical investigation. Variations, additions, and alternatives were derived from operant and cognitive learning theories. These challenged the benchmarks established by Wolpe's methods and greatly expanded the reach of behavior therapy beyond the 'neurotic' disorders which were his focus. Wolpe accommodated modeling, exposure, and reinforcement technologies, but stood firm against the wholesale cognitivization of behavior therapy, as well as attempts to integrate it with dynamic or insight approaches. Wherever one stood within the behavior and cognitive therapy camps, however, the watchword was empirical outcome data. If progress is promoted by competition, behavior therapy, indeed all of psychotherapy, owes much to the competitive stance of Joseph Wolpe.

5

The Overall Influence of Joseph Wolpe

This chapter addresses Wolpe's impact in each of four interrelated dimensions of psychotherapy: conceptual, technical, effectual, and institutional. The conceptual or philosophical foundation of a psychotherapy system delineates its view of the nature of human existence. Theories of psychotherapy suggest ways of untangling the problems of living to which humans are prone. The technical dimension includes what psychotherapists actually do in their interactions with persons seeking their assistance. Techniques are drawn from the conceptual system and reflect its view of human nature. The effectual dimension refers to how well psychotherapy succeeds in carrying out its ministrations. Effectiveness is conventionally employed as the criterion by which to validate the techniques and theory of a psychotherapeutic system, although it is widely agreed that procedures may be effective for reasons other than the theory which generated them. Finally, the institutional dimension refers to the establishment of educational facilities and professional organizations to propagate the psychotherapy system within a professional group and to a wider society. Its ultimate impact depends upon the degree to which a therapy system becomes institutionalized and thus outlives the personal influence of its founder.

Conceptual Contributions

Theories of psychotherapy generally include a broad focus concerning general properties of human nature and a narrower focus concerning problematic features of patients' daily lives. Therapists employ a philosophy of human nature which provides both the context for understanding the clinical features of their patients and the foundation for more specific theories of pathology and treatment.

A Natural Science–Hermeneutic Continuum
In their broad view of human nature, psychotherapy systems may be arrayed along a continuum ranging from a natural science

paradigm to a hermeneutic approach. Wolpe provides the anchor on the natural science pole of this continuum. The tenets of this position include the following: all that exists is the physical universe; it is possible to observe the operation of parts of the universe and describe these operations in terms of systematic (preferably mathematic) relationships; this process of systematic observation and description is termed 'science'; scientific knowledge is cumulative and corrective; animals, including humans, are parts of this universe; principles of animal behavior are relevant for human behavior; 'cognitive' activities (such as perceiving, thinking, feeling, and remembering) are continuous with phylogenic precursors and are consistent with the principles governing overt behavior; behavior is determined entirely by biologic and environmental variables, both past and current.

Historically, Freud was credited as the Darwinian revolutionary, demoting humans from their status as God's special creation to that of creatures harboring unconscious animalistic lusts. He proposed a determinism of biologic drives and infantile experiences and placed his therapy within the biological science tradition. However, Freud's system also suggested a discontinuity between humans and lower animals, in which the 'beast' within could be subdued by higher faculties (Gellner, 1992). In taking as its subject matter the veiled depths of the unconscious, psychodynamic therapies abandoned the possibility of objective observation and developed a secular mysticism that soon fractionated into competing sects. Further distancing psychodynamic therapy from natural science principles was a decided reluctance to formulate empirical evaluation of the methods derived from its concepts. Wolpe's conception of therapy displaced psychodynamic approaches toward the middle of the psychotherapy spectrum.

The hermeneutic pole of the continuum, based on existential philosophies, includes the following tenets: there is a non-physical or 'spiritual' dimension which resides within each person and throughout the universe; the goal of life is to become attuned to this dimension, and a teleologic principle drives humans toward such realization; humans possess non-material or spiritual faculties which transcend physical, biological and environmental processes, resulting in each individual creating his or her own reality; 'science' is a social system of belief by 'scientists,' having no validity greater than any other socially constructed belief system (Packer, 1985). The existential and humanist therapies occupy this end of the continuum, holding that humans are essentially free of physical determinism and have the ability to choose their own experience and behavior. Developed for the most part by persons trained in psychoanalysis, such as Rollo May and Carl Rogers, they objected to Freudian and behaviorist determinism. In contrast to Wolpe's cats, even persons who have experienced traumatic events are free to choose the extent of their trauma.

Hermeneutic therapies have generated a Babel of languages describing psychic factors, forces, and structures, but they are united in a view of humans as creators of their own experiences, demigods who forge their own individually unique existences (Vitz, 1977). For these therapies, as with psychodynamic ones, observation is largely a matter of inferences about structures and forces, unseen and unseeable. Evaluation is essentially a matter of consensus among the initiated based on illustrative anecdotes, similar to testimonials at religious services, rather than any attempt at quantification and mathematical analysis. The trend toward a religion model finds its apotheosis in the recent development of transcendental and mystical therapies, which seek to make contact with spiritual forces beyond humanity's mortal existence (Edwards, 1991).

Wolpe's Natural Science Legacy. Wolpe acceded to the natural science pole by adopting concepts from experimental animal learning to account for human behavior. His fundamental assumption was that all behavior, adaptive and maladaptive, was comprised of responses to current environmental stimuli in the context of prior experience and genetic constitution. The 'laws of learning' suggested the means for acquiring and changing responses and he instigated behavior therapy by developing new interventions based on these principles. (While Wolpe favored Pavlovian and Hullian accounts of learning, the natural science tradition is not restrictive and promotes change based on new facts and ways of organizing knowledge.) In this vein, he saw patients as more or less pervasive collections of 'habits' requiring systematic relearning, not as basically disordered personalities requiring major reconstruction. Patients were seen as 'normal' in many areas of their lives but saddled with maladaptive baggage in other areas. Behavior therapy maintains this focus on responses-to-situations rather than on global personality constructs.

Wolpe's natural science position promoted the assumption that the events of interest, behavior and its environmental context, can be directly observed – by both the therapist and, with some tutelage, the patient. Indeed, Wolpe's patient is the primary observer of his or her behavior and the everyday situations related to it. Direct observation was implied even for subjective events, in that the patient's self-reports of thoughts and feelings were taken at face value, although training to improve accuracy was provided and corroborative evidence was sought. This stood in deliberate contrast to the concept of the unconscious, which could be observed only indirectly through dreams and symptoms, or to transcendent states which could be experienced only through extra-sensory intuition. This belief in the validity of direct observation by oneself and others remains fundamental to behavior and cognitive therapies.

Quantitative assessment followed naturally from the focus on behavior and environment. Wolpe's stimulus hierarchies and subjective unit of disturbance scales were early manifestations of the presumption that the environment, behavior, and the relationships between them, could be measured. Furthermore, such assessment was the basis for gauging the progress of treatment, making changes when progress was unsatisfactory, and deciding when treatment goals had been accomplished.

Early critics of Wolpe objected that learning theory concepts such as 'stimulus,' 'response,' 'reinforcement,' 'generalization,' and so on, were poor metaphors, overextended from whatever usefulness they might have in the animal laboratory and irrelevant for human experience. Essentially, these were arguments for the special status of humans, whose complex experiences and behaviors could not be captured by banal concepts from the animal laboratory but required special appreciation of cognitive faculties.

Behavior therapy's shift from bedrock behaviorism has been described as a 'cognitive revolution' (see Chapter 4). But when the whole spectrum of psychotherapies is viewed, this change is more evolutionary than revolutionary. Cognitive therapies emphasized internal processes which interpret stimuli and choose responses, thus borrowing a page from the humanist catechism and dis-engaging humans from strict genetic and environmental deter-minism. The focus of cognitive–behavior therapy remained on responses to environmental events, but proposed that by altering their own environment people could change their course of behavior (for example, Bandura's 'reciprocal determinism', 1974; but see Skinner's account of 'self-control', 1953, pp. 228–9). Still, in keeping with the natural science viewpoint, cognitive–behavior therapy emphasized observation and quantitative assessment, and sought to link internal events to empirical referents.

In summary, to the extent that psychotherapy is concerned with directly observing behavior and the environment (whether termed 'response' and 'stimulus' or something else), specifying the relation-ships between them, quantifying these factors, and using these measures to guide treatment, the influence of Wolpe's natural science conceptual foundation can be seen. Even those who denigrate such formulations as naive, simplistic, mechanistic, robotic, or lacking in appreciation of what it means to be truly human, find such a formulation useful for stating their contrary positions.

Specific Clinical Constructs

Based on the natural science foundation, Wolpe's stimulus–response theory of anxiety, and its alleviation through reciprocal inhibition, provided new and influential ways of addressing maladaptive behavior and its treatment.

Anxiety.   Wolpe's concept of anxiety as the key factor in neurotic behavior owed much to Freud. Nor was Wolpe the first to suggest that anxiety was a response acquired according to learning principles; O.H. Mowrer (1939) was a notable precedent. Wolpe's contribution was to take the construct of anxiety out of the toileting experiences of early childhood and the electric shock apparatus of the laboratory and place it in the everyday existence of ordinary people. Neurotic anxiety could be learned at any time in any person's life in any number of upsetting circumstances. Its means of acquisition and modes of expression were continuous with 'normal' fear, which was an adaptive response to the hazards of daily living. Anxiety crossed the boundary into 'neurotic' fear when it interfered with effective living and persisted in the face of its maladaptive consequences. For Wolpe, 'neurotics' existed as a class different from 'normals' only in that they were unfortunate enough to have experienced frightful situations, including those mediated by social instruction, and were genetically disposed towards reacting strongly to them.

Parenthetically, it should be recalled that Wolpe excluded 'psychotic' disorders from his system on the grounds that their etiology was entirely biologic rather than based on anxiety conditioning. He acknowledged that learning procedures were useful in ameliorating some psychotic behavior problems but that a learning-based 'cure' was not possible. Most behavior and cognitive therapies retain this dichotomy, while many psychodynamic and humanist therapies do not make such a distinction.

Wolpe's model of anxiety conditioning has been narrowly interpreted and widely disputed. Other than post-traumatic stress disorder, many therapists found little evidence for events analogous to Wolpe's cats in their patients' histories. However, Wolpe recognized from the beginning that for humans, verbal and other social representations of aversive events were potent producers of anxiety. And as new evidence became available, he accepted the importance of modeling. Thus, a person need not be beaten but verbal admonishments or expressions of alarm would serve as well. All that was necessary for conditioning to occur was that a situation evoke the anxiety response, which could then be maintained by additional learning factors such as generalization and higher-order conditioning. Wolpe also promoted the view that 'insight' into the original neurotogenic circumstances might be helpful, but was neither necessary nor sufficient for behavior change.

Wolpe held that the multifarious symptoms of neurosis were the direct manifestation of the anxiety response, as opposed to the operation of unconscious mechanisms of defense against it. This had the important and influential effect of changing the focus of treatment to a direct attack on the patient's symptoms. His theory that anxiety was, at its core, a response of the autonomic (predominantly sympathetic) nervous system has not found wide acceptance but it generated a great deal of research and remnants of it remain in the currently popular tripartite theory of anxiety and in conceptualizations of stress disorders. For his part, Wolpe recognized that maladaptive motoric and cognitive behaviors may be responses to autonomic anxiety. There is little practical effect of this distinction; the emphasis in behavior and cognitive therapies remains on discerning the patient's symptoms in all their variety, be they autonomic, cognitive, or motoric, and their relation to the patient's environment.

The stimulus side of the stimulus–response equation led to a focus on the here-and-now rather than engaging in psychological archaeology. Following Wolpe, the behavior and cognitive therapies are concerned with determining the present daily circumstances under which symptoms occur as opposed to uncovering infantile fixations. It is also widely accepted that gradations in symptom severity are related to variations in features of the patient's environment, in accordance with Wolpe's adoption of the concept of stimulus generalization along various stimulus dimensions. That the stimulating 'environment' may be internal as well as external follows from Wolpe's learning theory concepts of interoceptive or 'response-produced' stimuli. The concept of higher-order conditioning leads the therapist to look for the spread of anxiety to new stimulus dimensions. While not as labyrinthine as psychodynamic defense mechanisms, such concepts lend complexity to Wolpe's therapy system commensurate with the complexity shown by patients' behavior.

Reciprocal Inhibition.   Just as anxiety was Wolpe's key concept for the origin and maintenance of neurotic behavior, reciprocal inhibition was his key concept for its undoing. The basic premise of his therapy was to oppose anxiety responses with antagonistic alternative responses. The reciprocally inhibitory relationship between the sympathetic and parasympathetic branches of the autonomic nervous system provided Wolpe with a useful heuristic for this mechanism, but he soon expanded the concept beyond an easily discerned competition between autonomic branches. As noted in Chapter 4, this concept generated considerable research. Evidence for the peripheral autonomic theory is inconsistent at best, though difficulties in observing autonomic activity allowed Wolpe to postulate the operation of unmeasured pathways. The possibility of more central reciprocally inhibitory neural mechanisms has received scant attention but recent interest in neural pathways and neurotransmitters may revive interest in central nervous system mechanisms of reciprocal inhibition.

For the practicing therapist, whether the mechanism of action takes place at a peripheral or central neurological level is less important than the metaphor that reciprocal inhibition provides for the broader behavioral principle of counterconditioning. Along with concepts such as reinforcement and discrimination, counter-conditioning has passed into the behavioral zeitgeist and Wolpe is rarely cited. The notion of treating a dysfunctional response by training an opposing adaptive one is the foundation of most behavioral and cognitive procedures, whether that response is relaxation, a motor skill, or a verbal appraisal.

Stress. Wolpe's model of anxiety and reciprocal inhibition con-tributed greatly to the conceptualization and treatment of 'stress.' The reactions of Wolpe's cats to electric shock were obviously similar to Cannon's (1929) observations of the 'fight or flight' response, which were recognized as the first phase of the complex neuroendocrine reaction known as stress (Budzynski et al., 1980; Selye, 1956). Later research revealed many similarities between anxiety and stress with respect to both physiologic characteristics and precipitating conditions (see review by Barlow, 1988, p. 158–208, 215–20). 'Stress-related disorders' were recognized as physical or medical conditions resulting from the chronic activation of specific organ systems. Chronic activation, in turn, was related to inherited susceptibility, environmental demands, and learned ways of meeting those demands. The concept of stress replaced the older notion of 'psychosomatic illness,' reflecting the emergence of 'behavioral medicine' in the 1970s, as an offshoot of behavior therapy, and the resultant leveraging of stress disorders from the psychodynamic realm (Pomerleau and Brady, 1979).

Given the overlap between stress and anxiety, Wolpe's inter-ventions were adapted easily for treatment of stress disorders. For example, controlled research has shown the effectiveness of systematic desensitization in the treatment of asthma (Moore, 1965), risk factors in 'Type-A' coronary patients (Suinn, 1974; 1990), and migraine headache (Mitchell and Mitchell, 1971). The reciprocal inhibition model can be seen in the widespread use of relaxation training as the foundation for most stress management programs. Wolpe's adaptation and promotion of Jacobson's progressive muscle relaxation had gained wide currency through desensitization research and practice, so it was readily at hand for application to stress disorders by behavioral clinical researchers. Notable examples include relaxation-based treatment of essential hypertension (Agras, 1981; Agras et al., 1983) and headache (Blanchard et al., 1980; 1990a). Such studies indicate that relaxation is an effective antidote to the chronic arousal presumed to cause these disorders.

Another major contributor to the behavioral treatment of stress was the development of biofeedback (Birk, 1973; Budzynski et al., 1980). Aided by electronic amplification of physiologic activity, patients are able to learn to control the arousal related to disorders such as tension and migraine headache and essential hypertension (Blanchard et al., 1980; 1990a,b; Wittrock et al., 1988). Relaxation remains an integral component of most biofeedback programs and, in many instances, biofeedback can be regarded as a means of training general relaxation (Poppen, 1988; Silver and Blanchard, 1978). Regardless of its use as a means of teaching control of a specific physiologic response or producing generalized relaxation, biofeedback follows the counterconditioning model, in which pathogenic arousal is replaced by its calm, restorative alternative (Budzynski et al., 1980; Poppen, 1988).

It should be noted that the role of cognitive factors in stress, similar to their role in anxiety, has been emphasized by many clinicians and researchers (Lazarus and Folkman, 1984). Accordingly, cognitive procedures have been employed in stress treatment programs, usually in conjunction with relaxation or biofeedback (Keefe and Beckham, 1993). To date, the contribution of cognitive procedures over and above relaxation or biofeedback has not been demonstrated in package treatment programs (Blanchard et al., 1990a,b). Just as in anxiety and depression disorders, the addition of cognitive treatments for stress-related disorders has not demonstrated a decided advantage for treatment outcome.

Anger. Wolpe initially conceptualized anger as an emotion reciprocally inhibitory to social anxiety. The appropriate expression of anger was a cornerstone of his assertiveness training procedures.

However, it was soon recognized that timidity, or 'over-controlled' anger, was only half the picture, and that aggression, or 'under-controlled' anger was also a problem for which assertiveness training was applicable (Alberti and Emmons, 1970; Rimm, 1977). A number of studies demonstrated that teaching assertiveness skills decreased verbal and physical aggression by adults with anger control problems (Rimm and Masters, 1979, pp. 83–8). Another approach employed modified desensitization – teaching patients to relax while imagining anger-provoking scenes (Suinn, 1990, pp. 313–18; Warren and McLellarn, 1982). Cognitive procedures were also incorporated, addressing patients' self-statements in provocative situations. All these anger control programs were consistent with the counterconditioning model – teaching adaptive alternatives for the autonomic, verbal, or motor components of anger. Research and application of this approach has lagged far behind the work on anxiety and stress. Given the societal importance of anger and aggression, this is an area for which the full impact of Wolpe's counterconditioning model has yet to be realized.

Technical Contributions

Wolpe conducted his therapy in a manner markedly different from prevailing psychoanalytic therapies and concurrently developing humanistic ones. These differences have become standard operating procedure for behavioral and cognitive therapies and have influenced other systems as well. First, Wolpe was active and directive as opposed to the 'blank screen,' interpretive, reflective, or non-directive styles of other therapies. Wolpe asked directly concerning things he wanted to know about and recommended directly things he wanted the patient to try. Secondly, Wolpe employed an explicit sequential plan for therapy: assessment, diagnosis, intervention, and evaluation. His medical training and natural science philosophy led him to begin each case with a specific assessment phase aimed at diagnosis. Diagnosis was not simply a labeling process of placing a patient in a category, but a highly individualized 'stimulus–response analysis' leading to a formulation of treatment goals. On the basis of the particular needs of the individual, Wolpe prescribed an intervention from among the many he developed, adapted, or borrowed, based on a combination of his conceptual formulation of the patient's problem and empirical evidence on what had worked for similar patients. He opposed simple eclecticism and always sought to integrate techniques into his theoretical system. Evaluation continued informally throughout intervention and served as the guide to decisions about continuing a procedure, changing to another one, or concluding treatment.

Contributions to Assessment and Diagnosis

Assessment Techniques. Wolpe began each case with a systematic amnestic survey of important areas in the patient's life. The patient's story was taken at face value, allowing for the foibles of memory and social convention, rather than as a surface covering for hidden meanings and feelings. The material gathered in the history served to flesh out the patient's presenting complaints, indicate other areas needing attention, and show areas of competence. The history interview also served to enlist the patient as an observer and reporter from the outset, providing him or her with a relatively straightforward therapeutic task in what otherwise might be a strange or upsetting situation. It also allowed the therapist to establish him or herself as a caring, noncritical listener. The interview content and method developed by Wolpe has continued to guide behavior and cognitive therapy assessment (Turkat, 1986).

Wolpe was an early advocate of self-report questionnaires for gathering clinical information. In keeping with his natural science patient-as-observer model, he used tests as direct requests for information rather than as indirect or projective measures of phenomena of which the patient was unaware. He was involved in the development of two instruments, a fear survey schedule (Wolpe and Lang, 1964; 1969) and an assertiveness inventory (Wolpe and Lazarus, 1966). These can be termed 'stimulus' questionnaires, consisting of lists of situations in which respondents rated their discomfort or other reactions. As described in Chapter 3, numerous iterations of fear surveys and assertiveness inventories followed, varying the situations listed and the rating methods, but employing the same format and philosophy laid down by Wolpe.

Another type of instrument may be termed 'response' question-naires, such as the Manifest Anxiety Scale (Spence and Taylor, 1953), the State–Trait Anxiety Inventory (Speilberger et al., 1970), and the Beck Depression Inventory (Beck, 1972). These list various feelings or reactions, with little regard to stimulus situations, which respondents are asked to endorse or rate. Such instruments are usually employed to place persons in categories based on nomothetic scoring, which Wolpe felt was insufficient at best. He strongly favored idiographic scoring of questionnaires, that is, the examination of each item to derive specific information for a particular patient. However, the greatest use of tests in the research literature has been for assigning subjects to groups and in measuring group pre- to post-intervention changes based on total scores. Wolpe felt that his advice on the use of questionnaires was not heeded and that behavior therapists often performed insufficient assessments, resulting in deficient therapy (Wolpe and Wright, 1988).

The life history and idiographic questionnaire scores provided contextual information for what Wolpe called a 'stimulus–response' analysis. In this, Wolpe sought a full description of patients' current symptoms and the circumstances under which they occurred. Response analysis encompassed patients' feelings, perceptions, thoughts, and actions, as well as the frequency, intensity, and duration of these events. The 'subjective unit of disturbance' (*suds*) scale has been widely adopted for self-report of many subjective responses in addition to anxiety. Analysis of stimuli included physical location, social surroundings, and temporal factors. Wolpe held that even 'free-floating' anxiety was related to pervasive external or internal cues. Responses often served as stimuli for further responses, and stimulus–response analysis sought to unravel the concatenation of thoughts, feelings, and actions as they fed off one another, sometimes escalating into overwhelming panic.

Wolpe's patient-as-observer approach to assessment was elaborated in the development of the 'self-control' models of therapy (Cautela, 1969; Kanfer, 1970; Thoreson and Mahoney, 1974). In this approach, patients were asked to write down specific instances of problematic occurrences as they occurred, using checklists and structured diaries, in addition to amnestic reports. Self-monitoring not only served to aid initial assessment, but continued during intervention to gauge progress and to enhance treatment by means of reactivity (Nelson, 1976).

Diagnosis as Case Formulation. Wolpe combined the history, questionnaire information, and the stimulus–response analysis, to provide a unique picture of each patient. This 'case formulation' model consisted of a narrative description of the patient's problems, the contexts in which they occurred, and their origin and development over time (Turkat, 1986; Wolpe and Turkat, 1985). This stood in marked contrast to traditional diagnosis according to *DSM* criteria or other psychotherapeutic formulations. One difference was that the case formulation was shared with the patient in order to confirm its accuracy and completeness. This had the effect of building an empathetic and constructive therapeutic relationship as the patient realized that he or she was 'understood.' Wolpe and Turkat (1985) contrasted this with the non-directive, reflection-of-feeling approach of Rogerian therapy, which may demonstrate empathy but does not contribute to delineating therapeutic goals. It was also different from psychodynamic therapies, in which the patient, at great length, developed 'insight' into his or her pathogenic conflict which the therapist had known all along but had hinted at only indirectly through interpretations.

Presenting the case formulation was also different from sharing a *DSM* category label with a patient, which might convey some professional expertise but was likely to be followed by the question, 'What can be done?' Following the nomothetic model, the answer is a statistical one; the *DSM* by definition suggests the usual treatment for the usual patient in each category. In contrast, Wolpe's case formulation prescribed an individualized treatment regime. It indicated specific treatment goals, addressing the particular behavior problems of each patient, and suggested particular inter-vention strategies to achieve those goals, addressing the particular etiologic and maintaining factors. Furthermore, it provided a treatment rationale for the client over and above a generic state-ment of effectiveness. Providing the patient with a straightforward account of treatment goals, methods and rationale was a major step toward accountability (see below).

Finally, Wolpe (1977; 1986; 1989a) held that tailoring treatment to the patient on the basis of individual case formulation was more effective than the practice of applying a standard intervention on the basis of membership in a diagnostic category, and that most outcome research was flawed by neglect of this factor. Persons (1991) has presented a similar analysis, arguing that case formu-lation is the basis for the clinical practice of a variety of psycho-therapies, psychodynamic and cognitive as well as behavioral, and that outcome studies do not reflect actual practice. In addition, the development of 'brief psychotherapy' indicates a movement toward recognition of the utility of specific treatment goals by psycho-dynamic therapies.

Intervention: Application of Techniques
After assessment and individualized diagnosis, Wolpe got to the business of intervention. His general approach to treatment charted the course for current behavior and cognitive therapies, and his specific procedures have been adopted or adapted by therapists of all persuasions.

General Therapy Contributions. One of Wolpe's major technical contributions was the conduct of psychotherapy by selecting from a palette of procedures, analogous to the medical model of selecting particular drug and surgical interventions for particular conditions. An observer of behavior therapy sessions would see many different procedures employed by the therapist depending on the particular case and the stage of treatment, in contrast to psychoanalytic and humanist therapies where the observer would see much the same thing from patient to patient and session to session – the patient talks, the therapist listens and provides occasional comments. Cognitive therapies initially were limited to verbal discussion, albeit more interactive than psychoanalytic and non-directive approaches, but later expanded their repertoires in the behavioral direction to include a variety of procedures, such as relaxation training, role-plays, homework assignments, and the like.

Wolpe's therapeutic repertoire of multiple techniques was sometimes criticized as a 'bag of tricks.' It is possible to employ procedures in this manner, and some of Wolpe's early cases gave the impression of trial-and-error as he struggled to devise interventions for patients who proved recalcitrant to usual methods. But this is not the true spirit of Wolpe's psychotherapy and he continued to work toward the goal of specific case formulation which would indicate the appropriate interventions for each patient. Gordon Paul's oft-cited question ('Which therapy for which patient, by which therapist, in which circumstances?') was not a rhetorical one for Wolpe; he felt it could be answered through careful assessment and appreciation of etiologic factors. He was critical of 'technical eclecticism,' which suggested an answer to Paul's question by means of statistical empiricism. Wolpe felt that such a cookbook approach would be less effective and add less to the understanding of neurotic behavior than one which was based on a conceptual analysis of the patient's behavior and a carefully prescribed intervention. This argument seemed reminiscent of Meehl's classic work (1954) on statistical versus clinical prediction in psychometric assessment – which strongly favored the statistical approach. It should be noted that 'seat-of-the-pants' eclecticism has far to go before achieving a valid empirical foundation. The statistical eclectic and the case formulation approaches are hypotheses which await future research.

Despite differences and disagreements, all subsequent behavior and cognitive therapy procedures follow the general procedural framework upon which Wolpe built his techniques. This procedural framework, as distinct from conceptual explanations, consists of the following: (1) present the critical situation to the patient in a controlled fashion; (2) weaken the undesirable responses; (3) strengthen the adaptive responses; (4) continue in a progressive manner until adaptive behavior occurs readily in everyday situations. Controlled presentation of critical stimuli could be accomplished by verbal descriptions, role-plays, display of items in the office, and supervised or instructed contacts in the natural environment. Undesirable responses could be weakened by attenuating the stimulus presentation, prolonging the stimulus presentation, response prevention through instruction or environmental arrangement, and punishment by social disapproval or other aversive stimuli. Adaptive responses could be established and strengthened by verbal instruction, modeling, performance feedback, and social approval. Explicit or implicit 'homework' assignments mediated behavior change from the office to the outside world. Various behavior and cognitive therapists disagreed on how best to present the critical stimuli, which adaptive and maladaptive responses to address, the most effective ways to strengthen or weaken them, and what hypothetical neurologic, learning, or cognitive mechanisms account for the process. Nonetheless, these four basic elements, first established by Wolpe, provided the foundation for all behavior and cognitive therapy procedures.

Specific Therapy Contributions. Wolpe's techniques provided basic tools for a large number of behavior, cognitive, and eclectic therapists. Even psychodynamic therapists have employed systematic desensitization, assertiveness training, and sexual therapy, although with their own theoretical interpretations. The impact of these most enduring of Wolpe's procedures is discussed briefly.

Systematic Desensitization. This remains the technique most strongly identified with Wolpe. Almost all introductory psychology textbooks include a section on Wolpe and desensitization. Desensitization provides a paradigmatic example of Wolpe's general principles and it retains the virtues he originally claimed for it: it is widely accepted by patients as a benign way to confront troubling situations; it is relatively easily conducted in an office environment; and, when employed in a sophisticated rather than superficial manner, it is highly effective for a wide variety of complex problems. Its disadvantages are that it is not effective with certain general classes of anxiety-related problems, such as obsessive–compulsive disorders, or for certain individuals. (It should be noted that the ability to detect failure to progress and the need to try a different procedure, rather than persisting in the same course, often for years, is a major contribution in itself.) As discussed in Chapter 4, systematic desensitization stimulated hundreds of researchers to test its theoretical and procedural foundations and provided the benchmark by which to measure the effectiveness of new methods.

Most of the 'new and improved' methods retain some features of desensitization, and all of them adhere to the general framework outlined above.

Most new methods challenged the notion of gradual progress up a strictly graded stimulus hierarchy to prevent the occurrence of anxiety. In 'flooding' procedures, highly anxiety-provoking stimuli were presented for lengthy periods. In 'exposure' procedures, situations evoking moderate discomfort were presented first and then a rough hierarchy was followed. In all of these procedures, as in desensitization, stimulus presentation was controlled: the patient agreed beforehand on what was to transpire and stimuli were presented in a therapeutic context – there were no surprises and no overwhelming anxiety. Most of the new methods employed relaxation, as in desensitization, to counteract anxious arousal; the difference was that anxiety was first evoked and then overcome rather than completely prevented. Finally, many new methods added a 'cognitive' component, in which patients were taught to remind themselves to engage in relaxation, employ problem-solving skills, or challenge irrational thoughts, when faced with anxiety stimuli.

As noted in Chapter 4, evidence comparing the newer methods with systematic desensitization and each other is often equivocal. Much work remains in sorting out 'which method for which patient.' There is a general consensus that anxiety-evoking methods are superior to desensitization for patients in which the primary problem is 'fear of fear,' a debilitating concern over the feelings of arousal, as in many agoraphobics and obsessive–compulsive disorders. Exposure methods are also useful in cases in which routine confrontation with upsetting events is unavoidable, resulting in 'resensitization.' Even if desensitization ultimately should be superseded, it remains the evolutionary ancestor of the later procedures and the original stimulus for comparative research.

Assertiveness Training. Wolpe adapted Salter's 'excitatory' exercises, naming the procedure assertiveness training. He developed it initially as a technique to overcome anxiety in interpersonal situations. A number of clinical researchers quickly saw it as a means of overcoming deficits in interpersonal skills and Wolpe agreed that the skill training and emotional reconditioning aspects were 'inextricably intertwined.'

Second only to systematic desensitization as a topic for clinical research, a long list of authors contributed to the development of assertiveness training, resulting in many procedural variations. Textbooks routinely include a statement to the effect that there is no single set of procedures which define the technique. Nevertheless, the essence of assertiveness training is contained in the broad outline originally sketched by Wolpe, in which the patient and therapist collaborate in defining difficult interpersonal situations, identifying appropriate responses, rehearsing the responses, and implementing them in daily life in progressively more difficult situations. Others have filled in technical details such as education on personal rights, coaching, modeling, performance feedback, self-instructions, self-reinforcement, cultural factors, and group training, to list but a few. Following Wolpe, many therapists have found that assertiveness training is immensely useful in overcoming the interpersonal distress that contributes to a panoply of problems, including depression, agoraphobia, sexual dysfunction, stress-related disorders, aggression, and familial discord.

Sexual Therapy. Wolpe's early work with patients having sexual problems was overshadowed by the extensive and highly publicized efforts of Masters and Johnson (1970). These investigators maintained an atheoretical stance, avoiding extant psychodynamic, behavioral, or cognitive models, and cited few precedents. Largely because of their program, sexual therapy became a speciality area rather than a component of behavioral or other psychotherapies. However, the techniques and principles developed by Wolpe are relevant for the therapist with patients presenting complaints of sexual dysfunction, either as a primary problem or, as is often the case, in conjunction with other difficulties. By integrating sexual therapy into a broader behavioral framework, Wolpe reminded psychotherapists that sexual anxiety, misconceptions and skill deficits are conceptually no different than other interpersonal problems and that interventions appropriate for other disorders are also effective for sexual problems. In addition, he reminded us that sexual dysfunctions often occur in the context of other problems (such as depression, marital discord, generalized anxiety, or social anxiety), and that these must be addressed in addition to the directed sexual training that forms the core of sexual therapy.

Other Techniques. Wolpe developed or adopted a variety of procedures that have not been researched as extensively as desensitization, assertiveness training, or sexual therapy. The current status of these techniques is briefly noted.

'Aversion therapy' refers to a collection of procedures designed to reciprocally inhibit inappropriate attraction or arousal to stimuli which are related to socially sanctioned or self-destructive behaviors. Reports of its use in the literature have declined markedly from a peak of popularity in the 1970s, although it continues to be routinely employed in some treatment programs for alcoholism and sexual deviance. The use of electric shock in aversion therapy is generally concluded to be ineffective, while nausea-inducing procedures have produced better results (Emmelkamp, 1986). 'Covert sensitization' (Cautela, 1967), which employs verbal descriptions of unpleasant scenes, is technically much simpler than electrical or chemical stimuli and has achieved at least as good results. 'Aversion relief,' in which appropriate stimuli are paired with the termination of the aversive stimulus, is sometimes employed as part of aversion therapy programs. It is widely agreed that aversion therapy is most effective within the context of a program to teach appropriate skills in place of the deviant behavior (see, for example, Brownell and Barlow, 1980).

'Thought stopping' may be regarded as an aversion procedure. It continues to be employed with some frequency in the treatment of obsessive or intrusive thoughts, usually in conjunction with other procedures (Spiegler and Guevremont, 1992, p. 297).

Wolpe recommended carbon dioxide inhalation for the treatment of generalized anxiety. It has recently received strong support in the treatment of panic disorder as well. Whereas Wolpe proposed that carbon dioxide inhalation directly inhibited anxiety, Barlow and colleagues found that it actually evoked anxious arousal and appears to be an exposure procedure (Barlow, 1988, pp. 447–60). Exposure to interoceptive anxiety stimuli in a safe, controlled setting, combined with education about the disorder and breathing retraining, has resulted in a highly effective treatment package.

Effectual Contributions

Wolpe's key contribution to psychotherapy was to insist that it should be demonstrably effective. He asserted that he was one of the first to achieve results over and above the nonspecific effects of hope and attention. As a clinician, he successfully treated numerous patients who had undergone years of psychoanalysis to no avail, producing an unassailable certainty of the superiority of his methods. But as a researcher, setting out to prove the validity of his claims, he was less successful. Unschooled in the grantsmanship that was the life force of psychotherapy research in the United States, he did not mount a sustained research or training program of his own. Although his theories and procedures provided grist for the research mills of hundreds of academic and clinical researchers, they owed him no special allegiance. Thus he was dependent on the ways others formulated their research questions and procedures, and was subject to their biases and agendas, for data concerning the effectiveness of his methods and the soundness of his theories. This insured that results favorable to his approach were fairly impartial but afforded him little opportunity for experimental follow-up of data that were not favorable. There was one matter, though, on which all agreed. Based on the natural science territory staked out by Wolpe, the conviction that systematic observation and measurement of outcome provided a pathway to better understanding of human nature and more effective treatment of human maladies became a fundamental tenet of behavior therapy. In addition, even though unsophisticated in experimental methodology, the investigations in which Wolpe participated were milestones in outcome research.

Legacies of Wolpe's Research
Wolpe's experimental foray with cats marked the end of an era begun by Pavlov, in which researchers narratively reported their observations of animals in the laboratory. Wolpe employed no group or single-subject research design, no quantitative assessment, no statistical analysis. Yet his anecdotal reports conveyed one compelling fact – he had created and cured 'experimental neurosis' in each of his animals. The drama of this accomplishment convinced him that he could effectively treat human neuroses as well. And the elegance of Hull's learning theory, combined with his own hypotheses about neural organization, convinced him that he was on the path of a true science of behavior.

His cat experiment inspired a few other animal studies (such as Poppen, 1970), but the animal model for psychopathology declined as researchers found increasing opportunity for the direct study of humans (Plaud and Vogeltanz, 1991). It is to the everlasting benefit of psychotherapy that Wolpe was unable to find a position as a Hullian researcher and was forced to earn his way as a psychotherapist. As soon as he began to accomplish successful outcomes, in the face of opposition from the entrenched psychoanalytic community, he published his findings. In keeping with his estranged relations with professional colleagues, he reported his outcomes in a confrontational manner – the new therapy based on the science of behavior was much superior to that based on archaic speculations about psychosexual development. Wolpe's challenge coincided with the conclusions of the combative Hans Jurgen Eysenck (1952), who had weighed psychotherapy in the balance and found it wanting. Wolpe presented tallies of successful therapy that were far superior to any that could be mustered for the other side (Wolpe, 1952b; 1958). The glove-slap across the face of psychotherapy was to prove his figures wrong or come up with better evidence for its own effectiveness.

Wolpe's second experimental endeavor was the supervision of Arnold Lazarus' doctoral research (1961), comparing group desensitization with group 'insight' therapy in the treatment of various phobic disorders. While no paragon of methodological rigor, this study was one of the first to arrange a contest between therapies. Success was measured by direct observation of the patients in anxiety-provoking situations – like Wolpe's cats that finally had to face the 'hooter.' Critics easily dismissed the overwhelming superiority of desensitization as experimenter bias, even though Lazarus reported that he found desensitization boring and was far more involved and interested in the insight groups. After their split, both Wolpe and Lazarus ceased to mention this study and its only legacy seemed to be as an example of poor design. However, two features – random assignment of comparable phobic patients to different therapeutic conditions and the observation of their behavior in problematic circumstances – became the defining characteristics of hundreds of studies that were to follow.

As detailed in Chapter 4, the catalyst that brought about the explosion of desensitization research was the discovery of large numbers of 'analogue' phobic college students, allowing psychology doctoral candidates ready access to 'clinical' populations. Early studies addressed the methodologic deficits of Lazarus' dissertation. They verified Wolpe's propositions that relaxation coupled with a gradually ascending hierarchy was necessary and sufficient for effective desensitization, and that relief of phobic problems did not result in 'symptom substitution' but often led to improved functioning in other areas of living. Once established as the benchmark treatment for phobic disorders, desensitization became the target for others to surpass. A positive outcome of this intramural competition was the development of effective treatment alternatives, such as modeling, flooding, and coping skill training, for individuals or categories of problems not amenable to desensitization. Analogue studies of desensitization and these alternative procedures formed the bulk of the research which meta-analyses, excepting statistical shenanigans, showed to be more effective than psychodynamic or humanistic therapies (Smith et al., 1980; see Chapter 4).

But analogue research also had a negative impact in the form of trivializing desensitization. The treatment of simple fears by employing simple spatial or temporal hierarchies promoted the view that that was all there was to it. The subtlety and complexity which Wolpe had described in treating individual patients was lost as researchers developed standardized protocols. Subjects were marched through one-size-fits-all therapies and group averages were compared after a small number of sessions with no regard for individual differences or complete recovery as a goal. In addition, the use of relatively low anxious subjects, eager to fulfill course credit requirements, made suggestion and expectancy factors especially salient, so that desensitization often fared no better than placebo procedures. Wolpe supported early analogue studies by citing them in his books and articles, but with no research base of his own he could address the derogatory studies only by gleaning supportive data whenever they appeared and by criticizing opposing data. This gave his later professional writing and speaking a defensive and contrary tone.

Assertiveness training also underwent extensive analogue research in a manner similar to desensitization (Fodor, 1980). As described previously, Wolpe's model of anger reciprocally inhibiting social anxiety was soon superseded by concern for social skill deficits, maladaptive self-statements, personal rights, and aggressive behavior, so that he is sometimes seen only as a transitory figure between Andrew Salter and later programs. However, Wolpe must be credited for transforming and publicizing Salter's work (as he had done for Jacobson), and incorporating it within a coherent system of psychotherapy. Wolpe was responsible for laying out the basic assertiveness training procedures which form the foundation of all later programs. He recognized and supported many of the variations in the focus and practice of assertiveness training. Above all, the purpose of assertiveness training research was to obtain objective evidence relating training to effective performance in problematic situations, fulfilling Wolpe's vision for a scientific psychotherapy

Wolpe's major concern was with 'real' neurotic patients, not analogue subjects, and he had the opportunity to participate in a definitive attempt to compare behavior therapy with psychoanalytic therapy when he was recruited to Temple University (Sloane et al., 1975). Whereas Lazarus' dissertation could be regarded as a Wright brothers flyer, the Temple project resembled a jumbo jet. A unique feature of this study was that each therapist was free to develop an intervention program that he thought best fit the needs of the individual patient, limited only by time constraints. Such an approach was appropriate for the psychoanalytic model, in which 'techniques' are at best only vaguely specified, as well as Wolpe's model of behavior therapy, in which procedures may be varied depending on their effectiveness with each individual. This controlled research project was probably the closest to psychotherapy as usually practiced.

There were four widely accepted conclusions from this study: first, significant improvement occurred for substantial numbers of people receiving only assessment and placement on a waiting-list; second, both behavior therapy and psychoanalytic therapy were equally effective in producing improvements greater than waiting-list; third, behavior therapy could therefore be regarded as a legitimate therapy; fourth, the factors responsible for effective therapy lie in the commonalities between various therapies and not the specific procedures or theories which distinguish them. Wolpe, of course, rejected the second and fourth of these conclusions, and he had known the first and third all along. As detailed in Chapter 4, there were in fact numerous instances where behavior therapy was shown to be superior to psychotherapy in this study. From a behavioral point of view, the greatest shortcoming of this project was its reliance on ratings and verbal reports rather than direct behavioral observation which, it is presumed, would have shown even more striking differences in favor of behavior therapy.

'Equal effectiveness' became the rallying cry of many traditional psychotherapy researchers, who continued to press for the investigation of factors common to all therapeutic endeavors (Frank, 1973; Luborsky et al., 1975; Bergin and Lambert, 1978; Smith et al., 1980; Lambert et al., 1986). 'Common factors' research can be regarded as a continuation of the older 'process' research which, presuming the effectiveness of psychotherapy, asked the question, 'How does it work?' (Garfield, 1992; Lambert and Bergin, 1992; Strupp and Howard, 1992). Methodologically, this research analyzed transcripts and tapes of therapy sessions for relationship variables – such as 'warmth, empathy, and genuineness' and 'therapeutic alliance' – and also studied personality factors that therapists and patients brought to their sessions. Ratings of these factors were correlated with ratings of outcomes. Particularly prized were findings of significant correlations within behavior therapy (see review by Lambert et al., 1986). For example, in the Temple project, the behavior therapists were rated as more empathetic than the psychoanalysts, and 'warmth' has been found to be related to outcome in studies of desensitization (such as Morris and Suckerman, 1974). The inference drawn from such findings is that Wolpe's procedures involved *nothing but* features common to all therapies.

From his first days as a therapist, Wolpe recognized the role of nonspecific factors in psychotherapy outcome. What he promised was *something more* – namely, specific therapy procedures added to these effects. This is his legacy to psychotherapy research, as investigators have continued to search for procedural factors that explain and enhance therapeutic outcome. However, the Temple model, in which therapists developed interventions for each individual patient, has been rejected by most researchers because it did not allow specification and control of the independent variable. Instead, the 'treatment manual' approach became standard operating procedure. First developed in analogue desensitization research, it allowed the same treatment to be administered across different patients by different therapists, and it permitted precise variations in a treatment variable in order to measure its effects (Lambert et al., 1986). A drawback of this approach is that it ignores or attempts to control for nonspecific, patient, and therapist variables rather than study them.

Wolpe (1977; 1986; 1989a,b) was increasingly critical of research which employed standardized protocols with people grouped into diagnostic categories. Not only was it different from the way therapy is practiced, threatening the external validity of research findings, but it detracted from the outcome of treatment in that procedures might be employed with individuals for whom they were ineffective or even counterproductive. This accounts for the common finding of similar average improvement across different treatment groups, which means that some patients improved and some did not. Wolpe insisted that those not improving had received inappropriate treatment even though they met broad diagnostic criteria. Some researchers have begun to address this issue, calling for a finer-grain analysis of patient needs within larger diagnostic categories, and matching treatment programs to those needs – just as Wolpe advocated (Eifert et al., 1990; Mersch et al., 1989; Persons, 1986; 1991). This is a labor-intensive process, and to date only a few studies have appeared which support this approach (for example Heiby, 1986; McKnight et al., 1984). Despite the difficulties, this is likely to be an important area of continuing research.

Just as in the Temple project itself, the aggregation of psychotherapy research has produced no overwhelming winners with respect to therapy effectiveness. Proponents of behavioral and cognitive therapies, while realizing there is room for improvement, see the research data as supporting their superiority over traditional psychodynamic and insight therapies (see Eysenck, 1993; Giles et al., 1993). Traditional therapy proponents assert that the issues are much too complicated for detecting any advantage, question the epistemology of the scientific approach, or draw the 'equal effectiveness' conclusion (see Elliot et al., 1993). No one, it seems, finds support for the superiority of psychodynamic and humanistic methods, and even some traditional psychotherapy investigators are willing to cede a 'significant increment' of effectiveness to behavioral and cognitive procedures, particularly with more difficult problems (Lambert et al., 1986).

Accountability

Psychotherapy remains an esoteric enterprise, far removed from the concerns of society at large. The debate over therapeutic effectiveness is largely a professional one, taking place in books, journal articles, and conventions. Documentation not only of ineffectiveness but of physical and psychological harm caused by psychoanalytic therapy in general, or by individual therapists (see Eysenck, 1992; Masson, 1988; 1992; Mays and Franks, 1985) has had little impact within the profession and less outside it. As psychotherapy is a profession that provides debatable gain and possible harm, it is perhaps fortunate that less than a quarter of the population with conditions that psychotherapy purports to treat gain access to services, and more than half of those that begin treatment drop out quickly (see review by Pekarik, 1993). Wolpe's approach has much to contribute to increasing the accountability and acceptability of psychotherapy.

Consumer Expectations. People seeking mental health services tend to expect concrete definition of their problems and an active, direct problem-solving approach (Benbenishty and Schul, 1987; Llewelyn, 1988). This view is inconsistent with many psychotherapies and their practitioners often go to some lengths to disabuse patients of such notions (Heitler, 1976). Wolpe's focus on patients' symptoms as the target of treatment and criterion for judging success, and his directness in explaining his methods and their relationship to patients' symptoms, was a major step toward meeting consumer preferences. Recall the critique of desensitization as 'nothing but' an especially effective means of raising patients' expectancies (Kazdin and Wilcoxon, 1976). Perhaps this is not a criticism so much as a lesson; namely, to be effective, procedures must make sense to the recipients.

One reason that patients drop out of treatment is its failure to meet their expectations (Pekarik, 1993). Thus one would expect higher retention rates for programs following Wolpe's model. There are scant data on this issue. For example, the Temple project found very low attrition rates for both behavior therapy and psychoanalytic groups. However, this study employed highly selected and informed participants, making it unrepresentative of therapy as usually practiced. Another reason given for early termination is alleviation of symptoms (Pekarik, 1993), which would suggest higher drop-out rates for symptom-focused treatments. Clearly, more research is needed on attrition rates and the reasons for dropping out among various types of psychotherapy.

Treatment Duration. Another reason that psychotherapy reaches only a small fraction of people who require services is that it can be very lengthy. Classic psychoanalysis required hundreds of hours across many years, which is clearly unfeasible for all but the moneyed leisure class. After World War II, there were some efforts to develop abbreviated psychoanalytic therapy, stimulated in part by the large number of soldiers and civilians who had suffered traumas (Alexander and French, 1946; Grinker and Spiegel, 1945). The goals of treatment were release of repressed memories and emotions, and techniques included hypnosis and narcotics. The reader may recall that Wolpe's dissatisfaction with this approach to treatment led to his development of an alternative. A decade later, he lauded the relative efficiency of his therapy, estimating about 40 sessions to be sufficient, with many patients requiring far less (Wolpe, 1958, p. 205). Shortly thereafter, Lazarus (1961; 1963) reported positive outcomes with less than half this number of sessions. His figures were in line with later studies of behavior therapy program duration (Wilson, 1981).

The field known as 'brief psychotherapy' has grown within traditional psychotherapy and is gradually changing its reputation as an inferior form of treatment. Ironically, one of the major contributors to this development has been behavior therapy, from which many goals and procedures have been adopted, including symptom-focused assessment and treatment, attention to current functioning, highly directive therapist activity, homework assignments, and flexible use of a variety of techniques (Koss and Butcher, 1986). Thus behavior therapy may be considered a *de facto* form of brief psychotherapy, but as a profession it has resisted inclusion under this rubric. This is because the remaining psychodynamic concepts are seen as counterproductive (Wolpe, 1990, p. 341), and, unlike in brief psychotherapy, the short time period is not an inherent goal but is regarded as a by-product of effective treatment.

Studies reveal that patients expect treatment to last only about five to 10 sessions. The average number of sessions attended by outpatients is about five in community mental health settings, and about 12 in private practice, with the median number of sessions in both settings around four (Pekarik, 1993). These small numbers are largely the result of patient drop-out rather than rapidly completing treatment goals. Thus both brief psychotherapy and behavior therapy, with their programs of about 20 sessions, far exceed what most patients are willing to endure. To date, behavior therapy has failed to investigate briefer forms of treatment, while psychodynamic and insight therapists have pushed ahead with programs of one or two sessions. Pekarik (1993, p. 430) concludes, 'It is indeed ironic that those who have led the field in the search for the most effective treatment under ideal circumstances seem to have conceded to others the search for delivery of the most cost-effective treatments in the real world of standard practice.' He warns that, in the rapidly changing world of reimbursement policy, behavior therapy may be left behind.

Cost.   Until recently, the marketplace for psychotherapy services promoted ineffectiveness and inefficiency (Giles, 1993). The longer a paying patient could be kept in treatment the better. The limited number of providers relative to demand seemed to insure a steady supply of customers regardless of their satisfaction. The dramatic increase in mental health workers in the United States since the 1960s has been more than matched by the demand for services. This situation is largely the result of the fee-for-service payment system of insurance and governmental agencies, in which private-practice providers are paid for how much they do and not how well they do it. Even in agencies where mental health workers are paid a fixed salary, there are no contingencies for positive outcomes.

However, there is increasing recognition that this state of affairs cannot continue (Giles, 1993). Since the introduction of Medicare in the United States in 1965, the demand for health services has risen over 1000 percent and health care costs have grown from about 6 percent to almost 20 percent of the gross national product. Mental health services comprise the third largest component of health costs and have risen even more rapidly than other areas in the past decade. Accordingly, cost-containment programs are proliferating.

Giles (1993) described the development of managed mental health care programs, in which 'preferred practices,' based on outcome data, are identified for various disorders in order to deliver the most cost-effective services. Such practices resemble treatment-manual based service delivery, calling to mind Wolpe's warning about the futility of treating everyone within a diagnostic category the same. Pekarik (1993) described the possibility of reimbursement agencies providing brief, low-intensity services to all patients by the lowest bidder, regardless of needs or outcomes. Nevertheless, this approach might represent a major advance in both cost management and service provision, if the majority of patients needing very brief treatment could be identified and served, allowing cost offsets for those requiring costlier intervention. This would require assessment and treatment directed toward specific problems rather than diagnostic categorization, and the continuous evaluation of both procedures and therapists, which is fully consistent with Wolpe's approach to therapy. What has eluded philosophical speculation and scientific investigation may be achieved finally by practical necessity.

Institutional Contributions

Joseph Wolpe was the first practicing 'behavior therapist,' formulating the theories and procedures that legions of other behavioral clinicians and researchers have built upon. Yet he constructed no lasting Behavior Therapy Institute, as was his early dream, nor did he maintain a close cadre who could be identified as 'Wolpian' adherents. For that reason, some may regard him only as a historical figure, like Mary Cover Jones or Andrew Salter, having little bearing on modern cognitive–behavior therapy. But Wolpe served as more than a milestone on the road to the current state of behavior therapy. He not only set the direction this new therapy would take, but his ideas and procedures are embedded in each step of its development. He left his imprint on the various educational and professional organizations that have emerged, and his publications have preserved his own thoughts and promoted the contributions of others.

Organizations

The June Institutes which Wolpe began in Charlottesville in 1965, and continued at the Behavior Therapy Unit in Philadelphia, were the closest he came to running a formal training program. These were carried on every summer for 15 years, providing direct training or supervision by Wolpe for, cumulatively, a few hundred persons. Participants included psychology graduate students and psychiatric residents as well as established academicians and clinicians from all over the United States and many other countries. This first-hand experience taught skills and ideas which they took back to their clinics, laboratories, and classrooms, to develop further in their own research and practice, producing the vitality and diversity which was so important to the evolution of an emerging discipline. Although Wolpe preferred that people remain orthodox to his teachings, he did not have the control that, for example, a major professor has over graduate assistants. It was inevitable that this bright and diverse group would try to improve on what they had learned.

The Behavior Therapy Unit at Eastern Pennsylvania Psychiatric Institute of Temple University was Wolpe's home base for 20 years. Following the Sloane et al. project (1975), Temple became one of the first centers for systematic clinical research in behavior therapy in the United States. The investigatory focus changed from competition with psychoanalytic therapy to one of developing and improving behavior therapy procedures for difficult-to-treat disorders. Although Wolpe did not participate directly in these projects, he provided the imprimatur for this enterprise, contributing greatly to the empirical foundation of behavior therapy. His writing and speaking promoted the data-based approach of the BTU and other research centers.

Wolpe's work was incorporated into the curricula of scores of clinical graduate programs in psychology, intermixed with theories and practices of others. It is the nature of educational programs, unlike training institutes, to present multiple sides of issues, challenge orthodoxies, and create new ones. As early as 1969, Bandura's classic *Principles of Behavior Modification*, widely employed as a textbook and as a model for later ones, showed the admixture of Wolpe's Pavlovian/Hullian conditioning approach with those of operant conditioning and cognitive processing. These three approaches formed the legs upon which behavior therapy stands, with endless disputes among their proponents about which is most important or fundamental. Later embellishments ranged from neuropsychology to social systems theory, with some opting for an atheoretical eclecticism. While such diversity is profitable for academics, whose stock-in-trade is research grants and publications, Wolpe argued that it has done little for practicing clinicians and their patients, whose outcomes were not demonstrably better than, and in some cases inferior to, those obtained by 'traditional' behavior therapy. What is certain is that the matter will be resolved not by argumentation but by societal demands for greater accountability from practicing therapists and the programs that train them. Perhaps such forces will bring about the evolution of training programs such as Wolpe envisioned, but the day when there is anything close to a standard curriculum regarding the causes and cures of maladaptive behavior remains far over the horizon.

The Association for the Advancement of Behavior Therapy (AABT), organized by Cyril Franks in 1967, quickly became the premier professional organization in the United States for the new therapy. Wolpe participated in the discussions leading to its founding, served as its second president after Franks, and made presentations at its annual convention every year since its founding. But it is a far more catholic organization than Wolpe may have envisioned. For example, AABT provided a forum for his crusade against cognitivism but the membership repeatedly elected to office those promoting cognitive–behavioral approaches. Its journal, *Behavior Therapy*, published much of the research on large-scale packaged treatment programs that Wolpe felt was antithetical to his individualized approach. On the whole, the diversity and energy of AABT members, whether 'for' or 'against' Wolpe's orthodoxy, have contributed to the growth and vitality of behavior therapy as an academic and professional discipline. Wolpe's own efforts to form a professional behavior therapy interest group within the psychiatric profession was not notably successful, and AABT has been the main forum for meetings of his Behavior Therapy and Research Society. The primary function of this Society centered on maintaining a roster of Clinical Fellows and publishing the *Journal of Behavior Therapy and Experimental Psychiatry*.

Publications

Wolpe and Reyna began publication of the *Journal of Behavior Therapy and Experimental Psychiatry* in 1970. They have maintained a distinguished editorial board across the cognitive–behavioral spectrum, although he and Reyna remain as chief editors. As the title implies, the journal has striven to include a psychiatric audience. Compared to its staid sister *Behavior Therapy*, this journal is notable for its innovative content. It regularly publishes case studies and transcripts as well as more rigorous formal research. Reports of new procedures and comments on interesting features of a particular disorder or an individual patient are found regularly in its pages. It also provides Wolpe with an editorial platform to comment on the behavior therapy scene. In this writer's opinion, it remains the most interesting and thought-provoking of the dozen or so cognitive and behavior therapy journals. It reflects Wolpe's continuing zest, indeed his love, for the field in which he was such a seminal figure.

Wolpe's most concrete legacy, of course, is his written work. Wolpe realized this early on, and from the beginning published his efforts for professional scrutiny. However, his goal was much different from the 'publish or perish' ethic that permeated academic psychology and medicine. Wolpe had a message, a gospel to deliver to the world of psychotherapy, and his books and articles were a powerful medium. He was also a reader, attending to the publications of others who were working the same territory. The development and debates that marked behavior therapy and its role within the larger psychotherapy spectrum have been documented in his published works, as described in the preceding chapters.

One legacy that remains undeveloped is the hundreds of hours of audio tape and film of Wolpe's practice with patients. These comprised training materials for participants at EPPI, and could provide a valuable resource for current and future students. They await archival organization and documentation.

Summary and Conclusions

Joseph Wolpe was a major force in steering psychotherapy in the direction of empirical science. To be sure, Freud had claimed scientific status for psychodynamic theory and psychoanalytic procedures, but traditional psychotherapists were notably reluctant to engage in empirical specification and evaluation of their enterprise. Wolpe's claims of measurable therapeutic success in the face of psychoanalytic failure (amplified greatly by Hans Eysenck) focused attention on accountability, an item which, some four decades later, is increasingly demanded by market forces. Wolpe inspired and encouraged the direct comparison of carefully specified psychotherapy procedures on measurable outcome variables. Systematic desensitization and assertiveness training stimulated a generation of researchers and provided the benchmarks for the development of additional methods. Wolpe himself was a key participant in landmark investigations establishing the scientific foundations of the new behavior therapy.

It cannot be said, however, that scientific psychotherapy has won the day. Strong anti-science movements also developed, proclaiming mystical connections to metaphysical worlds beyond the reach of objective rationality. Psychodynamic approaches, though fractionated by schisms led by charismatic individuals, and veiled in cloistered consulting rooms, remain a dominant power. In the tumultuous realm of psychotherapy, as in religion, flamboyant personalities and esoteric practices often command more attention than do cool appeals to data, and, indeed, may arouse more effectively the 'faith' which many hold to be a key element in the healing experience. While personable and persuasive, Wolpe could not be considered charismatic; the acceptance of his methods was not based on a cult of personality but on respect for reason and data.

At the conceptual level, Wolpe redirected psychotherapy from the unconscious to the conscious world and from the analysis of symbolic or hidden meanings to a direct focus on patients' complaints, on an objective analysis of current and historic etiologic factors, and on the therapeutic goal of teaching alternative adaptive behaviors. To accomplish this redirection he employed concepts of learning from the experimental laboratories of Pavlov and Hull that have proven decidedly robust and influential. Indeed, even the computer-based metaphors which characterize current cognitive–behavior therapy are refinements of, rather than replacements for, these basic concepts, inserting various 'central processing' mechanisms between stimulus input and response output. Recent trends indicate movement towards resolution of many areas of disagreement within cognitive and behavioral science (Plaud and Vogeltanz, 1991; Tryon, 1993a,b; Zinbarg, 1993). While these developments may supersede Wolpe's early twentieth-century learning constructs, they are consistent with the direction in which he pointed and are characteristic of the evolution that marks scientific progress. Above all, the focus of the scientific end of the psychotherapy spectrum remains where Wolpe aimed it, on observable behavior which is adaptive to the person's current environment.

In practice, Wolpe's assessment and therapy techniques have made lasting contributions at several levels: as a body of effective procedures in themselves; as benchmarks and stimuli for the development of more effective or efficient procedures; and as models for the specification of such procedures. The techniques of systematic desensitization and assertiveness training are part of the repertoire of thousands of therapists within the behavioral and cognitive areas of the psychotherapy spectrum, extending even to those in the psychodynamic area. Notable modifications of these techniques include coping-skill formulations of relaxation and assertion, the explicit use of modeling to instigate adaptive behavior and ameliorate anxiety, more aggressive exposure of patients to upsetting stimulus situations, and verbal correction of patients' appraisals of their environment and behavior. In addition, relaxation training has spun off from systematic desensitization to become the foundation of numerous stress and pain management programs. Wolpe embraced many of these modifications and opposed others on theoretical or empirical grounds. But what ties them all together is an implicit acceptance of the counter-conditioning model – the job of therapy is to teach adaptive behavior which is incompatible with maladaptive responses to situations encountered in daily life. Whereas Wolpe initially framed the issue in terms of anxiety and autonomic arousal, the principle of counterconditioning has been greatly extended to include the emotions of depression and anger, verbal and other interpersonal repertoires, and complex motor skills.

The unfinished task for Wolpe and therapies at the scientific end of the spectrum remains to find an efficient answer to the 'What therapy for what patient?' question first posed by Gordon Paul

(1967b). Several strategies have emerged in the ensuing decades which have begun to suggest some answers. Wolpe advocated an inductive strategy based on individual case formulation. In contrast is the 'package' approach, in which an amalgamation of treatments is provided for patients meeting broad diagnostic criteria. In between these two strategies, a 'sub-grouping' approach may be discerned, in which narrower bands of patients are clustered together on the basis of particular symptoms and life-history features. All have much to contribute: the package approach is useful at early stages of finding *something* that works and for large-scale field trials; case formulation addresses the idiosyncrasies of each patient and is the practice with which most clinicians are familiar; sub-group analysis may combine the best of both approaches, permitting empirically-validated cost-effective interventions for numerous person/problem groupings. As psychotherapy begins its second century, Wolpe has provided it with a clear choice between the cumulative progress of science or the continuous contentiousness of religion.

Select Bibliography of Wolpe's Works

Wolpe, J. (1952) Experimental neuroses as learned behaviour, *British Journal of Psychology*, 43, 243–68.

Wolpe, J. (1952) Objective psychotherapy of the neuroses, *South African Medical Journal*, 26, 825–9.

Wolpe, J. (1954) Reciprocal inhibition as the main basis of psychotherapeutic effects, *Archives of Neurologic Psychiatry*, 72, 205–6.

Wolpe, J. (1958) *Psychotherapy by reciprocal inhibition*. Stanford, CA: Stanford University Press.

Wolpe, J. (1963) Psychotherapy: the nonscientific heritage and the new science, *Behaviour Research and Therapy*, 1, 23–38.

Wolpe, J. (1964) Behaviour therapy in complex neurotic states, *British Journal of Psychiatry*, 110, 28–34.

Wolpe, J. (1966) The conditioning and deconditioning of neurotic anxiety. In C.D. Speilberger (ed.), *Anxiety and behavior*. New York: Academic Press.

Wolpe, J. (1969) *The practice of behavior therapy*. New York: Pergamon Press.

Wolpe, J. (1970) Transcript of initial interview in a case of depression, *Journal of Behavior Therapy and Experimental Psychiatry*, 1, 71–8.

Wolpe, J. (1970) The instigation of assertive behavior: transcripts from two cases, *Journal of Behavior Therapy and Experimental Psychiatry*, 1, 145–51.

Wolpe, J. (1970) Behavioral analysis of a case of hypochondriacal anxiety: transcript of first interview, *Journal of Behavior Therapy and Experimental Psychiatry*, 1, 217–24.

Wolpe, J. (1976) Behavior therapy and its malcontents: 1. Denial of its bases and psychodynamic fusionism, *Journal of Behavior Therapy and Experimental Psychiatry*, 7, 1–5.

Wolpe, J. (1976) Behavior therapy and its malcontents: 2. Multimodal eclecticism, cognitive exclusivism and exposure empiricism, *Journal of Behavior Therapy and Experimental Psychiatry*, 7, 109–16.

Wolpe, J. (1977) Inadequate behavior analysis: the achilles heel of outcome research, *Journal of Behavior Therapy and Experimental Psychiatry*, 8, 1–3.

Wolpe, J. (1978) Cognition and causation in human behavior and its therapy, *American Psychologist*, 33, 437–46.

Wolpe, J. (1978) Self-efficacy theory and psychotherapeutic change: a square peg for a round hole, *Advances in Behavior Research and Therapy*, 1, 231–6.

Wolpe, J. (1981) Behavior therapy versus psychoanalysis: therapeutic and social implications, *American Psychologist*, 36, 159–64.

Wolpe, J. (1981) The dichotomy between directly conditioned and cognitively learned anxiety, *Journal of Behavior Therapy and Experimental Psychiatry*, 12, 35–42.

194   *Joseph Wolpe*

Wolpe, J. (1986) Individualization: the categorical imperative of behavior therapy practice, *Journal of Behavior Therapy and Experimental Psychiatry*, 17, 145–53.

Wolpe, J. (1989) The derailment of behavior therapy: a tale of conceptual misdirection, *Journal of Behavior Therapy and Experimental Psychiatry*, 20, 3–15.

Wolpe, J. (1990) *The practice of behavior therapy* (4th ed.). New York: Pergamon Press.

Wolpe, J. and Lang, P.J. (1964) A fear survey schedule for use in behavior therapy, *Behaviour Research and Therapy*, 2, 27–30.

Wolpe, J. and Rachman, S. (1960) Psychoanalytic evidence: a critique based on Freud's case of little Hans, *Journal of Nervous and Mental Disease*, 131, 135–48.

Wolpe, J. and Taylor, J.G. (1963) Mind as a function of neural organization. In J. Scher (ed.), *Theories of the mind.* New York: Macmillan.

Wolpe, J. and Wright, R. (1988) The neglect of data-gathering instruments in behavior therapy practice, *Journal of Behavior Therapy and Experimental Psychiatry*, 19, 5–9.

References

Agras, W.S. (1967) Transfer during systematic desensitization therapy, *Behaviour Research and Therapy*, 5, 193–9.

Agras, W.S. (1981) Behavioral approaches to the treatment of essential hypertension, *International Journal of Obesity*, 5, 173–81.

Agras, W.S., Southam, M.A., and Taylor, C.B. (1983) Long-term persistence of relaxation-induced blood pressure lowering during the working day, *Journal of Consulting and Clinical Psychology*, 51, 792–4.

Alberti, R.E. and Emmons, M.L. (1970) *Your perfect right*. San Luis Obispo, CA: Impact Press.

Alexander, F. and French, T.M. (1946) *Psychoanalytic therapy*. New York: Roland Press.

Allyon, T. (1963) Intensive treatment of psychotic behavior by stimulus satiation and food reinforcement, *Behaviour Research and Therapy*, 1, 53–62.

American Psychiatric Association (1980) *Diagnostic and statistical manual of mental disorders* (3rd ed.). Washington, DC: American Psychiatric Association.

Amsel, A. (1962) Frustrative nonreward in partial reinforcement and discrimination learning: some recent history and a theoretical extension. *Psychological Review*, 69, 306–18.

Anderson, A.C. and Liddell, H.W. (1935) Observations on experimental neurosis in sheep, *Archives of Neurological Psychiatry*, 34, 330.

Andrews, G. and Harvey, R. (1981) Does psychotherapy benefit neurotic patients? *Archives of General Psychiatry*, 38, 1203–8.

Arkowitz, H. (1992) Integrative theories of therapy. In D.K. Freedheim (ed.), *History of psychotherapy: a century of change* (pp. 261–303). Washington, DC: American Psychological Association.

Ascher, L.M. (1980) Paradoxical intention. In A. Goldstein and E.B. Foa (eds.), *Handbook of behavioral interventions* (pp. 266–321). New York: Wiley.

Azrin, N.H. and Holz, W.C. (1966) Punishment. In W.K. Honig (ed.), *Operant behavior: areas of research and application* (pp. 380–447). New York: Appleton.

Azrin, N.H. and Nunn, R.G. (1973) Habit reversal: a method of eliminating nervous habits and tics, *Behaviour Research and Therapy*, 11, 619–28.

Bachrach, A.J. (1964) Some applications of operant conditioning to behavior therapy. In J. Wolpe, A. Salter, and L.J. Reyna (eds.), *The conditioning therapies* (pp. 62–75). New York: Holt, Rinehart, & Winston.

Bachrach, A.J., Erwin, W.J., and Mohr, J.P. (1965) The control of eating behavior in an anorexic by operant conditioning techniques. In L.P. Ullmann and L. Krasner (eds.), *Case studies in behavior modification* (pp. 153–63). New York: Holt, Rinehart, & Winston.

Baer, D.M., Wolf, M.M., and Risely, T.R. (1968) Some current dimensions of applied behavior analysis, *Journal of Applied Behavior Analysis*, 1, 91–7.

Bandura, A. (1965) Vicarious processes: a case of no-trial learning. In L. Berkowitz (ed.), *Advances in experimental social psychology* (Vol. 2, pp. 1–55). New York: Academic Press.

Bandura, A. (1969) *Principles of behavior modification*. New York: Holt, Rinehart, & Winston.

Bandura, A. (1971) Psychotherapy based upon modeling principles. In A.E. Bergin and S.L. Garfield (eds.), *Handbook of psychotherapy and behavior change: an empirical analysis* (pp. 653–708). New York: Wiley.

Bandura, A. (1974) Behavior theory and the models of man. *American Psychologist*, 29, 859–69.

Bandura, A. (1977) Self-efficacy: toward a unifying theory of behavior change, *Psychological Review*, 84, 191–215.

Bandura, A. (1978) On paradigms and recycled ideologies, *Cognitive Therapy and Research*, 2, 79–103.

Bandura, A. (1982) Self-efficacy mechanism in human agency, *American Psychologist*, 37, 122–47.

Bandura, A. and Adams, N.E. (1977) Analysis of self-efficacy theory of behavior change, *Cognitive Therapy and Research*, 1, 287–308.

Bandura, A., Blanchard, E.B., and Ritter, B. (1969) The relative efficacy of desensitization and modeling approaches for inducing behavioral, affective, and attitudinal changes, *Journal of Personality and Social Psychology*, 13, 173–99.

Bandura, A., Reese, L., and Adams, N.E. (1982) Microanalysis of action and fear arousal as a function of differential levels of perceived self-efficacy, *Journal of Personality and Social Psychology*, 43, 5–21.

Barlow, D.H. (1988) *Anxiety and its disorders*. New York: Guilford.

Beck, A.T. (1963) Thinking and depression, *Archives of Clinical Psychiatry*, 9, 324–33.

Beck, A.T. (1970) Cognitive therapy: nature and relation to behavior therapy, *Behavior Therapy*, 1, 184–200.

Beck, A.T. (1972) *Depression: causes and treatment*. Philadelphia, PA: University of Pennsylvania Press.

Beck, A.T. (1976) *Cognitive therapy and the emotional disorders*. New York: International Universities Press.

Beck, A.T. and Emery, G. (1985) *Anxiety disorders and phobias: a cognitive perspective*. New York: Basic Books.

Beck, A.T. and Mahoney, M.J. (1979) Schools of 'thought,' *American Psychologist*, 34, 93–8.

Beck, A.T., Rush, A.J., Shaw, B.F., and Emery, G. (1979) *Cognitive therapy of depression: a treatment manual*. New York: Guilford.

Bellack, A.S. and Hersen, M. (1977) The use of self-report inventories in behavioral assessment. In J.D. Cone and R.P. Hawkins (eds.), *Behavioral assessment: new directions in clinical psychology* (pp. 52–76). New York: Brunner/Mazel.

Benbenishty, R. and Schul, Y. (1987) Client–therapist congruence of expectations over the course of therapy, *British Journal of Clinical Psychology*, 26, 17–24.

Bergin, A.E. (1971) The evaluation of therapeutic outcomes. In A.E. Bergin and S.L. Garfield (eds.), *Handbook of psychotherapy and behavior change: an empirical analysis* (pp. 217–70). New York: Wiley.

Bergin, A.E. and Lambert, M.J. (1978) The evaluation of therapeutic outcomes. In

A.E. Bergin and S.L. Garfield (eds.), *Handbook of psychotherapy and behavior change: an empirical analysis* (2nd ed., pp. 217–70). New York: Wiley.

Bernreuter, R.G. (1933a) The measurement of self sufficiency, *Journal of Abnormal and Social Psychology*, 28, 291–300.

Bernreuter, R.G. (1933b) The theory and construction of the personality inventory, *Journal of Social Psychology*, 4, 387–405.

Bernstein, D.A. and Paul, G.L. (1971) Some comments on therapy analogue research with small animal 'phobias,' *Journal of Behavior Therapy and Experimental Psychiatry*, 2, 225–37.

Bersh, P.J., Notterman, J.M., and Schoenfeld, W.N. (1956) Extinction of a human cardiac response during avoidance conditioning, *American Journal of Psychology*, 69, 244–51.

Bijou, S.W. (1957) Methodology for an experimental analysis of child behavior, *Psychological Reports*, 3, 161–8.

Bijou, S.W., Birnbrauer, J.S., Kidder, J.D., and Teague, C. (1966) Programmed instruction as an approach to the teaching of reading, writing, and arithmetic to retarded children, *Psychological Record*, 16, 505–22.

Birk, L. (1973) *Biofeedback: behavioral medicine*. New York: Grune & Stratton.

Birk, L. and Birk, A.W. (1974) Psychoanalysis and behavior therapy, *American Journal of Psychiatry*, 131, 499–510.

Black, A.H. (1959) Heart rate changes during avoidance learning in dogs, *Canadian Journal of Psychology*, 13, 229–42.

Blanchard, E.B., Andrasik, F., Ahles, T.A., Teders, S.J., and O'Keefe, D. (1980) Migraine and tension headache: A meta-analytic review, *Behavior Therapy*, 11, 613–31.

Blanchard, E.B., Applebaum, K.A., Radnitz, C.L., Michultka, D., Morrill, B., Kirsch, C., Hillhouse, J., Evans, D.D., Guarnieri, P., Attanasio, V., Andrasik, F., Jaccard, J., and Dentinger, M.P. (1990a) Placebo-controlled evaluation of abbreviated progressive muscle relaxation and of relaxation combined with cognitive therapy in the treatment of tension headache, *Journal of Consulting and Clinical Psychology*, 58, 210–15.

Blanchard, E.B., Applebaum, K.A., Radnitz, C.L., Morrill, B., Michultka, D., Kirsch, C., Guarnieri, P., Hillhouse, J., Evans, D.D., Jaccard, J., and Barron, K.D. (1990b) A controlled evaluation of thermal biofeedback and thermal biofeedback combined with cognitive therapy in the treatment of vascular headache, *Journal of Consulting and Clinical Psychology*, 58, 216–24.

Boring, E.G. (1940) Was this analysis a success? *Journal of Abnormal and Social Psychology*, 35, 4–10.

Borkovec, T.D. (1972) Effects of expectancy on the outcome of systematic desensitization and implosive treatments of analogue anxiety, *Behavior Therapy*, 3, 29–40.

Borkovec, T.D. (1973) The role of expectancy and physiological feedback in fear research: a review with special reference to subject characteristics, *Behavior Therapy*, 4, 491–505.

Borkovec, T.D. and Nau, S.D. (1972) Credibility of analogue therapy rationales, *Journal of Behavior Therapy and Experimental Psychiatry*, 3, 257–60.

Bowers, T.G. and Clum, G.A. (1988) Relative contribution of specific and nonspecific treatment effects: meta-analysis of placebo-controlled behavior therapy research, *Psychological Bulletin*, 103, 315–23.

Boyd, J.H., Rae, D.S., Thompson, J.W., Burns, B.J., Bourdon, K., Locke, B.Z., and

Regier, D.A. (1990) Phobia: prevalence and risk factors, *Social Psychiatry and Psychiatric Epidemiology*, 25, 314–23.

Brady, J.P. (1966) Brevital-relaxation treatment of frigidity, *Behaviour Research and Therapy*, 4, 71–7.

Breger, L. and McGaugh, J.L. (1965) Critique and reformulation of 'learning-theory' approaches to psychotherapy and neurosis, *Psychological Bulletin*, 63, 338–58.

Brownell, K.D. and Barlow, D.H. (1980) The behavioral treatment of sexual deviance. In A. Goldstein and E.B. Foa (eds.), *Handbook of behavioral interventions* (pp. 604–72). New York: Wiley & Sons.

Budzynski, T.H., Stoyva, J.M., and Pfeffer, K.E. (1980) Biofeedback techniques in psychosomatic disorders. In A. Goldstein and E.B. Foa (eds.), *Handbook of behavioral interventions: a clinical guide* (pp. 186–265). New York: Wiley & Sons.

Cannon, W.B. (1929) *Bodily changes in pain, hunger, fear, and rage*. New York: Appleton.

Carlson, N.J. and Black, A.H. (1959) Traumatic avoidance learning: Note on the effect of response prevention during extinction, *Psychological Reports*, 5, 409–12.

Cautela, J.R. (1967) Covert sensitization, *Psychological Reports*, 74, 459–68.

Cautela, J.R. (1969) Behavior therapy and self-control: techniques and implications. In C.M. Franks (ed.), *Behavior therapy: appraisal and status* (pp. 323–40). New York: McGraw-Hill.

Cautela, J.R. (1972) Covert conditioning. In A. Jacobs and L.B. Sachs (eds.), *The psychology of private events* (pp. 109–30). New York: Academic Press.

Cautela, J.R. (1990) The shaping of behavior therapy: an historical perspective, *The Behavior Therapist*, 13, 211–12.

Cautela, J.R. and Wall, C.C. (1980) Covert conditioning in clinical practice. In A. Goldstein and E.B. Foa (eds.), *Handbook of behavioral interventions* (pp. 152–85). New York: Wiley & Sons.

Chambless, D.L. and Goldstein, A. (1980) The treatment of agoraphobia. In A. Goldstein and E.B. Foa (eds.), *Handbook of behavioral interventions* (pp. 322–415). New York: Wiley & Sons.

Cheek, D.K. (1976) *Assertive black . . . puzzled white*. San Luis Obispo, CA: Impact Press.

Chomsky, N. (1959) Review of B.F. Skinner's *Verbal Behavior*. *Language*, 35, 26–58.

Cooper, J.E. (1963) A study of behaviour therapy in 30 psychiatric patients, *The Lancet*, 1, 411–15.

Cooper, J.E., Gelder, M.G., and Marks, I.M. (1965) Results of behaviour therapy in 77 psychiatric patients, *British Medical Journal*, 1, 1222–5.

Curran, J.P. (1975) Social skills training and systematic desensitization in reducing dating anxiety, *Behaviour Research and Therapy*, 13, 65–8.

Curran, J.P. (1977) Skills training as an approach to the treatment of heterosexual-social anxiety: a review, *Psychological Bulletin*, 84, 140–57.

Davison, G.C. (1968) Systematic desensitization as a counter-conditioning process, *Journal of Abnormal Psychology*, 73, 91–9.

Davison, G.C. (1976) Homosexuality: the ethical challenge, *Journal of Consulting and Clinical Psychology*, 44, 157–62.

Dawidowicz, L.S. (1989) *From that place and time*. New York: W.W. Norton.

De Charms, R., Levy, J., and Wertheimer, M. (1954) A note on attempted evaluations of psychotherapy, *Journal of Clinical Psychology*, 10, 233–5.

Dimmick, F.L., Ludlow, N., and Whiteman, A. (1939) A study of 'experimental neurosis' in cats, *Journal of Comparative Psychology*, 28, 39–43.

Distinguished Scientific Award for the Applications of Psychology: 1979 (1980), *American Psychologist*, 35, 44–51.

Dollard, J. and Miller, N.E. (1950) *Personality and psychotherapy: an analysis in terms of learning, thinking, and culture.* New York: McGraw-Hill.

Donovan, T.R. and Gershman, L. (1979) Experimental anxiety reduction: systematic desensitization versus a false-feedback expectancy manipulation, *Journal of Behavior Therapy and Experimental Psychiatry*, 10, 173–9.

Dryden, W. and Ellis, A. (1988) Rational–emotive therapy. In K.S. Dobson (ed.), *Handbook of cognitive–behavioral therapies* (pp. 214–72). New York: Guilford.

Edwards, G. (1991) *Living magically: a new vision of reality.* London: Piatkus.

Eifert, G.H., Evans, I.M., and McKendrick, V. (1990) Matching treatments to client problems not diagnostic labels: a case for paradigmatic behavior therapy, *Journal of Behavior Therapy and Experimental Psychiatry*, 21, 163–72.

Elkin, I., Parloff, M.B., Hadley, S.W., and Autrey, J.H. (1985) NIMH treatment of depression collaborative research program, *Archives of General Psychiatry*, 42, 305–16.

Elliot, R., Stiles, W.B., and Shapiro, D.A. (1993) Are some therapies more equivalent than others? In T.R. Giles (ed.), *Handbook of effective psychotherapy* (pp. 3–20). New York: Plenum.

Ellis, A. (1957) Outcome of employing three techniques of psychotherapy, *Journal of Clinical Psychology*, 13, 344–50.

Ellis, A. (1962) *Reason and emotion in psychotherapy.* New York: Lyle Stuart.

Ellis, A. (1979) On Joseph Wolpe's espousal of cognitive–behavior therapy, *American Psychologist*, 34, 98–9.

Ellis, A. (1980) Rational–emotive therapy and cognitive behavior therapy: similarities and differences, *Cognitive Therapy and Research*, 4, 325–40.

Ellis, A. (1983) The philosophic implications and dangers of some popular behavior therapy techniques. In M. Rosenbaum, C.M. Franks, and Y. Jaffe (eds.), *Perspectives on behavior therapy in the eighties* (pp. 138–51). New York: Springer.

Ellis, A. and Harper, R.A. (1965) *A new guide to rational living.* North Hollywood, CA: Wilshire.

Emmelkamp, P.M.G. (1982) Obsessive–compulsive disorders; a clinical-research approach. In I. Hand (ed.), *Obsessions and compulsions – recent advances in behavioral analysis and modification.* New York: Springer.

Emmelkamp, P.M.G. (1986) Behavior therapy with adults. In S.L. Garfield and A.E. Bergin (eds.), *Handbook of psychotherapy and behavior change* (3rd ed.). New York: Wiley.

Emmelkamp, P.M.G., Mersch, P.P., and Vissia, E. (1985) The external validity of analogue outcome research: evaluation of cognitive and behavioral interventions, *Behaviour Research and Therapy*, 23, 83–6.

Eysenck, H.J. (1952) The effects of psychotherapy: an evaluation, *Journal of Consulting Psychology*, 16, 319–24.

Eysenck, H.J. (1957) *Dynamics of anxiety and hysteria: an experimental application of modern learning theory to psychiatry.* London: Routledge & Kegan Paul.

Eysenck, H.J. (1959a) Learning theory and behaviour therapy, *Journal of Mental Science*, 105, 61–75.

200   *Joseph Wolpe*

Eysenck, H.J. (1959b) *The Maudsley Personality Inventory*. London: University of London Press.

Eysenck, H.J. (ed.) (1960) *Behaviour therapy and the neuroses: readings in modern methods of treatment derived from learning theory*. London: Pergamon.

Eysenck, H.J. (1961a) Classification and the problem of diagnosis. In H.J. Eysenck (ed.), *Handbook of abnormal psychology* (pp. 1–31). New York: Basic Books.

Eysenck, H.J. (1961b) The effects of psychotherapy. In H.J. Eysenck (ed.), *Handbook of abnormal psychology* (pp. 697–725). New York: Basic Books.

Eysenck, H.J. (1970) The classification of depressive illness, *British Journal of Psychiatry*, 117, 241–50.

Eysenck, H.J. (1978) An exercise in mega-silliness, *American Psychologist*, 33, 517.

Eysenck, H.J. (1992) The outcome problem in psychotherapy. In W. Dryden and C. Feltham (eds.), *Psychotherapy and its discontents* (pp. 124–30). Buckingham: Open University Press.

Eysenck, H.J. (1993) Forty years on: the outcome problem in psycho-therapy revisited. In T.R. Giles (ed.), *Handbook of effective psychotherapy* (pp. 3–20). New York: Plenum.

Feather, B.W. and Rhoads, J.M. (1972a) Psychodynamic behavior therapy I. Theory and rationale, *Archives of General Psychiatry*, 26, 496–502.

Feather, B.W. and Rhoads, J.M. (1972b) Psychodynamic behavior therapy II. Clinical aspects, *Archives of General Psychiatry*, 26, 503–11.

Feldman, M.P. and MacCulloch, M.J. (1965) The application of anticipatory avoidance learning to the treatment of homosexuality. 1. Theory, technique, and preliminary results, *Behaviour Research and Therapy*, 2, 165–83.

Ferster, C.B. and Skinner, B.F. (1957) *Schedules of reinforcement*. New York: Appleton-Century-Crofts.

Fisher, E.B., and Winkler, R.C. (1975) Self control over intrusive experiences, *Journal of Consulting and Clinical Psychology*, 43, 911–16.

Foa, E.B., Blau, J., Prout, M., and Latimer, P. (1977) Is horror a necessary component of flooding (implosion?), *Behaviour Research and Therapy*, 15, 397–402.

Foa, E.B., Grayson, J.B., Steketee, G., Doppelt, H.G., Turner, R.M., and Latimer, P.L. (1983) Success and failure in the behavioral treatment of obsessive-compulsives, *Journal of Consulting and Clinical Psychology*, 15, 287–97.

Fodor, I.G. (1980) The treatment of communication problems with assertiveness training. In A. Goldstein and E.B. Foa (eds.), *Handbook of behavioral interventions* (pp. 501–603). New York: Wiley & Sons.

Frank, J.D. (1961) *Persuasion and healing*. New York: Shocken Books.

Frank, J.D. (1973) *Persuasion and healing: a comparative study of psychotherapy*. Baltimore, MD: Johns Hopkins University Press.

Frankl, V.E. (1960) Paradoxical intention: a logotherapeutic technique, *American Journal of Psychotherapy*, 14, 520–35.

Franks, C.M. (1993) Archives, *The Behavior Therapist*, 16, 133.

Franks, C.M. and Rosenbaum, M. (1983) Behavior therapy: Overview and personal reflections. In M. Rosenbaum, C.M. Franks, and Y. Jaffe (eds.), *Perspectives on behavior therapy in the eighties* (pp. 3–14). New York: Springer.

Galassi, J.P., DeLo, J.S., Galassi, M.D., and Bastien, S. (1974) The College Self-Expression Scale: a measure of assertiveness, *Behavior Therapy*, 5, 165–71.

Gambrill, E.D. and Richey, C.A. (1975) An assertive inventory for use in assessment and research, *Behavior Therapy*, 6, 550–61.

Garcia, J. and Koelling, R.A. (1966) Relation of cue to consequence in avoidance learning, *Psychonomic Science*, 4, 123–4.

Garfield, S.L. (1992) Major issues in psychotherapy research. In D.K. Freedheim (ed.), *History of psychotherapy: a century of change* (pp. 335–59). Washington, DC: American Psychological Association.

Geer, J.H. (1965) The development of a scale to measure fear, *Behaviour Research and Therapy*, 3, 45–53.

Gelder, M.G. and Marks, I. (1966) Severe agoraphobia: a controlled prospective trial of behaviour therapy, *British Journal of Psychiatry*, 112, 309–19.

Gelder, M.G., Marks, I., and Wolff, H.H. (1967) Desensitization and psychotherapy in the treatment of phobic states: a controlled enquiry, *British Journal of Psychiatry*, 113, 53–73.

Gellner, E. (1992) Psychoanalysis, social role and testability. In W. Dryden and C. Feltham (eds.), *Psychotherapy and its discontents* (pp. 41–63). Buckingham: Open University Press.

Gershman, L. and Stedman, J. (1971) Oriental defense exercises as reciprocal inhibiters of anxiety, *Journal of Behavior Therapy and Experimental Psychiatry*, 2, 117–19.

Giles, T.R. (1983a) Probable superiority of behavioral interventions I: Traditional comparative outcome, *Journal of Behavior Therapy and Experimental Psychiatry*, 14, 29–32.

Giles, T.R. (1983b) Probable superiority of behavioral interventions II: Empirical status of the equivalence of therapies hypothesis, *Journal of Behavior Therapy and Experimental Psychiatry*, 14, 189–96.

Giles, T.R. (1993) Consumer advocacy and effective psychotherapy: the managed care alternative. In T.R. Giles (ed.), *Handbook of effective psychotherapy* (pp. 481–8). New York: Plenum.

Giles, T.R., Neims, D.M., and Prial, E.M. (1993) The relative efficacy of prescriptive techniques. In T.R. Giles (ed.), *Handbook of effective psychotherapy* (pp. 455–79). New York: Plenum.

Goldfried, M.R. (1971) Systematic desensitization as training in self-control, *Journal of Consulting and Clinical Psychology*, 37, 228–34.

Goldfried, M.R. (1979) Anxiety reduction through cognitive–behavioral intervention. In P. Kendall and S. Hollon (eds.), *Cognitive–behavioral interventions: theory, research, and procedures* (pp. 117–52). New York: Academic Press.

Goldfried, M.R. (ed.) (1980) Some views on effective principles of therapy, *Cognitive Therapy and Research*, 4, 271–306.

Goldfried, M.R. and Trier, C. (1974) Effectiveness of relaxation as a coping skill, *Journal of Abnormal Psychology*, 83, 348–55.

Goldiamond, I. (1975) Toward a constructional approach to social problems, *Behaviorism*, 2, 1–84.

Goldstein, A.J., Serber, M., and Piaget, J. (1970) Induced anger as a reciprocal inhibitor of fear, *Journal of Behavior Therapy and Experimental Psychiatry*, 1, 67–70.

Grencavage, L.M. and Norcross, J.C. (1990) Where are the commonalities among the therapeutic common factors? *Professional Psychology: Research and Practice*, 21, 372–8.

Grings, W.W. and Lockhart, R.A. (1966) Galvanic skin response during avoidance learning, *Psychophysiology*, 3, 29–34.

Grinker, R.R. and Spiegel, J.P. (1945) *War neuroses*. Philadelphia, PA: Blakiston.

202   Joseph Wolpe

Guthrie, E.R. (1935) *The psychology of learning.* New York: Harper.

Hain, J.D., Butcher, R.H., and Stevenson, I. (1966) Systematic desensitization therapy: an analysis of results in twenty-seven patients, *British Journal of Psychiatry*, 112, 295–307.

Harris, B. (1979) Whatever happened to Little Albert? *American Psychologist*, 34, 151–60.

Hawkins, R.M.F. (1992) Self-efficacy: a predictor but not a cause of behavior, *Journal of Behavior Therapy and Experimental Psychiatry*, 23, 251–6.

Heiby, E.M. (1986) Social versus self-control deficits in four cases of depression, *Behavior Therapy*, 17, 158–63.

Heide, F.J. and Borkovec, T.D. (1984) Relaxation-induced anxiety: mechanisms and theoretical implications, *Behaviour Research and Therapy*, 22, 1–12.

Heitler, J.B. (1976) Preparatory techniques in initiating expressive psychotherapy with lower class, unsophisticated patients, *Psychological Bulletin*, 83, 339–52.

Hersen, M. (1971) Fear scale norms for an in-patient population, *Journal of Clinical Psychology*, 27, 375–8.

Hersen, M. (1973) Self-assessment of fear, *Behavior Therapy*, 4, 241–57.

Herzberg, A. (1945) *Active psychotherapy.* New York: Grune & Stratton.

Hestand, R., Howard, D., and Gregory, R. (1971) The Willoughby Schedule: a replication, *Journal of Behavior Therapy and Experimental Psychiatry*, 2, 111–12.

Hilgard, E.R. (1956) *Theories of learning* (2nd ed.). New York: Appleton-Century-Crofts.

Hodgson, S., Rachman, S., and Marks, I. (1972) The treatment of chronic obsessive–compulsive neurosis: follow-up and further findings, *Behaviour Research and Therapy*, 10, 181–9.

Hollon, S.D. and Carter, M.M. (1994) Depression in adults. In L.W. Craighead, W.E. Craighead, A.E. Kazdin, and M.J. Mahoney (eds.), *Cognitive and behavioral interventions* (pp. 89–104). Boston: Allyn & Bacon.

Hull, C.L. (1933) *Hypnosis and suggestibility: an experimental approach.* New York: Appleton-Century.

Hull, C.L. (1943) *Principles of behavior.* New York: Appleton-Century-Crofts.

Jacobson, E. (1938) *Progressive relaxation: a psychological and clinical investigation of muscular states and their significance in psychological and medical practice.* Chicago: University of Chicago Press.

Jansson, L., Jerremalm, A., and Ost, L.G. (1986) Follow-up of agoraphobic patients treated with exposure in-vivo or applied relaxation, *British Journal of Psychiatry*, 149, 486–90.

Jensen, B.J. and Haynes, S.N. (1986) Self-report questionnaires and inventories. In A.R. Ciminero, K.S. Calhoun, and H.E. Adams (eds.), *Handbook of behavioral assessment* (2nd ed., pp. 150–75). New York: Wiley.

Jones, H.G. (1956) The application of conditioning and learning techniques to the treatment of a psychiatric patient, *Journal of Abnormal and Social Psychology*, 52, 414–19.

Jones, M.C. (1924) A laboratory study of fear. The case of Peter, *Pedigogigal Seminary*, 31, 308–15.

Kanfer, F.H. (1970) Self-regulation: research, issues, and speculations. In C. Neuringer and J.L. Michael (eds.), *Behavior modification in clinical psychology* (pp. 178–220). New York: Appleton-Century-Crofts.

Kazdin, A.E. (1979) *History of behavior modification: experimental foundations of contemporary research*. Baltimore, MD: University Park Press.

Kazdin, A.E. and Wilcoxon, L.A. (1976) Systematic desensitization and nonspecific treatment effects: a methodological evaluation, *Psychological Bulletin*, 83, 729–58.

Kazdin, A.E. and Wilson, G.T. (1978) *Evaluation of behavior therapy: issues, evidence, and research strategies*. Cambridge, MA: Ballinger.

Keefe, F.J. and Beckham, J.C. (1993) Behavioral medicine. In L.W. Craighead, W.E. Craighead, A.E. Kazdin, and M.J. Mahoney (eds.), *Cognitive and behavioral interventions: an empirical approach to mental health problems* (pp. 197–213). Boston, MA: Allyn & Bacon.

Klein, M.H., Dittman, A.T., Parloff, M.B., and Gill, M.M. (1969) Behavior therapy: observations and reflections, *Journal of Consulting and Clinical Psychology*, 33, 259–66.

Knight, R.P. (1941) Evaluation of the results of psychoanalytic therapy, *American Journal of Psychiatry*, 98, 434–46.

Koss, M.P. and Butcher, J.N. (1986) Research on brief psychotherapy. In S.L. Garfield and A.E. Bergin (eds.), *Handbook of psychotherapy and behavior change* (3rd ed., pp. 627–70). New York: Wiley.

Kruger, D.W. (1969) *The making of a nation: a history of the Union of South Africa*. London: Macmillan.

Lacey, J.I. and Lacey, B.C. (1958) Verification and extension of the principle of autonomic response specificity, *American Journal of Psychology*, 71, 50–73.

Lacey, J.I., Bateman, D.E., and VanLehn, R. (1953) Autonomic response specificity: an experimental study, *Psychosomatic Medicine*, 15, 8–21.

Lambert, M.J. and Bergin, A.E. (1992) Achievements and limitations of psychotherapy research. In D.K. Freedham (ed.), *History of psychotherapy: a century of change* (pp. 360–90). Washington, DC: American Psychological Association.

Lambert, M.J., Shapiro, D.A., and Bergin, A.E. (1986) The effectiveness of psychotherapy. In S.L. Garfield and A.E. Bergin (eds.), *Handbook of psychotherapy and behavior change* (3rd ed., pp. 157–212). New York: Wiley & Sons.

Landis, C.L. (1937) A statistical evaluation of psychotherapeutic methods. In S.E. Hinsie (ed.), *Concepts and problems in psychotherapy* (pp. 155–65). New York: Columbia University Press.

Landis, C.L. (1940) Psychoanalytic phenomena, *Journal of Abnormal and Social Psychology*, 35, 17–28.

Landman, J.T. and Dawes, R.M. (1981) Psychotherapy outcome: Smith and Glass' conclusions stand up under scrutiny, *American Psychologist*, 37, 504–16.

Lang, P.J. (1964) Experimental studies of desensitization psychotherapy. In J. Wolpe, A. Salter, and L.J. Reyna (eds.), *The conditioning therapies* (pp. 38–50). New York: Holt, Rinehart, & Winston.

Lang, P.J. (1968) Fear reduction and fear behavior: problems in treating a construct. In J.M. Shlien (ed.), *Research in psychotherapy* (Vol. 3, pp. 90–102). Washington, DC: American Psychological Association.

Lang, P.J. (1969) The mechanics of desensitization and the laboratory study of human fear. In C.M. Franks (ed.), *Behavior therapy: appraisal and status* (pp. 160–91). New York: McGraw-Hill.

Lang, P.J. and Lazovik, A.D. (1963) The experimental desensitization of a phobia, *Journal of Abnormal and Social Psychology*, 66, 519–25.

Lang, P.J., Lazovik, A.D., and Reynolds, D.J. (1965) Desensitization, suggestibility, and pseudo-therapy, *Journal of Abnormal Psychology*, 70, 395–402.

Lange, A.J. and Jakubowski, P. (1976) *Responsible assertive behavior: cognitive/behavioral procedures for trainers.* Champaign, IL: Research Press.

Lazarus, A.A. (1958) New methods in psychotherapy: a case study, *South African Medical Journal*, 32, 660–4.

Lazarus, A.A. (1961) Group therapy of phobic disorder by systematic desensitization, *Journal of Abnormal and Social Psychology*, 63, 505–10.

Lazarus, A.A. (1963) The results of behavior therapy in 126 cases of severe neurosis, *Behaviour Research and Therapy*, 1, 69–79.

Lazarus, A.A. (1964) Crucial procedural factors in desensitization therapy, *Behaviour Research and Therapy*, 2, 65–70.

Lazarus, A.A. (1966) Broad-spectrum behaviour therapy and the treatment of agoraphobia, *Behaviour Research and Therapy*, 4, 95–7.

Lazarus, A.A. (1967) In support of technical eclecticism, *Psychological Reports*, 21, 415–16.

Lazarus, A.A. (1971) *Behavior therapy and beyond.* New York: McGraw-Hill.

Lazarus, A.A. (1973) Multimodal behavior therapy: treating the BASIC ID, *Journal of Nervous and Mental Disease*, 156, 404–11.

Lazarus, A.A. (1974) Desensitization and cognitive restructuring, *Psychotherapy: Theory, Research, and Practice*, 11, 98–102.

Lazarus, A.A. (1976) *Multimodal behavior therapy.* New York: Springer.

Lazarus, A.A. (1977) Has behavior therapy outlived its usefulness? *American Psychologist*, 32, 550–4.

Lazarus, A.A. (1980) Toward delineating some causes of change in psychotherapy, *Professional Psychotherapy*, 11, 863–70.

Lazarus, A.A. and Abramovitz, A. (1962) The use of 'emotive imagery' in the treatment of children's phobias, *Journal of Mental Science*, 108, 191–5.

Lazarus, A.A. and Rachman, S.J. (1957) The use of systematic desensitization in psychotherapy, *South African Medical Journal*, 31, 934–7.

Lazarus, A.A. and Rachman, S.J. (1960) The use of systematic desensitization in psychotherapy. In H.J. Eysenck (ed.), *Behaviour therapy and the neuroses.* London: Pergamon.

Lazarus, R.S. and Folkman, S. (1984) *Stress, appraisal, and coping.* New York: Springer.

Lazovik, A.D. and Lang, P.J. (1960) A laboratory demonstration of systematic desensitization psychotherapy, *Journal of Psychological Studies*, 11, 238–47.

Lee, C. (1989) Theoretical weaknesses lead to practical problems: the example of self-efficacy theory, *Journal of Behavior Therapy and Experimental Psychiatry*, 20, 115–23.

Leitenberg, H., Agras, S., Butz, R., and Wincze, J. (1971) Relationship between heart rate and behavioral change during treatment of phobia, *Journal of Abnormal Psychology*, 78, 59–68.

Levis, D.J. (1980) Implementing the technique of implosive therapy. In A. Goldstein and E.B. Foa (eds.), *Handbook of behavioral interventions* (pp. 92–151). New York: Wiley & Sons.

Levis, D.J. and Boyd, T.L. (1985) The CS exposure approach of implosive (flooding) therapy. In R.M. Turner and L.M. Ascher (eds.), *Evaluating behavior therapy outcome* (pp. 56–94). New York: Springer.

Levis, D.J. and Hare, N. (1977) A review of the theoretical, rational and empirical support for the extinction approach of implosive (flooding) therapy. In M. Hersen, R.M. Eisler, and P.M. Miller (eds.), *Progress in behavior modification* (pp. 152–202). New York: Academic Press.

Ley, R. (1985) Agoraphobia, the panic attack, and the hyperventilation syndrome, *Behaviour Research and Therapy*, 23, 79–81.

Ley, R. (1987) Panic disorder and agoraphobia: fear of fear or fear of the symptoms produced by hyperventilation? *Journal of Behavior Therapy and Experimental Psychiatry*, 18, 305–16.

Lick, J.R., Sushinsky, L.W., and Malow, R. (1977) Specificity of fear survey schedule item and the prediction of avoidance behavior, *Behavior Modification*, 1, 195–203.

Liddell, H.S. (1964) The challenge of Pavlovian conditioning and experimental neurosis in animals. In J. Wolpe, A. Salter, and L.J. Reyna (eds.), *The conditioning therapies* (pp. 127–47). New York: Holt, Rinehart, & Winston.

Lindsley, O.R. (1956) Characteristics of the behavior of chronic psychotics as revealed by the free operant conditioning methods, *Diseases of the Nervous System, Monograph Supplement*, 21, 66–78.

Llewelyn, S.P. (1988) Psychological therapy as viewed by clients and therapists, *British Journal of Clinical Psychology*, 27, 223–37.

Lohr, J.M., Kleinknecht, R.A., Conley, A.T., DalCerro, S., Schmidt, J., and Sontag, M.E. (1992) A methodological critique of the current status of Eye Movement Desensitization (EMD), *Journal of Behavior Therapy and Experimental Psychiatry*, 23, 159–68.

London, P. (1972) The end of ideology in behavior modification, *American Psychologist*, 27, 913–20.

LoPiccolo, J. (1977) From psychotherapy to sex therapy, *Society*, 14, 60–8.

Luborsky, L. (1954) A note on Eysenck's article 'The effects of psychotherapy: an evaluation,' *British Journal of Psychology*, 45, 129–31.

Luborsky, L., Singer, B., and Luborsky, L. (1975) Comparative studies of psychotherapy: is it true that 'everyone has won and all must have prizes?' *Archives of General Psychiatry*, 32, 995–1008.

Mahoney, M.J. (1971) The self-management of covert behavior: a case study, *Behavior Therapy*, 2, 575–8.

Mahoney, M.J. (1977) Reflections on the cognitive-learning trend in psychotherapy, *American Psychologist*, 32, 5–13.

Mahoney, M.J. and Thoreson, C.E. (1974) *Self-control: power to the person.* Monterey, CA: Brooks/Cole.

Maier, S.E., Seligman, M.E.P., and Solomon, R.L. (1970) Pavlovian fear conditioning and learned helplessness. In B.A. Campbell and R.M. Church (eds.), *Punishment* (pp. 299–342). New York: Appleton-Century-Crofts.

Malinowski, B. (1927) *Sex and repression in savage society.* London: K. Paul, Trench,Trubner, & Co.

Marks, I.M. (1978) Behavioral psychotherapy of adult neurosis. In A.E. Bergin and S.L. Garfield (eds.), *Handbook of psychotherapy and behavior change: an empirical analysis* (2nd ed., pp. 493–547). New York: Wiley.

Marks, I.M. and Gelder, M.G. (1965) A controlled retrospective study of behaviour therapy in phobic patients, *British Journal of Psychiatry*, 111, 561–73.

Marks, I.M. and Gelder, M.G. (1966) Common ground between behaviour therapy and psychodynamic methods, *British Journal of Medical Psychology*, 39, 11–23.

Marmor, J. (1969) Neurosis and the psychotherapeutic process: similarities and differences in the behavioral and psychodynamic conceptions, *International Journal of Psychiatry*, 7, 514–19.

Marmor, J. (1971) Dynamic psychotherapy and behavior therapy: are they irreconcilable? *Archives of General Psychiatry*, 24, 22–8.

Marmor, J. (1980) Recent trends in psychotherapy, *American Journal of Psychiatry*, 137, 409–16.

Marshall, W.L., Gauthier, J., Christie, M., Currie, D., and Gordin, A. (1977) Flooding therapy: effectiveness, stimulus characteristics, and the value of brief in vivo exposure, *Behaviour Research and Therapy*, 15, 79–87.

Masserman, J. (1943) *Behavior and neurosis*. Chicago: University of Chicago Press.

Masson, J. (1988) *Against therapy: emotional tyranny and the myth of psychological healing*. New York: Atheneum.

Masson, J. (1992) The tyranny of psychotherapy. In W. Dryden and C.Feltham (eds.), *Psychotherapy and its discontents* (pp. 7–29). Buckingham: Open University Press.

Masters, W.H. and Johnson, V.E. (1966) *Human sexual response*. Boston, MA: Little, Brown Co.

Masters, W.H. and Johnson, V.E. (1970) *Human sexual inadequacy*. Boston, MA: Little, Brown Co.

Mays, D.T., and Franks, C.M. (1985) *Negative outcomes in psychotherapy*. New York: Springer.

McFall, R.M. and Twentyman, C. (1973) Four experiments on the relative contribution of rehearsal, modeling and coaching to assertion training, *Journal of Abnormal Psychology*, 81, 199–218.

McGlynn, F.D. (1971) Experimental desensitization following three types of instructions, *Behaviour Research and Therapy*, 9, 367–9.

McGuire, R.J. and Vallance, M. (1964) Aversion therapy by electric shock, a simple technique, *British Medical Journal*, 1, 151–2.

McKnight, D.L., Nelson, R.O., Hayes, S.C., and Jarrett, R.B. (1984) Importance of treating individually assessed response classes in the amelioration of depression, *Behavior Therapy*, 15, 315–35.

Meehl, P. (1954) *Clinical versus statistical prediction*. Minneapolis, MN: University of Minnesota Press.

Meichenbaum, D.H. (1973) Cognitive factors in behavior modification: modifying what clients say to themselves. In C.M. Franks and G.T. Wilson (eds.), *Annual review of behavior therapy* (Vol. 1, pp. 416–31). New York: Brunner/Mazel.

Meichenbaum, D.H. (1977) *Cognitive behavior modification: an integrative approach*. New York: Plenum Press.

Meichenbaum, D.H. and Cameron, R. (1974) The clinical potential of modifying what clients say to themselves. In C. Thoreson and M. Mahoney (eds.), *Self-control: power to the person*. Monterey, CA: Brooks/Cole.

Mersch, P.P.A., Emmelkamp, P.M.G., Bogels, S.M. and van der Sleen, J. (1989) Social phobia: individual response patterns and the effects of behavioral and cognitive interventions, *Behaviour Research and Therapy*, 27, 421–34.

Meyer, V. (1957) The treatment of two phobic patients on the basis of learning principles, *Journal of Abnormal and Social Psychology*, 55, 261–6.

Meyer, V, and Crisp, A.H. (1966) Some problems in behaviour therapy, *British Journal of Psychiatry*, 112, 367–81.

Miller, G.A., Galanter, E., and Pribram, K.H. (1960) *Plans and the structure of behavior*. New York: Holt, Rinehart, & Winston.

Miller, N.E. (1948) Studies of fear as an acquirable drive: I. Fear as motivation and fear-reduction as reinforcement in the learning of new responses, *Journal of Experimental Psychology*, 38, 89–101.

Miller, N.E. (1951) Learnable drives and rewards. In S.S. Stevens (ed.), *Handbook of experimental psychology* (pp. 435–72). New York: Wiley.

Miller, R.E., Murphy, J.V., and Mirsky, I.A. (1957) Persistent effects of chlorpromazine on extinction of an avoidance response, *Archives of Neurological Psychiatry*, 78, 526–32.

Miller, S.B. (1972) The contribution of therapeutic instructions to systematic desensitization, *Behaviour Research and Therapy*, 10, 159–70.

Mitchell, K.R. and Mitchell, D.M. (1971) Migraine: an exploratory treatment application of programmed behavior therapy techniques, *Journal of Psychosomatic Research*, 15, 137–57.

Moore, N. (1965) Behavior therapy in bronchial asthma: a controlled study, *Journal of Psychosomatic Research*, 9, 257–76.

Moreno, J.L. (1946) *Psychodrama*. New York: Beacon House.

Morris, R.J. and Suckerman, K.R. (1974) The importance of therapeutic relationship in systematic desensitization, *Journal of Consulting and Clinical Psychology*, 42, 148.

Mowrer, O.H. (1939) A stimulus–response analysis of anxiety and its role as a reinforcing agent, *Psychological Review*, 45, 553–65.

Mowrer, O.H. (1940) Anxiety reduction and learning, *Journal of Experimental Psychology*, 27, 497–516.

Mowrer, O.H. (1947) On the dual nature of learning: a re-interpretation of 'conditioning' and 'problem solving', *Harvard Educational Review*, 17, 102–48.

Mowrer, O.H. (1950) *Learning theory and personality dynamics*. New York: Ronald Press.

Mowrer, O.H. (1960) *Learning theory and behavior*. New York: Wiley.

Mowrer, O.H. and Viek, P. (1948) An experimental analogue of fear from a sense of helplessness, *Journal of Abnormal and Social Psychology*, 83, 193–200.

Murray, M.E. (1976) A dynamic synthesis of analytic and behavioral approaches to symptoms, *American Journal of Psychotherapy*, 30, 561–9.

Neisser, U. (1967) *Cognitive psychology*. New York: Appleton-Century-Crofts.

Nelson, R.O. (1976) Methodological issues in assessment via self-monitoring. In J.D. Cone and R.P. Hawkins (eds.), *Behavioral assessment: new directions in clinical psychology* (pp. 217–40). New York: Brunner/Mazel.

Notterman, J.M., Schoenfeld, W.N., and Bersh, P.J. (1952) Conditioned heart rate in humans during experimental anxiety, *Journal of Comparative and Physiological Psychology*, 45, 1–4.

Packer, M.J. (1985) Hermeneutic inquiry in the study of human conduct, *American Psychologist*, 40, 1081–93.

Page, H.A. (1955) The facilitation of experimental extinction by response prevention as a function of the acquisition of a new response, *Journal of Comparative and Physiological Psychology*, 48, 14–16.

Paul, G.L. (1966) *Insight vs. desensitization in psychotherapy*. Stanford, CA: Stanford University Press.

Paul, G.L. (1967a) Insight versus desensitization in psychotherapy two years after termination, *Journal of Consulting Psychology*, 31, 333–48.

Paul, G.L. (1967b) Strategy of outcome research in psychotherapy, *Journal of Consulting Psychology*, 31, 109–18.

Paul, G.L. (1968) Two-year follow-up of systematic desensitization in therapy groups, *Journal of Abnormal and Social Psychology*, 73, 119–30.

Paul, G.L. (1969) Outcome of systematic desensitization I: Background, procedures, and uncontrolled reports of individual treatment. In C.M. Franks (ed.), *Behavior therapy: appraisal and status* (pp. 63–104). New York: McGraw-Hill.

Paul, G.L. and Shannon, D.T. (1966) Treatment of anxiety through systematic desensitization in therapy groups, *Journal of Abnormal and Social Psychology*, 71, 124–35.

Pavlov, I.P. (1927/1960) *Conditioned reflexes* (translated by G.V. Anrep). New York: Dover Publications.

Pekarik, G. (1993) Beyond effectiveness: uses of consumer-oriented criteria in defining treatment success. In T.R. Giles (ed.), *Handbook of effective psychotherapy* (pp. 409–36). New York: Plenum.

Persons, J.B. (1986) The advantages of studying psychological phenomena rather than psychiatric diagnoses, *American Psychologist*, 41, 1252–60.

Persons, J.B. (1991) Psychotherapy outcome studies do not accurately represent current models of psychotherapy: a proposed remedy, *American Psychologist*, 46, 99–106.

Phelps, S. and Austin, N. (1975) *The assertive woman*. San Luis Obispo, CA: Impact Press.

Plaud, J.J. and Vogeltanz, N. (1991) Behavior therapy: lost ties to animal research, *The Behavior Therapist*, 14, 89–93.

Polin, A.T. (1959) The effects of flooding and physical suppression as extinction techniques on an anxiety motivated avoidance locomotor response, *Journal of Psychology*, 47, 235–45.

Pomerleau, O.F. and Brady, J.P. (1979) Introduction: the scope and promise of behavioral medicine. In O.F. Pomerleau and J.P. Brady (eds.), *Behavioral medicine: theory and practice* (pp. xi–xxvi). Baltimore, MA: Williams & Wilkins.

Poppen, R. (1970) Counterconditioning of conditioned suppression in rats, *Psychological Reports*, 27, 659–71.

Poppen, R. (1976) Review of R.B. Sloane, F.R. Staples, A.H. Cristol, N.J. Yorkston, and K. Whipple (eds.), *Psychotherapy Vs. Behavior Therapy*, *Journal of Behavior Therapy and Experimental Psychiatry*, 7, 101.

Poppen, R. (1988) *Behavioral relaxation training and assessment*. New York: Pergamon Press.

Potter, S. (1971) *The complete upmanship* [including *Lifemanship* and *Gamesmanship*]. New York: Holt, Rinehart, & Winston.

Rachman, S. (1966a) Studies in desensitization – III: Speed of generalization, *Behaviour Research and Therapy*, 4, 7–15.

Rachman, S. (1966b) Studies in desensitization – II: Flooding, *Behaviour Research and Therapy*, 4, 1–6.

Rachman, S. (1971) *The effects of psychotherapy*. Oxford: Pergamon Press.

Rachman, S. (1973) The effects of psychological treatment. In H.J. Eysenck (ed.), *Handbook of abnormal psychology* (pp. 805–61). New York: Basic Books.

Rachman, S. and Eysenck, H.J. (1966) Reply to a 'critique and reformulation' of behavior therapy, *Psychological Bulletin*, 65, 165–9.

Rachman, S. and Hodgson, R. (1974) Synchrony and desynchrony in fear and avoidance: 1, *Behaviour Research and Therapy*, 12, 311–18.

Rachman, S. and Hodgson, R. (1980) *Obsessions and compulsions*. Englewood Cliffs, NJ: Prentice-Hall.

Rathus, S.A. (1973) A 30-item schedule for assessing assertive behavior, *Behavior Therapy*, 4, 398–406.

Rescorla, R.A. (1988) Pavlovian conditioning: it's not what you think it is, *American Psychologist*, 43, 151–60.

Reyna, L.J. (1946) Experimental extinction as a function of the interval between extinction trials. Unpublished doctoral dissertation, University of Iowa.

Rimm, D.C. (1973) Thought stopping and covert assertion in the treatment of phobias, *Journal of Consulting and Clinical Psychology*, 41, 466–7.

Rimm, D.C. (1977) Assertive training and the expression of anger. In R.E. Alberti (ed.), *Assertiveness: innovations, applications, issues* (pp. 83–92). San Luis Obispo, CA: Impact Press.

Rimm, D.C. and Masters, J.C. (1979) *Behavior therapy: techniques and empirical findings* (2nd ed.). New York: Academic Press.

Robins, L.N., Helzer, J.E., Weissman, M.M., Orvaxchel, H., Gruenberg, E., Burke, J.D. Jr., and Regier, D.A. (1984) Lifetime prevalence of specific psychiatric disorders in three sites, *Archives of General Psychiatry*, 41, 949–58.

Rosenthal, T.L. and Bandura, A. (1978) Psychological modeling: theory and practice. In S.L. Garfield and A.E. Bergin (eds.), *Handbook of psychotherapy and behavior change* (2nd ed., pp. 621–58). New York: Wiley.

Rosenzweig, S. (1936) Some implicit common factors in diverse methods of psychotherapy, *American Journal of Orthopsychiatry*, 6, 412–15.

Rosenzweig, S. (1954) A transvaluation of psychotherapy: a reply to Eysenck, *Journal of Abnormal Psychology*, 49, 298–304.

Rubin, M. (1972) Verbally suggested responses as reciprocal inhibition of anxiety, *Journal of Behavior Therapy and Experimental Psychiatry*, 3, 273–7.

Rush, A.S., Beck, A.T., Kovacs, M., and Hollon, S. (1977) Comparative efficacy of cognitive therapy and pharmacotherapy in the treatment of depressed outpatients, *Cognitive Therapy and Research*, 1, 17–37.

Ryle, G. (1949) *The concept of mind*. London: Hutchinson.

Sabaliunas, L. (1990) *Lithuanian social democracy in perspective, 1893–1914*. Durham, NC: Duke University Press.

Sallis, J.F., Lichstein, K.L., and McGlynn, F.D. (1980) Anxiety response patterns: a comparison of clinical and analogue populations, *Journal of Behavior Therapy and Experimental Psychiatry*, 11, 179–83.

Salter, A. (1944) *What is hypnosis?: studies in auto and hetero conditioning*. New York: R.R. Smith.

Salter, A. (1949) *Conditioned reflex therapy: the direct approach to the reconstruction of personality*. New York: Creative Age Press.

Schwartz, B. and Reisberg, D. (1991) *Learning and memory*. New York: W.W. Norton.

Seagraves, R.T. and Smith, R.C. (1976) Concurrent psychotherapy and behavior therapy: treatment of psychoneurotic outpatients, *Archives of General Psychiatry*, 33, 756–63.

Searles, J.S. (1985) A methodological and empirical critique of psychotherapy outcome meta-analysis, *Behaviour Research and Therapy*, 23, 453–63.

Seiden, D.Y. (1994) Behavior and cognitive therapies in France: an oral history, *Journal of Behavior Therapy and Experimental Psychiatry*, 25, 105–12.

Seligman, M.E.P. (1971) Phobias and preparedness, *Behavior Therapy*, 2, 307–20.

Selye, H. (1956/1976) *The stress of life*. New York: McGraw-Hill.

Semans, J.H. (1956) Premature ejaculation, a new approach, *Southern Medical Journal*, 49, 353–7.

Serber, M. (1972) Teaching the nonverbal components of assertive training, *Journal of Behavior Therapy and Experimental Psychiatry*, 3, 179–83.

Shapiro, D.A. and Shapiro, D. (1977) The 'double standard' in evaluation of psychotherapies, *Bulletin of the British Psychological Society*, 30, 209–10.

Shapiro, D.A. and Shapiro, D. (1982) Meta-analysis of comparative therapy outcome studies: a replication and refinement, *Psychological Bulletin*, 92, 581–604.

Shapiro, F. (1989a) Eye movement desensitization: A new treatment for post-traumatic stress disorder, *Journal of Behavior Therapy and Experimental Psychiatry*, 20, 211–17.

Shapiro, F. (1989b) Efficacy of the eye movement desensitization procedures in the treatment of traumatic memories, *Journal of Traumatic Stress*, 2, 199–23.

Shapiro, M.B. (1957) Experimental method in the psychological description of the individual psychiatric patient, *International Journal of Social Psychiatry*, 3, 89–102.

Shelton, J.L. (1973) Murder strikes and panic follows – can behavior modification help? *Behavior Therapy*, 4, 706–8.

Silver, B.V. and Blanchard, E.B. (1978) Biofeedback and relaxation training in the treatment of psychophysiological disorders: or are the machines really necessary? *Journal of Behavioral Medicine*, 1, 217–39.

Skinner, B.F. (1938) *The behavior of organisms: an experimental analysis*. New York: Appleton-Century.

Skinner, B.F. (1948) *Walden Two*. New York: Macmillan.

Skinner, B.F. (1950) Are theories of learning necessary? *Psychological Review*, 57, 193–216.

Skinner, B.F. (1953) *Science and human behavior*. New York: Macmillan.

Skinner, B.F., Solomon, H.C., and Lindsley, O.G. (1953) *Studies in behavior therapy*. Metropolitan State Hospital, Waltham, MA: Status Report No. 1.

Sloane, R.B., Staples, F.R., Cristol, A.H., Yorkston, N.J., and Whipple, K. (1975) *Psychotherapy versus behavior therapy*. Cambridge, MA: Harvard University Press.

Smith, M.L. and Glass, G.V. (1977) Meta-analysis of psychotherapy outcome studies. *American Psychologist*, 32, 752–60.

Smith, M.L., Glass, G.V., and Miller, T.I. (1980) *The benefits of psychotherapy*. Baltimore, MD: Johns Hopkins University Press.

Solomon, R.L. and Wynne, L.C. (1954) Traumatic avoidance learning: the principles of anxiety conservation and partial irreversibility, *Psychological Review*, 61, 353–85.

Solomon, R.L., Kamin, L.J., and Wynne, L.C. (1953) Traumatic avoidance learning: the outcome of several extinction procedures with dogs, *Journal of Abnormal and Social Psychology*, 48, 291–302.

Solyom, L. and Miller, S.A. (1965) A differential conditioning procedure as the initial phase of the behaviour therapy of homosexuality, *Behaviour Research and Therapy*, 3, 147–60.

Sparks, A. (1990) *The mind of South Africa*. New York: Knopf.

Speilberger, C.D., Gorsuch, R.L., and Lushene, R.E. (1970) *Manual for the state-trait anxiety inventory*. Palo Alto, CA: Counseling Psychologist Press.

Spence, K.W. and Taylor, J.A. (1953) The relation of conditioned response strength to anxiety in normal, neurotic, and psychotic subjects, *Journal of Experimental Psychology*, 45, 265–72.

Spiegler, M.D. and Guevremont, D.C. (1992) *Contemporary behavior therapy* (2nd ed.). Pacific Grove, CA: Brooks/Cole.

Stampfl, T.G. and Levis, D.G. (1967) Essentials of implosive therapy: a learning-theory-based psychodynamic behavioral therapy, *Journal of Abnormal Psychology*, 72, 496–503.

Stampfl, T.G. and Levis, D.G. (1968) Implosive therapy – A behavioral therapy? *Behaviour Research and Therapy*, 6, 31–6.

Steketee, G.S., Foa, E.B., and Grayson, J.B. (1982) Recent advances in the behavioral treatment of obsessive–compulsives, *Archives of General Psychiatry*, 39, 1365–71.

Stern, R.S. and Marks, I.M. (1973) A comparison of brief and prolonged flooding in agoraphobics, *Archives of General Psychiatry*, 28, 210.

Stevenson, I. and Wolpe, J. (1960) Recovery from sexual deviation through overcoming non-sexual neurotic responses, *American Journal of Psychiatry*, 116, pp. 737–42.

Stiles, W.G., Shapiro, D.A., and Eliot, R. (1986) Are all psychotherapies equivalent? *American Psychologist*, 41, 165–80.

Stoltz, S.B. (1977) *Report of the American Psychological Association Commission on Behavior Modification*. Washington, DC: American Psychological Association.

Strupp, H.H. (1978) Psychotherapy research and practice: an overview. In A.E. Bergin and S.L. Garfield (eds.), *Handbook of psychotherapy and behavior change: an empirical analysis* (2nd ed., pp. 3–22). New York: Wiley.

Strupp, H.H. (1982) The outcome problem in psychotherapy: contemporary perspectives. In J. Harvey and M. Parks (eds.), *Psychotherapy research and behavior change*. Washington, DC: American Psychological Association.

Strupp, H.H. and Howard, K.I. (1992) A brief history of psychotherapy research. In D.K. Freedheim (ed.), *History of psychotherapy: a century of change* (pp. 309–34). Washington, DC: American Psychological Association.

Stuart, R.B. (1969) Operant-interpersonal treatment for marital discord, *Journal of Consulting and Clinical Psychology*, 33, 675–82.

Subcommittee on Constitutional Rights, Committee on the Judiciary, United States Senate, 93rd Congress (1974) *Individual rights and the federal role in behavior modification*. Washington, DC: US Government Printing Office.

Suinn, R.M. (1974) Behavior therapy for cardiac patients, *Behavior Therapy*, 5, 569–71.

Suinn, R.M. (1990) *Anxiety management training: a behavior therapy*. New York: Plenum.

Suinn, R.M. and Richardson, F. (1971) Anxiety management training: a non-specific behavior therapy program for anxiety control, *Behavior Therapy*, 2, 498.

Sullivan, B.J. and Denny, D.R. (1977) Expectancy and phobic level: effects on desensitization, *Journal of Consulting and Clinical Psychology*, 45, 763–71.

Taylor, J.G. (1962) *The behavioral basis of perception*. New Haven, CT: Yale University Press.

Thoreson, C.E. and Mahoney, M.J. (1974) *Behavioral self-control*. New York: Holt, Rinehart, & Winston.

Thorpe, J.G., Schmidt, E., Brown, P.T., and Castell, D. (1964) Aversion relief

212 Joseph Wolpe

therapy: a new method for general application, *Behaviour Research and Therapy*, 2, 71–82.

Thurstone, L.L. and Thurstone, T.G. (1930) A neurotic inventory, *Journal of Social Psychology*, 1, 3–30.

Tori, C. and Worell, L. (1973) Reduction of human avoidant behavior: a comparison of counterconditioning, expectancy and cognitive information approaches. *Journal of Consulting and Clinical Psychology*, 41, 269–78.

Tryon, W.W. (1993a) Neural networks: I. Theoretical unification through connectionism, *Clinical Psychology Review*, 13, 341–52.

Tryon, W.W. (1993b) Neural networks: II. Unified learning theory and behavioral psychotherapy, *Clinical Psychology Review*, 13, 353–71.

Turkat, I.D. (1986) The behavioral interview. In A.R. Ciminero, K.S. Calhoun, and H.E. Adams (eds.), *Handbook of behavioral assessment* (2nd ed., pp. 109–49). New York: Wiley.

Turner, R.M., DiTomasso, R.A., and Murray, M.R. (1980) Psychometric analysis of the Willoughby personality schedule, *Journal of Behavior Therapy and Experimental Psychiatry*, 11, 185–94.

Ullman, L.P. and Krasner, L. (eds.) (1965) *Case studies in behavior modification.* New York: Holt, Rinehart, & Winston.

Valentine, C.W. (1943) *Psychology of early childhood: a study of mental development in the first years of life.* London: Methuen.

Valins, S. and Ray, A. (1967) Effects of cognitive desensitization on avoidance behavior, *Journal of Personality and Social Psychology*, 7, 345–50.

Vitz, P. (1977) *Psychology as religion: the cult of self-worship.* Grand Rapids, MI: Eerdmans.

Voegtlin, W. and Lemere, F. (1942) The treatment of alcohol addiction, *Quarterly Journal of Studies on Alcohol*, 2, 717–803.

Walker, E.A. (1957) *A history of southern Africa* (3rd ed.). London: Longmans, Green.

Warren, R. and McLellarn, R.W. (1982) Systematic desensitization as a treatment for maladaptive anger and aggression: a review, *Psychological Reports*, 50, 1095–102.

Watson, J.B. (1913) Psychology as the behaviorist views it, *Psychological Review*, 20, 158–77.

Watson, J.B. and Rayner, R. (1920) Conditioned emotional reactions, *Journal of Experimental Psychology*, 3, 1–4.

Weitzman, B. (1967) Behavior therapy and psychotherapy, *Psychological Review*, 74, 300–17.

Wilkins, W. (1971) Desensitization: social and cognitive factors underlying the effectiveness of Wolpe's procedure, *Psychological Bulletin*, 76, 311–17.

Willoughby, R.R. (1932) Some properties of the Thurstone Personality Schedule and a suggested revision, *Journal of Social Psychology*, 3, 401–24.

Willoughby, R.R. (1934) Norms for the Clark–Thurstone Inventory, *Journal of Social Psychology*, 5, 91–102.

Wilson, G.T. (1981) Behavior therapy as a short-term therapeutic approach. In S.H. Budman (ed.), *Forms of brief therapy* (pp. 131–66). New York: Guilford.

Wilson, G.T. and Evans, W.I.M. (1967) Behavior therapy and not the behavior 'therapies,' *AABT Newsletter*, 2, 5–7.

Wilson, G.T. and Rachman, S. (1983) Meta-analysis and the evaluation of psychotherapy outcome: limitations and liabilities, *Journal of Consulting and Clinical Psychology*, 51, 54–64.

Wittrock, D.A., Blanchard, E.B. and McCoy, G.C. (1988) Three studies on the relation of process to outcome in the treatment of essential hypertension with relaxation and thermal biofeedback, *Behaviour Research and Therapy*, 26, 53–66.

Wolberg, L. (1948) *Medical Hypnosis*. New York: Grune & Stratton.

Wolf, S. and Wolff, H.G. (1947) *Human gastric functions*. New York: Oxford.

Wolff, H.G. (1950) Life stress and cardiovascular disorders, *Circulation*, 1, 187–93.

Wolpe, J. (1948) An approach to the problem of neurosis based on the conditioned response. Unpublished MD thesis, University of the Witwatersrand.

Wolpe, J. (1949) An interpretation of the effects of combinations of stimuli (patterns) based on current neurophysiology, *Psychological Review*, 56, 277–83.

Wolpe, J. (1950) Need-reduction, drive-reduction, and reinforcement: a neurophysiological view, *Psychological Review*, 57, 19–26.

Wolpe, J. (1952a) Experimental neuroses as learned behaviour, *British Journal of Psychology*, 43, 243–68.

Wolpe, J. (1952b) Objective psychotherapy of the neuroses, *South African Medical Journal*, 26, 825–9.

Wolpe, J. (1952c) Primary stimulus generalization: a neurophysiological view, *Psychological Review*, 59, 8–10.

Wolpe, J. (1952d) The neurophysiology of learning and delayed reward learning, *Psychological Review*, 59, 192–9.

Wolpe, J. (1952e) Formation of negative habits: a neurophysiological view, *Psychological Review*, 59, 290–9.

Wolpe, J. (1953a) Learning theory and 'abnormal fixations,' *Psychological Review*, 60, 111–15.

Wolpe, J. (1953b) Theory construction for Blodgett's latent learning, *Psychological Review*, 60, 340–4.

Wolpe, J. (1954) Reciprocal inhibition as the main basis of psychotherapeutic effects, *Archives of Neurologic Psychiatry*, 72, 205–26.

Wolpe, J. (1955) The significance for psychotherapy of some animal experiments, *Leech*, 25, 31–3.

Wolpe, J. (1956a) Learning versus lesions as the basis of neurotic behavior, *American Journal of Psychiatry*, 112, 923–31.

Wolpe, J. (1956b) New facts and old misconceptions about neuroses, *South African Medical Journal*, 30, 542–4.

Wolpe, J. (1958) *Psychotherapy by reciprocal inhibition*. Stanford, CA: Stanford University Press.

Wolpe, J. (1960a) Truth about psychoanalysis, *British Medical Journal*, May 28, 1659.

Wolpe, J. (1960b) Efficacy of psychoanalysis, *British Medical Journal*, November 16, 1601.

Wolpe, J. (1961a) The claims of psychoanalysis, *New Statesman*, April 14, 584–5.

Wolpe, J. (1961b) Pavlov or Freud, *Lancet*, April 15, 824–5.

Wolpe, J. (1961c) The prognosis in unpsychoanalyzed recovery from neurosis, *American Journal of Psychiatry*, 117, 35–9.

Wolpe, J. (1963a) Psychotherapy: the nonscientific heritage and the new science, *Behaviour Research and Therapy*, 1, 23–38.

Wolpe, J. (1963b) Behavior therapy, *Lancet*, 1, 886–7.

Wolpe, J. (1963c) Quantitative relationships in the systematic desensitization of phobias, *American Journal of Psychiatry*, 119, 1062–8.

Wolpe, J. (1964a) Behaviour therapy in complex neurotic states, *British Journal of Psychiatry*, 110, 28–34.

Wolpe, J. (1964b) The resolution of neurotic suffering by behavioristic methods, *American Journal of Psychotherapy*, 18 (Supplement No. 1).

Wolpe, J. (1964c) Behavior therapy and publicity, *Canadian Medical Association Journal*, 90, 39.

Wolpe, J. (1964d) What is behavior therapy? *Listener*, 71, 149–50.

Wolpe, J. (1964e) New therapeutic methods based on a conditioned response, *Zeitschrift fur Psychologie*, 169, 173–96.

Wolpe, J. (1964f) Reply to Mowrer's comments on reciprocal inhibition therapy, *Behaviour Research and Therapy*, 1, 339–41.

Wolpe, J. (1964g) Review of G.K. Yacorzinski et al., *Investigation of carbon dioxide therapy*, *American Journal of Psychology*, 77, 170–1.

Wolpe, J. (1964h) New ways to treat sex disorders, *Sexology*, 31, 16–20.

Wolpe, J. (1965a) Behaviour therapy, *British Medical Journal*, 1, 1609–10.

Wolpe, J. (1965b) Behavior therapy, *Discovery*, August, 7–11.

Wolpe, J. (1965c) Comments on H.J. Eysenck's 'The effects of psychotherapy,' *International Journal of Psychiatry*, 1, 173–5.

Wolpe, J. (1965d) Review of J. Masserman (ed.), *Science and psychoanalysis – psychoanalytic education* (Vol. 5), *Journal of Nervous and Mental Disease*, 140, 473.

Wolpe, J. (1965e) Conditioned inhibition of craving in drug addiction: a pilot experiment, *Behaviour Research and Therapy*, 3, 185–9.

Wolpe, J. (1966a) Direct behavior modification therapies. In L.E. Abt and B.F. Riess (eds.), *Progress in clinical psychology* (Vol. 7). New York: Grune & Stratton.

Wolpe, J. (1966b) The conditioning and deconditioning of neurotic anxiety. In C.D. Speilberger (ed.), *Anxiety and behavior* (pp. 179–90). New York: Academic Press.

Wolpe, J. (1966c) Behavior therapy and stuttering: deconditioning the emotional factor, *Proceedings, International Seminar on Stuttering and Behavior Therapy*. Monterey, CA.

Wolpe, J. (1967) Parallels between animal and human neuroses. In J. Zubin and H.F. Hunt (eds.), *Comparative psychopathology*. New York: Grune & Stratton.

Wolpe, J. (1969) *The practice of behavior therapy*. New York: Pergamon Press.

Wolpe, J. (1970) The discontinuity of neurosis and schizophrenia, *Behaviour Research and Therapy*, 8, 179–87.

Wolpe, J. (1973) *The practice of behavior therapy* (2nd ed.). New York: Pergamon Press.

Wolpe, J. (1976a) *Theme and variations: a behavior therapy casebook*. New York: Pergamon Press.

Wolpe, J. (1976b) Behavior therapy and its malcontents: 1. Denial of its bases and psychodynamic fusionism, *Journal of Behavior Therapy and Experimental Psychiatry*, 7, 1–5.

Wolpe, J. (1976c) Behavior therapy and its malcontents: 2. Multimodal eclecticism, cognitive exclusivism and exposure empiricism, *Journal of Behavior Therapy and Experimental Psychiatry*, 7, 109–16.

Wolpe, J. (1977) Inadequate behavior analysis: the achilles heel of outcome research, *Journal of Behavior Therapy and Experimental Psychiatry*, 8, 1–3.

Wolpe, J. (1978a) Cognition and causation in human behavior and its therapy, *American Psychologist*, 33, 437–46.

Wolpe, J. (1978b) Self-efficacy theory and psychotherapeutic change: a square peg for a round hole, *Advances in Behavior Research and Therapy*, 1, 231–6.

Wolpe, J. (1979) The experimental model and treatment of neurotic depression, *Behaviour Research and Therapy*, 17, 555–65.

Wolpe, J. (1980) Behavior therapy for psychosomatic disorders, *Psychosomatics*, 21, 5.

Wolpe, J. (1981a) The dichotomy between directly conditioned and cognitively learned anxiety, *Journal of Behavior Therapy and Experimental Psychiatry*, 12, 35–42.

Wolpe, J. (1981b) Behavior therapy versus psychoanalysis: therapeutic and social implications, *American Psychologist*, 36, 159–64.

Wolpe, J. (1982) *The practice of behavior therapy* (3rd ed.). New York: Pergamon Press.

Wolpe, J. (1986) Individualization: the categorical imperative of behavior therapy practice, *Journal of Behavior Therapy and Experimental Psychiatry*, 17, 145–53.

Wolpe, J. (1989a) How indifference to individual differences has made a mockery of outcome research. Paper presented at the 23rd Annual Convention of the Association for the Advancement of Behavior Therapy, Washington, DC.

Wolpe, J. (1989b) The derailment of behavior therapy: a tale of conceptual misdirection, *Journal of Behavior Therapy and Experimental Psychiatry*, 20, 3–15.

Wolpe, J. (1990) *The practice of behavior therapy* (4th ed.). New York: Pergamon Press.

Wolpe, J. (1993) Commentary: the cognitivist oversell and comments on symposium contributions, *Journal of Behavior Therapy and Experimental Psychiatry*, 24, 141–7.

Wolpe, J. and Abrams, J. (1991) Posttraumatic stress disorder overcome by eye-movement desensitization: a case report, *Journal of Behavior Therapy and Experimental Psychiatry*, 22, 39–43.

Wolpe, J. and Ascher, L.M. (1976) Outflanking 'resistance' in a severe obsessional neurosis. In H.J. Eysenck (ed.), *Case histories in behavior therapy*. London: Routledge & Kegan Paul.

Wolpe, J. and Lang, P.J. (1964) A fear survey schedule for use in behavior therapy, *Behaviour Research and Therapy*, 2, 27–30.

Wolpe, J. and Lang, P.J. (1969) *Fear survey schedule*. San Diego, CA: Educational and Industrial Testing Service.

Wolpe, J. and Lazarus, A.A. (1966) *Behavior therapy techniques: a guide to the treatment of the neuroses*. New York: Pergamon Press.

Wolpe, J. and Rachman, S. (1960) Psychoanalytic evidence: a critique based on Freud's case of little Hans, *Journal of Nervous and Mental Disease*, 131, 135–48.

Wolpe, J. and Taylor, J.G. (1963) Mind as a function of neural organization. In J. Scher (ed.), *Theories of the mind* (pp. 218–40). New York: The Free Press.

Wolpe, J. and Turkat, I.D. (1985) Behavioral formulation of clinical cases. In I.D. Turkat (ed.), *Behavioral case formulation* (pp. 5–36). New York: Plenum.

Wolpe, J. and Wright, R. (1988) The neglect of data-gathering instruments in behavior therapy practice, *Journal of Behavior Therapy and Experimental Psychiatry*, 19, 5–9.

Wolpe, J., Groves, G.A., and Fischer, S. (1980) Treatment of narcotic addiction by inhibition of craving: contending with a cherished habit, *Comprehensive Psychiatry*, 21, 308.

Wolpe, J., Lande, S.D., McNally, R.J., and Schotte, D. (1985) Differentiation between classically conditioned and cognitively based neurotic fears: two pilot studies, *Journal of Behavior Therapy and Experimental Psychiatry*, 16, 287–93.

Wolpe, J., Salter, A., and Reyna, L.J. (eds.) (1964) *The conditioning therapies: The challenge in psychotherapy*. New York: Holt, Rinehart, & Winston.

Wolpin, M. and Raines, J. (1966) Visual imagery, expected roles and extinction as possible factors in reducing fear and avoidance behavior, *Behaviour Research and Therapy*, 4, 25–37.

Wynne, L.C. and Solomon, R.L. (1955) Traumatic avoidance learning: acquisition and extinction in dogs deprived of normal peripheral autonomic function, *Genetic Psychology Monographs*, 52, 241–84.

Yates, A.J. (1958a) Symptoms and symptom substitution, *Psychological Review*, 65, 371–4.

Yates, A.J. (1958b) The application of learning theory to the treatment of tics, *Journal of Abnormal and Social Psychology*, 56, 175–82.

Zinbarg, R.E. (1993) Information processing and classical conditioning: implications for exposure therapy and the integration of cognitive therapy and behavior therapy, *Journal of Behavior Therapy and Experimental Psychiatry*, 24, 129–39.

Index